Shades of Globalizat
Childhood Settings

Shades of Globalization in Three Early Childhood Settings

Views from India, South Africa, and Canada

Ailie Cleghorn
Concordia University, Montreal, Canada

Larry Prochner
University of Alberta, Edmonton, Canada

SENSE PUBLISHERS
ROTTERDAM/BOSTON/TAIPEI

A C.I.P. record for this book is available from the Library of Congress.

ISBN: 978-94-6091-099-9 (paperback)
ISBN: 978-94-6091-100-2 (hardback)
ISBN: 978-94-6091-101-9 (e-book)

Published by: Sense Publishers,
P.O. Box 21858,
3001 AW Rotterdam
The Netherlands
http://www.sensepublishers.com

Printed on acid-free paper

Cover photograph by Robert G. Myers

Dedication

To the children of the world
in the hope
that they may stay local
while going global

CONTENTS

ILLUSTRATIONS

FIGURES

TABLES

ACKNOWLEDGMENTS

Many people in India, South Africa, and Canada are to be thanked for their contributions to this book. *Shades of Globalization* could not have been written at all if the children, parents, teachers, and other educators in each country had not been so welcoming during the four years of our research in their preschool settings. To all of them, we are most grateful.

Next, the study that this book stems from would have been impossible without the support and collaboration of our colleagues both abroad and at home. Some contributed directly to particular chapters, others provided entry to the settings, and still others gently reminded us of local customs and regulations when our cross-cultural sensitivity failed to serve us well.

At the M.S. University of Baroda and at the University of Pretoria, several lecturers and students provided valuable assistance. They not only coordinated school visits but undertook or helped with classroom observations and the occasional need for translation. At Concordia University and the University of Alberta, a number of graduate research assistants helped out over the four years in a myriad of ways: organizing data, keeping files intact, sending emails, checking references, and so on. We hope their experience with the project has inspired them to venture out in similar ways, repaying them for their efforts in ways that their research assistant salaries could not. The manuscript was copyedited by Cardinal Consultants, Toronto; the references were cross-checked by Amanda Pichette and Jennifer Fletcher.

We are indebted to Professor Jessica Ball, University of Victoria, for the final touch that she has provided with the Afterword. Thanks also to Linda David-Cree for reading the manuscript and giving us some final tips as to how to communicate more effectively with the reader. Rinelle Evans' input on the historical minutiae of South Africa was invaluable as was Nkidi Phatudi's help in deciphering the many early childhood policy documents.

Without the friendly support of Peter de Liefde at Sense Publications this book would not be. Many thanks for the tolerance of our delaying tactics, grounded in the realities of life as they were.

Portions of chapters 3 and 5, previously published in *Research in Comparative and International Education*, and the *International Journal of Early Years Education*, are reprinted here with kind permission. Similarly, permissions have been granted from Sage, Routledge, and Taylor and Francis publishers for excerpts and modifications to tables in chapter 6.

Finally, last but definitely not least, our deep appreciation goes to the Social Sciences and Humanities Research Council of Canada, which funded *A comparison of early childhood thought and practice in Canada, India, and South Africa* for four years.

ABBREVIATIONS

AHS	Aboriginal Head Start (Canada)
AHSOR	Aboriginal Head Start On Reserve
AHSUNC	Aboriginal Head Start Urban and Northern Communities
AIHS	American Indian Head Start
ANHS	Alaska Native Head Start
AWC	Anganwadi centre
AWH	Anganwadi helper
AWW	Anganwadi worker
DoE	Department of Education
EC	early childhood
ECCE	early childhood care and education
ECD	early childhood development
ECE	early childhood education
FNMI	First Nations, Métis, and Inuit (Canada)
Grade R	Reception Year (South Africa)
ICDS	Integrated Child Development Services (India)
IEA	International Association for the Evaluation of Educational Achievement
INAC	Indian and Northern Affairs Canada
L1	First Language
LoI	Language of Instruction
MoE	Ministry of Education
NGO	Non-Governmental Organization
OBE	Outcomes-Based Education
UNESCO	United Nations Educational, Scientific, and Cultural Organization
UNICEF	United Nations Children's Fund

PREFACE

This book has been written for those who are interested in the diversity of children's lives and preschool experiences throughout the world. In addition to comparative and international education researchers, many readers are included: education and social policy makers, teacher educators, teachers, pre-service student teachers, day-care and preschool workers, parents, community leaders, governmental and non-governmental organizations and consultants, early childhood program planners and evaluators, community development workers, university lecturers, developmental psychologists—the list goes on. As chapter 1 outlines, each of the eight chapters touches on a different aspect of the three case study preschools, one each in India, South Africa, and Canada.

When a book is authored by more than one person, often the reader has no idea as to the actual contributions of each author. This book was most definitely a joint enterprise, thus to locate one author's name before the other on the cover is quite misleading. Larry and Ailie contributed equally to chapter 1, while Larry took the lead on chapters 3, 5 and 6, and Ailie took the lead on chapters 2, 4, 7 and 8. Dr. Prerana Mohite and Namita Bhatt at the M.S. University of Baroda in India were contributing authors on chapters 2 and 3, and in addition provided factual input on the other chapters whenever needed. Dr. Nkidi Phatudi at the University of Pretoria provided details for sections of chapter 2, as well as factual data concerning South Africa's many policies in early childhood education and other areas. Chapter 5 is an adaptation of an article jointly written by Larry, Ailie, and Nicole Green, first published in the *International Journal of Early Years Education*. Nicole was then at the National Institute of Education, Nanyang Technological University in Singapore, and is now on the faculty of the University of New England in Australia.

CHAPTER 1

THREE PRESCHOOLS: THREE COUNTRIES

INTRODUCTION

This book casts a socio-cultural and critical eye on early childhood policy and practice in three very different semi-rural settings, in India, South Africa, and a First Nations (Aboriginal) community in Canada. Our primary aim is to throw light on the myriad of ways in which two major trends intersect and play out in diverse ECCE settings. On the one hand, there is increased world-wide recognition of the validity of local, indigenous ways of knowing about, and working with, children. This is evident, for example, in the goals for quality education formulated by the United Nations Educational, Scientific, and Cultural Organization's Education for All initiative. On the other hand, the forces of globalization, coupled with the legacy of colonialism, appear to militate against the inclusion of local knowledge and activities in early childhood programs.

In the following chapters, we draw on the policy analysis and ethnographic fieldwork of a triple case study that we carried out between 2004 and 2008 in the three countries. The intention is to illuminate the ways in which apparent differences in practice reflect common societal concerns: past and present political injustices; changes in the social meaning attached to racial, ethnic, and linguistic difference; strategies for preparing children for school in a changing world. Although policy documents tend to obscure differences in early childhood education, we suggest that differentiation at the local, cultural level persists, sometimes subtly, sometimes intentionally, in day-to-day practice.

Another purpose of this book is to raise questions and to give the reader pause. Although we do not specifically take a post-modern stance, from time to time, and especially in chapter 8, we will cast a critical eye back to some of the issues that the chapters touch on, using straightforward, clear language to do so. Thus the following chapters will be of interest to readers who are concerned with policy-practice issues, inclined to question universal prescriptions for best practice in education in general and in early childhood education in particular, and apt to think through some of the prevailing taken-for-granted assumptions about how early childhood environments should be organized and how the activities within them should be carried out.

In each country, the research was carried out within formal early childhood settings, organized by communities and sponsored by their governments to promote early childhood development and early learning. Although each setting provided various services, their predominant identity was as a preschool. Chapter 2 describes the physical and other features of the case study preschools, including a description of a typical day in each, and draws on historical data to show how the preschools

1

arrived at the point where we began our study.[1] The following chapters then take up a particular theme, examining it from the perspectives of the authors' observations and those of our collaborators and the participants in each setting. Chapter 3 outlines the policy and curriculum contexts, homing in, for example, on policy-practice accord or discord as the case may be, with particular regard to the theme of preparing children for school and for a changing world. An analysis of curriculum policy documents illuminates not only ideas that have been imported from the West, but also each country's vision of the kind of adult that schooling, starting at the preschool level, is intended to produce. Chapter 4 talks about the children, teachers, parents, and other adults, how they interact and relate to each other in the various situations and contexts, and what language or languages they use for what purposes. In chapter 5, we turn to the topic of the preschool spaces, how they are organized, and how materials are used and displayed within them. Chapter 6 takes a close look at the interplay between care and formal teaching, what we refer to as the paediatric-pedagogical dimension, as suggested in the work of Robert LeVine and others (1994).

Chapter 7 shifts to an analytical reflection on the foregoing chapters, picking up some of the recurrent themes of difference across the three early childhood settings. The intention here is to show how overt differences may hide similarities in attitude, for example, while superficial similarities may conceal deeply rooted cultural differences. In addition to a further examination of the preschools' spaces, indoors and out, we take a comparative look at the daily schedules, especially for the proportions of time allotted to care as contrasted to teaching activities. Following this, the chapter returns to the topic of possible policy-practice gaps and a discussion of indigenous and western influences on practice.

Finally, in chapter 8 we take a critical look at some of the global issues that the previous chapters have implicitly or explicitly raised. In particular we ask: What do these three settings tell us about the current global academic discourse about quality in early childhood settings? What do they tell us about increasingly global prescriptions regarding curricula, and about transitions from preschool to regular school? That is, what do these chapters suggest about how best to prepare children in some of the majority world's less developed communities to move from one cultural and linguistic context, the home and preschool, to the cultural and linguistic context of the school? Then, in the concluding part of this chapter, the reader will find a few ideas as to how early childhood policy makers and educators might stay local while going global—by identifying and then integrating those aspects of the global that will best enhance the local. We suggest that the verdict is not yet in as to the direction early childhood care and education is moving: towards greater uniformity of practice due to the spread of western ideas through teacher education, through policy borrowing and through access to and use of westernized curriculum materials, towards a greater celebration of the local and of local identities, or a hybrid of both.

Before moving on to chapter 2, it is necessary to define our terms, the key concepts, and the theoretical and other considerations that this book concerns.

WHAT DOES GLOBALIZATION MEAN?

This book explores the extent to which and in what ways globalization is affecting early childhood policy and practice in diverse settings. To research this question with regard to policy was a fairly straightforward matter: we gathered as many policy documents as possible about education in general and about early childhood care and education (ECCE), sometimes going back several decades. As chapter 3 describes, these were analysed thematically and comparatively as well as in the light of historical trends in each setting. This analysis served to highlight such matters as cultural values, conceptions of the child and childhood, the goals of education, visions of the kind of adult citizen that the education system aims to produce, ideas about the role of the teacher in preschools and in school communities, and so on.

Practice, however, is quite a different and more complex research matter. In order to obtain a reading on the multiple influences on teachers' actions within classroom settings, a researcher could conceivably administer a survey questionnaire to thousands of teachers. We believe, however, that the reasons underlying much of what teachers do, when, how, and why, lie outside the realm of consciousness. That is, teachers are products of the culture that they have been raised and educated in and this has formed deeply rooted beliefs in the teacher about how children are to be raised, how they learn, how they are to behave, when they may play, how adults and children are to interact, and what it means to be a teacher. A better way to obtain insight into this complex issue is to use ethnographic techniques to observe in and out of classrooms over a long period of time, and to talk informally with teachers on many occasions. In such ways, the researcher arrives at an understanding of what has been observed that includes the perspective of the participants, the teachers. This was essentially how we carried out our study.

Globalization Defined

Globalization has many meanings. Anthony Giddens (1990) defines globalization as "the intensification of worldwide social relations which link distant localities in such a way that local happenings are shaped by events occurring many miles away and vice versa" (p. 64). Stated differently, McGrew and Lewis (1992) view globalization as a process in which events, decisions, activities, and products in one part of the world can significantly affect communities and individuals in other parts of the world. Globalization thus involves a change in the way we understand geography and experience localness. Many of the activities that previously involved face-to-face interaction at the local level are now conducted across great distances, due to the ease of telecommunications, at least for those living in the industrialized, minority parts of the world. Globalization thus has integrative as well as divisive dimensions. On the one hand, there is the possibility of the emergence of larger, collective identities and shared meanings; on the other hand, there is bound to be persistence of local identities and meanings, due to the apparent human need for face-to-face interaction in familiar situations, for a sense of belonging and personal identity. It was in this sense that we considered globalization in the study that informed the writing of this book.

There are, however, many aspects to globalization, thus it touches the educational domain in many ways; these include educational policy borrowing and formation, the influence of technology in the classroom, the content of the textbooks used in teacher education, teaching practice, the content of the curriculum, and the selection and use of available teaching materials. The influence of globalization thus creates considerable grounds for debate, for example, about what the view of the child should be, and what constitutes quality in early childhood settings. What should be the priorities, school readiness with the emphasis on behavioural norms as well as pre-reading and pre-math, or care, play, socialization, and healthy development? Globalization may have serious implications for the content of the curriculum in teacher education, especially if the curriculum and texts have been imported from the West. To the extent that such content may be at odds with indigenous (local) views of the child and how children develop and learn, the impact on classroom practice may be great.

To ask if globalization is a good thing or not, is not the point; globalization has had an impact, and is certain to continue to influence the experience of teachers and learners in unpredictable and sometimes conflicting ways. In this regard, we see the three case study settings engaged in a process of social change, each in their own way. For example, over the last 25 to 30 years, Canada's First Nations (Aboriginal) peoples have received wide recognition with regard to the harsh assimilative schooling conditions that previous generations suffered during a process of internal colonization (Battiste, 2000; Blauner, 1972; Indian and Northern Affairs Canada, 2003).[2] In South Africa, along with the end of apartheid in 1994 came the start of major changes in education policy, curricular reforms, the racial integration of schools, and the deployment of black teachers to formerly white schools, and white teachers to formerly all black schools. In India, relatively recent economic development has brought a plethora of technological changes to many communities and people's lives in the form of new media and communications.

Globalization, then, is often a code word for westernization and modernization, a phenomenon captured in the terms Disneyfication and McDonaldization (cf. Ritzer, 1993). As such, it has economic, social, cultural, and political elements. Of particular relevance here is the notion of universalization, a socio-cultural and economic process of spreading various objects, experiences, ideas and policies worldwide (Steiner-Khamsi, 2004). Thus values and attitudes associated with capitalism and free enterprise, competition and individualism, are thought to spread the world over, undermining pre-existing cultures and local self-determination in the process, in a kind of neo-colonialization (Apple, 2003). One of the central questions in our study asked to what extent we find evidence of this in the case study preschools in India, South Africa, and Canada. For instance, we had our eyes open for cultural shifts from a communal orientation in which individual identity is tied directly to membership in the extended family and community group, to an individualistic orientation as evidenced by an emphasis on individual achievement, competition, and ideas of getting ahead, of social mobility. Certainly, as the reader will find in chapter 3, the analysis of policy documents clearly tied investments in early childhood education with nation-building, progress, and competing on the world stage.

Globalization involves the spread of the corporate brand across the world so that products are developed and then marketed in Toronto, Mumbai, and Johannesburg, as well as in small Inuit communities in Canada's North and rural villages in Africa. Brands like Coca-Cola, Nike, Sony, Nestlé and a host of others have become part of the fabric of people's lives almost everywhere, sometimes with seemingly benign results and sometimes with disastrous results (Klein, 2003, as cited in Barakett & Cleghorn, 2007). It was not long ago, for instance, in several parts of the majority world and in Africa especially, that Nestlé marketed its baby formula so successfully that mothers abandoned breastfeeding in favour of bottle-feeding, but often the only water that was available to mix the formula was contaminated; the infant death rate rose dramatically (WHO, Nov. 24, 2001). Another example is found in Canada's Native (Aboriginal) communities, where the incidence of child diabetes has skyrocketed along with the consumption of soft drinks such as Coca-Cola (Aboriginal Health Newsletter, 2008). Further, with the influence of popular culture, there has been an increased commercial effort to condition children and young people to construct their identities around brands. In our triple case study these aspects of globalization were mainly evident in the Canadian and South African settings, in the kinds of materials that were available to decorate classrooms, as well as in the ways they were displayed in relation to the available space. The reader will find more about this topic in chapter 5.

Globalization Influences Teachers

Globalization has the potential to influence teachers and how they work with young children in many ways. For example, western-generated theories about child development often form the basis of teacher training courses, the assumption being that these theories are universally applicable (Nsamenang, 2007). Teachers are also influenced by the recommended use of a specific EC approach, such as High/Scope or Montessori, through imported learning materials, including children's storybooks, puzzles, and plastic blocks, donated by a foreign non-governmental organization, and by being required to use a foreign language with children. In addition, teachers themselves are increasingly exposed via the media to the commercial trappings of western culture.

It is not only teachers who are affected directly by globalization; they must also deal with children who come to the classroom with visions of a very different world than that of the parents. Gupta (2008, p. 18) reports the experience of a teacher in an urban preschool in India:

> Children are being exposed to a lot of animated media (games), which is making them more aggressive and their interest in reading books is being affected. With the western culture being brought to India, the value system of respect and thoughtfulness is gradually disappearing ... They try to copy that culture and parents are pressurized in this whole process.

Globalization also comes to educational settings through the remnants of the colonial era, post-colonialism, in India and South Africa. The experience of the Aboriginal peoples of Canada, as just stated, has been one of internal colonization, with significantly different effects which will be discussed in subsequent chapters. Post-colonial may be defined as "a juxtaposition, a continuing and complex interplay of ideas and practices between the colonizer and the colonized, between the West and the non-West, between the traditional and the modern, between the dominant and the marginalized" (Gupta, 2008, p. 13-14). Again with regard to her research of early childhood and primary school settings in urban India, Gupta notes the hybridity with which "teachers were interweaving elements of an ancient cultural philosophy that was still actively practiced, with elements of British colonial and American progressive educational perspectives" (p. 22).

Globalization Affects Families

Globalization directly affects the lives of families with young children. Myers (2001), for example, notes that programs for child care are nested in local, community, national, and cultural environments that affect the way children are cared for through various policies and laws, as well as through sets of beliefs about the ways children are to be raised. Majority world national and cultural contexts are in turn immersed in and influenced by globalization, through aid programs sponsored by international organizations such as UNICEF, the World Bank, and the Canadian International Development Agency (CIDA). Globalization thus stands to have an impact at the local level on the preschools and other institutions that are established for the care and early education of children. These were but a few of the issues that we cast our ethnographic eyes upon in the early childhood settings that this book discusses.

In sum, globalization is a favourite catchword of journalists and politicians, used mainly as a shorthand way of describing the spread and connectedness of production (Smith & Smith, 2002). It is not a new phenomenon; rather, it has been present and increasing for centuries, linked to industrialization, migration, and urbanization, as well as advances in technology and communication, all of which are trends that are continuing across the world. The situation today is significantly changed, however, due to the volume of international trade and the speed of communication and technological developments, particularly those associated with transportation and the media. Globalization is promoted and stimulated by these trends and, in turn, reinforces and has an impact on them.

POLICY

A detailed comparative description of early childhood policy in India, South Africa, and Canada will be found in chapter 3 and further discussed in chapter 7. For the moment we need to be clear about what is meant by policy. A policy is a statement, plan or guide for action; it is not a law, however policies can become laws. Policies set out the position that a governing body, such as a government, school board or parent organization, has decided to take on a particular matter, often a controversial one. At the national level, a policy sets out the goals, objectives and guiding principles for action to which it will commit resources. National policies may take the form of frameworks that provide a context for coordination and inter-sectoral priority setting, in a kind of top down/bottom up integration. In contrast, one finds stand-alone policies, especially in countries where social issues facing women and children are in urgent need of attention. In such cases policy development would be based, for instance, on studies of the situation of vulnerable children, on urban and rural differences in cultures and practice. In countries where economic constraints are severe, in the face of competition for scarce resources, it is sometimes a major challenge to garner the political will and to assign priority in the distribution of resources to the needs of young children, their care and early education.

INDIGENOUS KNOWLEDGE

The word 'indigenous' is used in the following chapters interchangeably with the word 'local' when the reference is to local knowledge or local culture. Our understanding of the term comes mainly from the field of anthropology; it is also of considerable interest to comparative educators. There are several definitions of indigenous knowledge. Below are two with which we concur. Indigenous knowledge refers to

> A body of knowledge associated with long-term occupancy of a certain place ... to traditional norms and social values as well as to mental constructs that guide, organize, and regulate the people's way of living. (Dei, Hall, & Rosenberg, 2000, p. 6)

> Indigenous knowledge reflects the dynamic way in which the residents of an area have come to understand themselves in relationship to their natural environment and how they organize that folk knowledge of flora, fauna, cultural beliefs and history to enhance their lives. (Semali & Kincheloe, 1999, p. 3)

Two concepts that facilitate our understanding of the way in which indigenous knowledge enters into teaching practice and teachers' work with children are surface culture and deep culture (Kuper, 1999). Surface culture refers to those aspects of culture that people are aware of and point to when asked what is particular about what they do or their way of life—language, symbols, stated beliefs, clothing, formal religion, rituals, holidays, artefacts, art, etcetera. Deep culture refers to the embedded meanings that are attached to surface culture elements through long-established attitudes, beliefs, values, procedures, patterns of behaviour, and norms. Deep culture may explain behaviours that appear to contradict stated beliefs, since behaviour stemming from deep culture may not be conscious, but can simply be what people consider normal or the way things are. One of the main reasons for using ethnographic research techniques is to obtain insight into the elements of deep culture, thus the concept is important to understanding evidently conflicting influences and seemingly opposing trends on teachers.

At the outset of this chapter, it was stated that the forces of globalization, along with post-colonial factors, appear to militate against the inclusion of local knowledge and activities in EC programs. Clearly, this book takes the position that local knowledge is important. Here are some reasons why we take this position.

Many international development experts are calling for educational programs that are rooted in the indigenous knowledge of local cultures while also providing the knowledge and skills that people now may need to live in a global world (Abdi & Cleghorn, 2005; Abagi, 2005; Anderson-Levitt, 2003; Cleghorn, 2005; Kendrick & Jones, 2008; Mkosi, 2005; Odora-Hoppers, 2002; Prochner & Cleghorn, 2005; Semali & Kincheloe, 1999; Shizha, 2005). This is because of the repeated and conclusive evidence that when there is a sharp discontinuity between the culture and language of the home and that of the school, children must cross many kinds of borders in the process of adapting to school. Border crossing refers to the ability to shift cognitively as well as culturally, and when possible, linguistically, from one worldview to another. Worldview refers to the taken-for-granted understandings that each cultural group holds about the world; it refers to a fundamental organization of the mind, a way of looking and of understanding (Aikenhead & Jegede, 1999; Anderson-Levitt, 2003; Cobern, 1998; Giroux, 1992; Heath, 1983; Nsamenang, 2004; Serpell, 1993). These borders are not only linguistic, cultural, and conceptual but social too, since teaching involves cultural transmission of the dominant, western ways of thinking as well as the transmission of behavioural norms into school settings (Apple, 1979; Mifflen & Mifflen, 1982; Waldrip & Taylor, 1999). Such home-school differences may thus place an exceptional cognitive load on the learner as they engage in what may be referred to as a process of 'triple translation' in order to understand the content and the routines of schooling. In turn, this process may also affect the role that the school can or should play in fostering individual and cultural identity, vastly increasing the risk of school failure (Leahy, Sweller, & Cooper, 2005; Merritt, Cleghorn, & Abagi, 1988; Nsamenang, 2008; Pence, Garcia & Evans, 2008; Sweller, 1994). We will return to these complex issues in chapter 8.

To elaborate a little more, increasingly throughout the world teachers are required to use English as the language of instruction (LoI). The LoI is often not yet known by the learners and moreover is not taught as a second or foreign language; rather, it tends to be used in the classroom in a 'submersion' manner, as if the learners are well on their way to knowing it.. This is particularly the case if the teacher is fluent in the LoI. In situations where the teacher is also a second language learner of the LoI, the situation is even more complex (Cleghorn, 2005; Cleghorn & Evans, 2009). In either case, since the students do not understand the classroom language, teachers may believe that they have no other choice but to resort to rote methods in order to have the children practice saying the words they do not yet understand. Such rote routines have been referred to as teachers' safetalk (Hornberger & Chick, 2001). While filling up teaching time, they tend to restrict the curriculum to disconnected bits of information, drastically affecting the emergent literacy abilities of the learners. Next, the behavioural norms of the school setting may have been imported along with the LoI and a colonial system of education. Thus for example, when at home children may be expected to remain quiet when visitors arrive and to seat themselves lower than the adults, at school they may be expected to jump to attention and call out loudly and in unison "Good morning M'am!" Similarly, what constitutes punishable behaviour at school may be totally at odds with parental expectations at home (Shizha, 2005). These examples reflect but a few of our concerns about the importance of tying instruction to the actual knowledge and abilities of children in order to build from what is there, not from what is not there. The situation is not so very different for immigrant children in the West as they integrate linguistically and otherwise to the North American system of education (Dachyshyn & Kirova, 2008).

WHY COMPARE ECCE IN INDIA, SOUTH AFRICA, AND CANADA?

The reader might well ask what can be learned from a triple ECCE case study in three such different regions of the world. One reason is to look at similarities and differences in order to facilitate the making of distinctions. What influences from abroad and what changes from within a country in terms of economics or demography have affected ECCE policy and practice? By comparing the three sites we also provide a check on the ethnocentric lens that most of us unavoidably employ when looking at our own situations. Comparative research allows us to see what is specific to a setting and what is more general. We hope that the reader will gain a sense of what can or cannot (or should not) be changed with regard to working with young children, for example, in terms of social policies that affect them.

Case studies inevitably raise questions in readers' minds with regard to how representative a single setting can be. In that this study was a qualitative comparison of three very different preschool settings, in India, South Africa, and Canada, it did not in any way pretend to generalize its findings; rather, the intention was to address some general issues in the field of ECCE and to provide insights with regard to the local and global issues and concerns that the study has centred on, as outlined here. Each of the preschools is thus unique in its own way; however each is also embedded in a particular historical and cultural context. Chapter 2 elaborates those contexts.

Although the study was not in any way a comparative evaluation relating to the quality of the three ECCE settings, it is important to point out that our observations raise questions about how educators in the West tend to think about early childhood quality issues. We will return to this matter in chapter 8. For the moment, we ask that the reader not consider the details of the three settings in an evaluative way, but rather with interest in how things simply differ from one place to another, what these differences in practice may mean to the participants, and why they may persist.

NOTES

[1] In this project the video-taping day was taken as a main source of information about what constituted 'a typical' day in each centre, with the data corroborated by observations on many other days, as well as through discussions with teachers and observations in several other preschools.

[2] Hicks (2004, pp. 4-5) refers to internal colonization as intra-national exploitation of distinct cultural groups. Referring to Robert Blauner's earlier work, Hicks notes that internal colonization starts with forced involuntary entry into the dominant society. This is more than the result of culture contact, but involves a policy of transforming or destroying a way of life.

CHAPTER 2

LEGACIES OF COLONIZATION

In order to locate each of the study preschools in its respective historical and cultural context, this chapter will first give a brief, thumbnail sketch of their colonial histories. This will expand what was said in the introduction about the ways in which the settings have been marked by social change. These histories are quite different from one another, however, they contain certain similar elements. They are important for the relatively similar roles they have played in establishing patterns of dominance, suppression of indigenous ways of socializing children, and eventually for laying the foundation for resistance to that dominance and the concomitant revival, at least in South Africa and in Canada, of indigenous languages, cultures, patterns of child-rearing, and schooling. The legacies of these histories can be seen in the content of curricula, in teacher training programs, in the expectations for children's readiness to read. Some would argue that certain aspects of colonization are perpetuated via the global spread of policies such as outcomes-based education (OBE) (Jansen, 2002; Nsamenang, 2004), thus linking to the particular aspects of globalization with which this book is concerned.

The study from which this book stems began with a hint at the consequences of those histories: we suggested, along with others in the field, that global trends in ECCE seem to be moving in two directions at once. On the one hand there is increasing recognition of the validity of local ways of knowing and doing. On the other hand, the legacies of colonialism, whether externally imposed or internally generated, and operating through the processes of globalization, appear still to discourage the inclusion of indigenous knowledge and activities in ECCE programs. Stated differently, ECCE programs in many parts of the world appear to be "taking their cues from imported models that reinforce value shifts towards the individualistic, production-oriented cultures of the West" (Myers, 1992. p. 29). Our position is that this represents a serious loss for the schooling as well as for the identities of children in each setting. It represents an institutionalized, formal, and official perpetuation of the intentions of colonization, a legitimized way to cut people off from their roots. This is legitimized because in the minds of many educational planners, a western form of schooling, even at the preschool level, represents modernity, progress, and hope for the future. In addition, when local knowledge, games, songs, and other activities are excluded from the curriculum it becomes impossible for teachers to connect with what the child brings from home to school, to move children from the familiar to what is not yet known, despite what may have been the teachers' modern training in Vygotskian and constructivist principles of teaching and learning. Thus one of our research goals was to try to identify ways that educators, parents, and communities might better prepare children for formal schooling, although increasingly western in style, while preserving the integrity of locally valued ways of knowing and of educating children. In each of the research settings, colonization has had an impact, at first on rudimentary and often socially or racially inequitable services provided for the care of children, and in due course but with marked variations, on the development of preschool programs whose primary purpose has become that of preparing children for a formal, western model of schooling. In the preschool in India, this was less the case than in Canada or South Africa.

THE THREE SETTINGS IN THE CONTEXT OF THEIR STORIES OF COLONIZATION

Canada – Little Lake Preschool

As outlined by Armitage (1995) with regard to Canada, Australia, and New Zealand, there are several quite similar stories to be told concerning the history of British colonization. In the West, colonization began with Columbus' 1492 arrival in the West Indies and the establishment of semi-permanent fishing settlements. By the early 1500s there were small permanent settlements for the extraction of natural resources and for trade with Aboriginal peoples. It was not until the seventeenth century that contact with Aboriginal peoples, in what later became Canada, began. By the early nineteenth century the process of colonization and expansion was worldwide. All European powers were involved, but Britain dominated the greatest amount of territory. By today's standards, Britain in the nineteenth century was very ethnocentric. It was a hierarchical society with strictly defined social class divisions, concerned with controlling those who were considered outside the accepted economic structure—the poor in Britain and Aboriginal peoples in the colonies. Laws and social policies were established to protect them, to prepare them via organized Christianity for full British citizenship through enfranchisement. These ideas fuelled the expansion of the British Empire, the nation-building of the colonies, and the felt need to preserve the colonizers' security within the colonial borders—by military force if necessary. At the time of contact with the British, Indigenous Nations were self-sustaining, self-governing Nation states. When direct conflicts arose many Aboriginal peoples were simply killed. If not killed, their lands were taken and their life-styles were controlled by missionaries in the effort to convert them to Christianity.

Britain's 1837 *Report from the Select Committee on Aborigines* exemplifies the attitudes of the day and the rationale behind the colonizers' actions.

It is not to be doubted that this country [Britain] has been invested with wealth and power, with arts and knowledge, with the sway of distant lands, and the mastery of restless waters, for some great purpose in the government of the world. Can we suppose otherwise than that it is our office to carry civilization and humanity, peace and good government, and above all, the knowledge of the true God, to the utmost ends of the earth? (as cited in Armitage, 1995, p. 3)

The 1837 House of Commons Select Committee on Aborigines set the stage for the treatment of First Nations children in Canada. It was believed that children offered the best means to ensure that Aboriginal peoples would be prepared for the responsibilities of Christianity, civilization, and British citizenship. Child welfare policy was used as a means of managing families by separating the children of paupers from their parents to provide children for domestic service and trade apprenticeships. These measures were extended to orphans, truants, children of unmarried mothers, abusive or neglectful parents, and Aboriginals. For children this meant life in boarding school, residential care, foster homes, or as an adoptee in Britain or in one of the colonies.

The children of Aboriginals were removed from their families so the dominant culture could attain its objectives—"to the utmost ends of the earth." It was only in the second half of the twentieth century that removing children from their parents in order to change a people and a culture came to be recognized as an act of oppression, a type of genocide, as established in the 1948 United Nations Convention on the Prevention and Punishment of the Crime of Genocide.[1] However, it is of note that on February 23, 2007, the Assembly of First Nations and the First Nations Child and Family Caring Society filed an official complaint with the Canadian Human Rights Commission based on the findings of the Wen:de study. The Wen:de report stated that there were three times the number of children in child welfare and foster care today than at the height of the residential schools, and that Aboriginal peoples are overrepresented in federal and provincial penal institutions. These institutions continue to cut people off from their families, language, culture, and local knowledge (First Nations Child and Family Caring Society of Canada, 2005).

The paternalistic 'save the child' philosophy was an inappropriate response to Aboriginal problems, perceived or real. While children were in care or residential schools they were separated from their own language, culture, and local knowledge, and they received only a rudimentary education. They were deprived of the influence of their own parents, and the chance to care for their siblings. Physical and sexual abuse was rampant in many institutions, thus creating patterns of violence between and towards children that became part of the parenting behaviour of subsequent generations, well into the present (Armitage, 1995).

The turning point came in the 1960s, along with Civil Rights and Feminist movements, including the Quiet Revolution in Quebec.[2] Aboriginal peoples became more vocal in their resistance to having their land rights extinguished and they rejected the child welfare policies that were imposed in the name of assimilation and integration. The results of this history are very much with us today. There are now comprehensive efforts among the First Nations and other Aboriginal peoples to establish alternative Aboriginal policies, to modify mainstream child welfare policies and, as can be seen in the aims, materials, and activities of this study's First Nations preschool, to re-establish roots and identity. There is however much recovery still to come, since relations with the federal government remain strained.

The Aboriginal peoples were robbed of their resources and confined to marginalised areas that were of little use to the settlers. They did not choose to live as a minority within an alien culture; in Ogbu's (1991) terms, they lived as an involuntary minority. To this day the general living conditions for immigrant groups (voluntary minorities) are better than those of Aboriginal peoples who still must fight for influence on the policies that are developed on their behalf by the federal government; these are constant reminders of the fact that their views have been consistently disregarded.

Little Lake's Location

The Little Lake preschool meets in several rooms of an administrative building in a First Nations community in western Canada. The community's right to the land was established as a result of treaty negotiations with the crown in the nineteenth century. It is designated an Indian reserve as defined by the *Indian Act* (Department of Justice Canada, 1985). The setting is distinctly rural, with individual residences separated by bush or farmland. A cluster of homes is situated near the centre of the community, which includes the administrative building, health clinic, child-care centre, and the preschool. The elementary and high school sits on its own about a kilometre distant from the administrative centre of the community. The building housing the preschool was constructed in the 1980s, and it is also used for community meetings, parent education groups, and other functions. There have been few modifications for its use by young children, though outdoors there is a large, fenced play area for the exclusive use of the preschool. The front door enters directly into the single classroom, with a large group meeting area on one side and various play centres located throughout the space. Child-sized tables and chairs are situated at the opposite side of the room near the kitchen. They are used for seating at breakfast and lunch time and for arts and crafts at other times. The other rooms in the preschool are a teachers' office with windows looking into the classroom, a washroom with a child-sized toilet, and a storage room.

The preschool operates two half-day programs with a total of approximately fifteen children enrolled in each. The focus for this study was the morning class, which was the younger group of children, mostly aged four. Many of the children in this class attended kindergarten in the community school in the afternoon. Subsequent to the study, the enrolment of the preschool has shifted to include two half-day classes with four-year-old children. This was done in response to a change at the community school, to implement a full-day kindergarten for five-year-olds and eliminate the kindergarten for the younger children.

Most children arrived at the preschool between 9:00 and 9:30 a.m.. The preschool staff, the coordinator, assistant teacher, and cook, arrive about 30 minutes before the children to prepare the classroom and the children's breakfast. The minibus driver works at the preschool as a second assistant teacher, coordinating the arts and crafts. The staff are employed ten months per year, with the preschool closed in July and August.

Little Lake preschool includes children with challenging behaviours, and staff have evolved strategies for working with them based on cultural knowledge combined with more conventional behavioural techniques, such as modelling. In some instances, children who have been suspended from the community school kindergarten for their behaviour have been accommodated at the preschool. The approach to accommodating and working with children with special needs reflects the coordinator's background as a health care provider and her training in child development, as well as community values that include all children.

The children all reside with their parents or extended family in the First Nations community. Most children speak English with their parents at home, and only a few parents are fluent in the local language. The coordinator, who is a local language speaker, uses English and the Aboriginal language with the children, both in formal teaching and informal situations. For example, labels for the days of the week and months would be said in English and then in the Aboriginal language.

A Typical Day at Little Lake[3]

The majority of the children are brought to the preschool by the minibus and have at most a 30 minute ride. The driver, a preschool staff member, accompanies the children into the classroom where they leave their outdoor clothing and bags in individually marked cubbies. The morning begins with breakfast, served to the children at their tables by the preschool staff. A second meal, a hot lunch, is served about two hours later before the children leave for home or the community school kindergarten. After breakfast, the program begins with a formal group-time including smudging and prayers. Smudging is a ceremony in which grasses are lit to produce some smoke. The container of smoking grass is presented to each child in turn, who use their hands to waft the smoke towards themselves in order to cleanse their hearts and minds.

A sample schedule of the morning activities is included below. However, it is not rigidly followed, and for much of the time children play at a variety of learning centres of their choice. Learning centres involving pre-academic work as well as the craft of the day are required for all children; the staff invite children individually to work with them at these centres over the course of the morning. Most mornings include play outdoors or a nature walk.

Table 1. Sample Schedule at Little Lake

Time	Activity
9:30 a.m.	Arrival
9:35	Snacks (breakfast)
9:45	Morning circle; sweet grass, prayer by Elder or director; greetings; songs; special announcements
10:35	School Readiness
10:50	Gross motor
11:10	Story time
11:20	Group work
11:45	Lunch
12:15 p.m.	Home time

Teaching at Little Lake

As an Aboriginal Head Start preschool, the staff does not require teacher certification, which in Canada is managed provincially. However, as a preschool program Little Lake is subject to licensing requirements for child care programs, including the same staff qualification requirements. Training for child care staff is assessed at different levels. At the time of the study, the basic requirement was a two-year college diploma in early childhood education. All staff at Little Lake have undertaken some course-work in early childhood education. The Director and classroom aide have nearly completed their diplomas through part-time studies over a period of several years. Whereas college training in ECCE is typically oriented toward developmentally appropriate practice, the Little Lake staff use a variety of methods, including direct instruction for teaching pre-academic skills during group time. Staff use culturally-appropriate teaching strategies purposefully, based on their understanding of learning styles, spirituality, and the importance of community and relationships.

In the Aboriginal Head Start program, curriculum is created by each community for its preschool, in consideration of recommendations in the standards guide (Health Canada, 2005). At Little Lake, this was achieved using a formal process of consultations with community leaders, with further input on a regular basis from parents and staff. The result is a curriculum which does not clearly follow a single approach. It is, however, future oriented; staff are keen to prepare children for later school success via skill-training. This is consistent with the official AHS education component which includes school readiness.

What Does the Future Hold?

The AHS program was established in 1995 as an early intervention program for Aboriginal children living off-reserve in urban and northern communities, and extended to children on-reserve in 1998. Little Lake preschool dates from this period. Currently, funds are available for existing AHS programs only. An extensive review of Urban and Northern AHS programs was completed in 2006, but the results have not been made public. There has been no large-scale review of on-reserve programs. In general, the program has not been subject to any type of critical attention or evaluation. This situation was noted by the OECD (2004) review team in their report on Canada, who recommended

> that independent and regular evaluations of large programmes be undertaken,
> e.g. of Aboriginal Head Start, urban Aboriginal or community services within
> a region or large city, with the intention both of raising standards and forming
> staff. (p. 13)

It is notable, however, that in the report of the National Dialogue on Federal Aboriginal Early Childhood Development Strategy (Aboriginal Research Institute of Six Nations Reserve, 2005), involving Aboriginal stakeholders from across Canada, increased funding and program coordination were priorities, whereas evaluation research received scant attention. More recently it appears that two trends are emerging. In early 2009, the INAC initiated projects on performance measurement, school success plans, and school evaluations, and secondly, there is apparent interest in establishing partnerships with provincial school boards as a possible means to off-load costs from the federal government to the provinces.

South Africa— Tshwane Preschool

South Africa was colonized first by the Dutch, soon after Jan van Riebeeck and 90 men landed in 1652 at the Cape of Good Hope. Within 10 years there was a small settlement of about 250 white people of Dutch origin (Beck, 2000). The Dutch made contact with the original Aboriginal peoples the San ('bushman') hunter-gatherers and the Khoi ('Hottentot') peoples, who herded livestock. In the early 1700s, Dutch farmers moved north and east, pushing the Khoi and San into service for the colonists while forcing them from their lands. Slaves were also brought in from East India, Madagascar, and Malaysia; a mixed-race population was eventually created through intermarriage. By the late eighteenth century, the Dutch had been joined by German and French Huguenots who were Protestants. An Afrikaner nation emerged as the Dutch colonizers, along with the less populous German and French, began to lose their attachment to Europe. There were many clashes with Bantu speaking groups, and between several of the Bantu groups themselves.

The British took over from the Dutch in 1795 and again in 1806 after a brief resurgence of Dutch control. Conflicts continued, especially with the Xhosa, one of the larger Bantu-speaking groups. With the arrival of British missionaries and the emancipation of slaves in 1834, British legal dominance began. The Afrikaners resisted British colonial rule along with its rather superficial form of racial egalitarianism. At about the same time, several black kingdoms, with whom there was much conflict, lost the struggle against white control. Reserves were created under traditional African law, but outside the reserves British control was the rule; it was non-racial in theory but excluded most people of colour in practice.

After nearly annihilating the San and Khoi, Bantu-speaking peoples and European colonists opposed one another in a series of ethnic and racial conflicts that continued until the democratic transformation of 1994. Conflict among Bantu-speaking chiefdoms was as common and severe as that between black and white. In resisting colonial expansion, black African rulers formed powerful kingdoms by incorporating neighbouring chieftaincies. The result was the consolidation of the Zulu, Xhosa, Pedi, Venda, Swazi, Sotho, Tswana, and Tsonga nations. Similarly formed was the fairly large Indian population that had developed as a result of the import of indentured labourers from India for the sugar cane plantations. Those of Dutch descent, although also white, began to see themselves as Afrikaners. Due to their disagreement with British legislation and control, they moved into the interior of the country by ox wagon. This white migration is commonly known as the Great Trek of 1835.

With the on-going conflicts between the Afrikaners and British, Afrikaners gained a degree of independence under Paul Kruger, president of the Transvaal (former name of the Zuid-Afrikaansche Republiek). However, when gold was discovered in 1886 and the arrival of large numbers of British, there was an increased threat to Afrikaner independence. This resulted in the Anglo-Boer/South African War in 1899, during which one half million British soldiers took on 65,000 Boers with black South Africans pulled in on both sides. The Boers engaged in guerrilla war tactics against the British who followed a scorched earth policy and introduced concentration camps as a measure to break the support the Boers were given by those on the farms. The result was that thousands of Boer women, children, blacks and coloureds died.

The Union of South Africa was established in 1910. There were 6 million inhabitants of which about 20% were white, 67% black, 9% coloured and 2.5% Asian. The African National Congress (ANC) came into being in 1912, beginning many years of resistance to white control. The 1913 Land Act reserved 90% of the land for white ownership. Skilled jobs were reserved for whites. The ANC supported Britain's role in the First World War in the hope of gaining their support; hundreds of black soldiers died. By the 1930s when blacks were moving into the cities, laws were passed to segregate black and white residents. In 1948 the Afrikaner Nationalist party came to power with the vote against British imperialism, introducing more and more repressive laws.

The 1950s saw increasing resistance led by the ANC and culminating in the jailing of leaders such as Nelson Mandela. The policy was one of separate development with the black populations divided into ethnic groups, each with its own restricted area or township from which they could not leave without 'passes.' A state of emergency came in 1960 when the ANC organized a passive anti-pass campaign that turned violent in Sharpeville, with many killed. When the Afrikaans leader Verwoerd took South Africa out of the British Commonwealth in 1961 the UN General Assembly imposed economic sanctions. Nelson Mandela, Walter Sisulu and others were sentenced in 1964 to life imprisonment for having led the underground resistance. The ANC continued to operate anyway. Verwoerd was assassinated, and segregation was more strictly enforced. In 1976 the youth of Soweto marched, ostensibly against being taught in Afrikaans. More violence followed, and in 1977 Steve Biko's murder by police brought the situation fully to the world's attention.

Apartheid finally ended when then President de Klerk lifted restrictions on the ANC and other opposition groups and released Mandela from prison. The first democratic election was held in 1994. The ANC won and Nelson Mandela became President of South Africa.

South Africa's history has moved quickly from near absolute white control and near complete division of the races to a more unified nation with the majority black population in charge—a nation whose dream is one of unity in the face of extreme diversity; there are now 11 official languages. The effects of this history on the schooling of black children in particular have been profound and they persist today. While white communities in South Africa had developed along the lines of the other colonies, with the establishment of western school systems and social welfare policies to protect children, little investment was put into educational services for black children. For example, in the 1970s about 2% of South Africa's education budget went to schools for black children (Beck, 2000). In addition to violent reaction against apartheid, one can still observe the legacy of colonization in the all-black township communities outside the major cities, within their schools and preschools. It is here we see a paucity of books within which children can find images of themselves or familiar situations portrayed. It is in the organization of classrooms and the presence of few materials that we see very little that says, "This is South Africa." It is here that we see a language-in-education policy that is meant to build and reinforce group and individual identities, while unity is being promoted through increasing teaching via English.

Although much more will be said about policy and curriculum matters in chapter 3, a little background is needed here. The dawn of the new democracy in 1994 brought children's rights to the centre stage of South African politics for the first time. The country's Constitution (Act 108 of 1996) guarantees all children equal rights. According to Section 29 (a) of the Bill of Rights, "everyone has the right to basic education." This statement opened the doors for all young children to participate actively in education. As the reader will see in chapter 3, the Department of Education developed legislation and policies that are critical in entrenching and sustaining the rights of the child. White Paper No. 1 on Education and Training (1995) paved the way for the introduction of the Interim Policy of Early Childhood Development, which gave rise to the launching of the three-year National Reception Year Pilot Project (1997-1999). This pilot project was undertaken to investigate a national system for a year-long program of public provisioning of early childhood development, namely the reception year[4] (Grade R) for five to six-year-olds (DoE, 1995) in disadvantaged areas. The long-term goal of the government was that by 2010 all learners entering Grade 1 should have participated in an accredited Reception Year program. In order to be accredited, a centre must comply with requirements of several government departments, including minimum staff qualifications. Achievement of the government's goal thus remains an ongoing challenge since the majority of centres are still unregistered and unlicensed.

The Nationwide Audit of ECD Provisioning in South Africa (DoE, 2001c) revealed that less than 26% of preschool teachers, most of whom were black, held qualifications recognized by the DoE, suggesting that many preschool teachers lacked the training and background experience to be effective practitioners in the new South Africa's burgeoning number of preschools. The preschools were and are being looked to as a means to improve children's readiness for school, and to combat what was perceived as a problem of 'maladjustment' on the part of many black children, in particular. There are two lingering problems however. One is that there has yet been little thinking at higher levels to adjust schools to children, rather than children to schools. As the following quote from a speech by the Minister of Education in 2005 suggests, the problem is seen to lie within the child.

Our particular challenge here is that nearly a quarter of our children under 5 are stunted and one in 10 underweight for their age. The youngest and those in rural areas are worst affected. We know that maternal education is the key to child survival and that women in rural areas have suffered most from the legacy of inadequate education under apartheid.

What this means is that many children are simply unprepared for the transition to formal schooling. And the evidence is clear for all to see in the results of the key competency tests, like the one last year that found more than 60% of Grade 3s in the Western Cape are not achieving literacy and numeracy levels required by the national curriculum and 15% could not read or calculate at the most basic level.[5]

Another problem is that the condition of the preschools varies enormously. This affects children's experience prior to entering Grade R where, at least theoretically, some form of equity can be reached via the Grade R curriculum (the Revised National Curriculum Statement of 2004) that was designed for all. The majority of teachers who are now responsible for teaching in Grade R have undergone retraining on the official mandated curriculum; the quality of that training, however, is reputed to be quite uneven (Phatudi, 2007).

As evidence that a colonial mindset continues, in May of 2003 the same Minister of Education stated, "We begin with the teaching and the understanding in early childhood of nursery rhymes, such as: Baa, Baa, Black Sheep...."[6] One might ask if there is not a more suitable rhyme to be found, perhaps in several of South Africa's languages.

Tshwane Preschool's Location

What does Tshwane preschool look like and to what extent is it similar to or different from other preschools in the region?[7] Tshwane is located on a large piece of property in a former black township (a town) about 45 kilometres from a major city. The roads are roughly paved and lined with small cement block or brick bungalow houses. There are few green spaces or trees. The preschool building is a solid, well-built single storey red brick structure. There is a large playground with some climbing equipment at the back and a small vegetable garden. Inside there are four classrooms, a large kitchen, a bathroom with child-sized toilets and sinks, an office for the principal, and a room which was being turned into a sick room. On the hallway walls there are many posters, six of which are about HIV/AIDS prevention.

Tshwane preschool evolved over the years from being housed in a church in 1985, then in a poorly-built small building (1987-1995), and eventually to its present location and solid condition. The initiative of establishing the school came from the principal, whom the school is named after. She is a qualified teacher who is registered with the teachers' professional organization, the South African Council of Educators (SACE). As a primary school teacher, the principal recognized that something needed to be done for the children who were seen to be loitering on the streets without adult supervision or anything to do. She raised her concerns with the local Lutheran church minister who then consulted the membership. Eventually, the church decided to use its building as a preschool since it was not used during week days. She became the first teacher and principal of the school. With the support of the school and local community, the preschool gradually raised sufficient funds to purchase a plot of land. The first structure close to its present location was, in the principal's words, a tin shack, very hot in the summer months and bitter cold in the winter. The principal embarked on a fundraising drive and by 1996 the walls of a brick structure were up. With the assistance of an Irish group who donated money for the roofing, the school was completed in time for the 1996 intake. Today the school boasts four classrooms including one for toddlers.

Within the preschool there is a fresco type of painting in the central hallway area depicting the principal's experience as a preschool teacher from her days in Botswana to the school as it is today in South Africa. During apartheid, the surrounding area was a homeland for the Batswana people. At that time, ECE enjoyed subsidization from the government. Tshwane preschool benefited from this arrangement. It had three qualified teachers, including the principal, who were paid by the government.

The classrooms each contain a teacher's table, small tables and chairs for children, a carpeted or linoleum area for the whole group to sit on the floor, small cupboards for their belongings, teacher-made posters of letters and numbers, as well as children's art work on the walls. Several of the posters depict white people or racially ambiguous people, such as the one displaying "Our body." The few dolls in play corners are white. More will be said about materials and space in chapter 5.

Tshwane served about 110 children from 18 months to age 6. The children were grouped into separate classrooms by age. The focal grade was Grade R (reception year), designated as the school preparation year. By the end of the study, the Grade R class had been moved into the local public school, in line with South Africa's policy of providing a reception year for all. The children arrive between 7 and 8 in the morning and leave around 1:00 p.m., while some stay for what is referred to as after care, until about 5:00 p.m. The after care program is mainly custodial, allowing children to take a nap and providing them with a snack. This costs 2 rand per day.

The principal arrives early in the morning to be there for the few children whose parents must leave them as they go into the city for work. Breakfast is provided by the preschool. Similarly, she alone stays until 6 p.m. most days until the few parents who work in the city are able to pick up their children. The principal was clearly very proud of the school and dedicated to it and its children. For example, when children are sick she takes them to a nearby clinic that is free. She also reported that parents who are too poor to pay the fees volunteer to do things at the centre—clean the grounds and windows, or look after the garden. They do not have to be asked. This suggests a strong community spirit and good school-parent relations. The school enjoys government support for teacher salaries—7000 rand per month (about $1000) for the Grade R teacher. The principal's salary is the same as that of a regular school principal.

Tshwane welcomes children with special needs. Approximately 10% of the children are AIDS orphans, being cared for by grandmothers. They are exempt from fees. During the years of the research project there were three children with Down Syndrome, one of whom was the size of a three-year-old though she was six at the start of the study, and still attending the preschool when the study ended four years later. When she came to the school at age 4, she could not walk. Now she walks and talks and is reported to be very active. All the children come from the neighbouring township where there is a high rate of unemployment. Parents are mainly working class with limited education, most often dropouts from high school or primary school. Many of the parents are younger women (18-25) who are on social grants (welfare) and not working. The principal reported that she sometimes has to prod the young mothers who receive their funds on the 18th of the month so that they can then pay the school fees of 170 Rand per month (about $30), the next day. The home language of the majority of the children is Setswana; this is also the language of learning and teaching, observed to have been mixed with some English in Grade R, to prepare the children for school where they will be taught via English.

A Typical Day at Tshwane

The school day at Tshwane commences as early as seven o'clock in the morning. Some parents drop off their children before catching the early train, bus, or taxi to town for work. Most of the children are however brought to the school by taxi vans and some by older school-going siblings. They are welcomed by the teachers at the entrance or go straight to class. As Table 2 suggests, the day starts with breakfast as most of the children come to school with empty stomachs.

Table 2. Sample Schedule at Tshwane, Morning Program

Time	Activity
7:00 a.m.	Staff arrival
8:00	Pupils arrive
8:10	Independent activity
9:00	Breakfast
9:30	Morning 'rug-time': greetings, devotion, weather, discussion
10:00	Activity (story, music, movement)
11:00	Developmental 'rug-time'
11:30	Pre-reading skill, pre-writing skill, number concepts
12:00	Lunch, rest
1:00 p.m.	Departure

Three meals are provided as the children spend most of the day at school. Breakfast is followed by a prayer and morning circle, a story telling or reading activity. This is followed by free choice activities, then creative activities done both inside and outside the classroom. The teacher reads a story from a big book. Due to the lack of African language books, the teacher sometimes reads from an English book with Setswana words pasted over the English text. The stories are normally discussed in Setswana. The normal daily program which teachers reported was obtained from NGOs is followed. This includes literacy, numeracy, and life skills time slots, free play activities, singing, outdoor play and creative activities. The formal program ends with a story and lunch. Those who go home are fetched by siblings, taxis, or parents, while those who remain behind are given small mats to sleep on. Rest time is followed by outdoor play or, if weather does not permit, free play indoors. The formal preschool schedule ends at 1:00 in the afternoon, however many stay afterwards for after care, as mentioned earlier. The schedule above was followed loosely.

Teaching in Grade R

During the time of the research project, the 2004 Revised National Curriculum was being trialled and implemented. Thus what we observed was in a state of transition, with elements of the new Grade R curriculum which emphasizes preliminary skills in literacy, numeracy and life skills mixed with the preschool daily program that preceded its implementation. Much of this program reflected the influence of non-governmental organizations that, during the apartheid days, kept early childhood development programs running in the townships. Thus one can identify elements of Montessori, High/Scope and Reggio Emilia principles, adapted at times to the culture, traditions, values, and backgrounds of the children. Purchased materials are complemented by home- and self-made materials.

Given the large number of unqualified and under-qualified teachers, implementing the official curriculum is a significant challenge. In studies conducted by Botha, Maree and De Witt (2005), which focused on mathematics activities and Phatudi (2007), which examined transitions, it was found that despite the teachers being in relatively well-resourced schools they still found it difficult to follow the curriculum. Botha et al. (2005) reported that although the curriculum change required teachers to specifically plan mathematics activities, teachers were ignoring it. Phatudi (2007) found formal activities, particularly the use of worksheets, prominent in Grade R classrooms.

Since preschools fall outside the jurisdiction of the education ministry, Grade R classes in preschool centres are not monitored by government officials, allowing them to adapt the curriculum and activities to local perceptions of the needs of the children. This appeared to be the case at Tshwane preschool, despite the fact that the Grade R teacher had undergone training provided by the Provincial DoE. With the development of a universal Grade R system within the public schools, subject to government monitoring, this local adaptability would appear to be lost.

Teacher Qualifications

According to the Nationwide Audit on ECD (2000), nearly 70% of South Africa's teaching corps has no formal, recognized qualifications. With the Skills Development Act of 2003 the government introduced funding to standardize qualifications and thus to upgrade teacher qualifications. Learnerships were offered via service providers such as NGOs by the Education, Training and Development Practices (ETDP) Sector Education and Training Authority (SETA) funded by compulsory contributions of 1% of employer payrolls. These learnerships are work-based and therefore compel whoever registers to complement her/his classroom teaching and learning with a practical component of teaching in a preschool. There is a stipend attached to the learnerships, so that teachers can earn a salary for its duration.

Physical Resources of Tshwane

Tshwane preschool, despite being located in a working class township, is relatively well resourced with posters, building blocks, puzzles, paint, crayons, swings, a jungle gym, and many other materials. These church and NGO-donated resources create room for a variety of activities which enrich learning so that Tshwane preschool is reputed to be of high quality. Our observations carried out in several other preschools for comparative purposes would concur with this view. As noted above, the Grade R teacher now holds formal qualifications due to recent upgrading made available at the provincial level, and the principal is a certificated primary school teacher. The introduction of the official Grade R curriculum has given teachers guidance and confidence in knowing that what they are doing is approved. One teacher referred to the 2005 Curriculum Guide as "her bible." Anecdotal reports from local primary schools suggest that Tshwane children are considered to be well prepared for formal schooling.

What Does the Future Hold?

Many Grade R classes have now been moved out of preschool settings and into government primary schools. This is a very recent key change in the preparation of South Africa's children for formal schooling that demands observation and description in light of the findings of studies such as the one this book is based on. Of note is the fact that educational policy in the post-apartheid South Africa has borrowed from a western model of outcomes-based education (OBE). This is reflected in the Grade R policy for assessment standards in which children are expected to "differentiate between play and useful tasks at home," and "participate in creative activities that will stimulate entrepreneurial thinking (e.g. drawing, cutting, singing, playing, talking)" (Dept. of Education, 2008).

Tshwane preschool provides a concrete example of the kind of social change that has taken place in South Africa since the end of apartheid; however, the viability of Tshwane preschool is, at this writing, precarious. Its location fell into the area that was reassigned to another province due to the government re-demarcation of provincial boundaries. This meant that all the privileges it previously enjoyed were withdrawn as new authorities assumed control. The Grade R class was moved from the preschool to the nearby public primary school, as per Ministry of Education policy to make Grade R accessible to all. Qualified teachers in preschools who were paid by the government are being relocated to primary schools. In addition, the number of children attending Tshwane is dropping as more and more children are bussed to city schools. With the end of apartheid parents in the townships started bussing their children to formerly all-white suburban schools that enjoyed good reputations for offering quality education. This has resulted in the depopulation of township schools with many closing their doors or merging with neighbouring ones, further reducing their quality and connectedness to local communities, local traditions and languages.

India— Sunbeam Anganwadi

British colonization of India remains as one of the most influential phases of her history. From the early sixteenth century, India witnessed a steady influx of foreigners. Their interests varied in purpose and approach. The Portuguese established the first European trading centre in Kollam, Kerala, followed by Vasco da Gama, a Portuguese sailor who established a trading centre in Goa in 1510. The Dutch, British, and French entered at the beginning of the seventeenth century, primarily for trade. The erstwhile Mughal Empire faced a decline in the early eighteenth century and the Europeans gradually took over certain regions of the country.

India had a fairly vast number of provinces, each functioning under a large or a small kingdom. The kingdoms were often wealthy, expansive, and lacked co-ordination and a unifying governing body. Battles frequently ensued, with assertion of power, capture and expansion of territories, and amassment of wealth as primary motives. The British forces in India at the time had a major task of guarding the British East India Company property. The Battle of Plassey on 23 June 1757 changed this. Although inferior in number to the Bengal armed forces, the British forces were approached by a commander in chief of the army of the Nawab of Bengal. The strategy was to demand logistical support to overthrow the Nawab in return for trade grants. Under the command of Robert Clive, the forces betrayed the Nawab and helped defeat him. The commander-in-chief was installed on the throne as a ruler, but not without a price. The potential to conquer smaller Indian kingdoms was soon realized by the British and served to mark the beginning of the colonial era. By the early nineteenth century, the British exerted direct or indirect control over all of present-day India. Consequently, the influence of the British extended in all spheres ranging from railroads and communications, education, and schooling to the social fabric of the society.

The colonial era of the British was popularly known as the *British Raj*. The extent of its impact on education is described by Chaudhary (2009), who reports that over the course of the nineteenth century, the indigenous system of schooling in British India was replaced by the new state system of education developed by the East

India Company until 1857, and was controlled by the British Crown from 1858 to 1919. The provision of primary education was decentralized and left to local governments, such as rural and urban municipal councils in the early 1880s. However, the pedagogy and philosophy guiding education during the colonial period remained as a debateable issue. The only opportunities for elementary education in the nineteenth century were provided by non-government schools established by western Christian missions and Indian social and religious reform organizations.

Oriental learning, which was a classical learning in local, indigenous languages, was promoted by a few eighteenth century officials who had become scholars of languages such as Persian, Tamil, and Sanskrit. The *anglicists* on the other hand, advocated the introduction of institutions for western learning based upon the British curriculum with English as the medium of instruction (Zastoupil & Moir, 1999). The anglicists outnumbered the orientals and by the early nineteenth century English was made the official language of government business. Scrase (1993) maintains that by the middle of the nineteenth century, colonial education policy had enforced the recommendations that schooling should be in English, with the promotion of European and British ideas and values, and that the state should control education at every stage. English still remains and maintains a dominant position in Indian social and commercial life.

Self-government was introduced in the 1860s by British officials representing direct rule by the Crown. This led to a shifting of financial responsibility for education to a growing Indian middle class. While the local educational spending was directed towards the education of urban boys for professions, rural and girl's education suffered a major setback. Families often chose to send their daughters to 'all girls' educational institutions where schools followed a general curriculum and the medium of instruction were the vernacular languages.

The twentieth century saw a growing nationalist movement gaining support from Indian leaders. One of the goals was to develop nationalist educational paradigms and challenge the colonial model of education. Mahatma Gandhi instilled the idea of teaching basic literacy in vernacular languages to the majority of the population. The slow but steady reform movement gradually developed into the Indian Independence Movement. The independence movement attained its objective with the independence of India on the 15 August 1947. The fight for freedom from colonialism meant that major decisions pertaining to a shift in educational ideologies waited until after 1947.

Addressing important issues related to education and schooling has been a significant part of the Indian constitution since independence. The need for early intervention on behalf of children, especially those from economically marginalized communities, has been well recognized. India reached a population of one billion in 2001. It has the largest child population in the world. However, the overall level of human development is considered to be quite low.

A National Focus Group on Early Childhood Education (2006) report notes that India has a wealth of traditional practices in ECCE that date back almost 5,000 years, although the formal documentation occurred only in the latter half of the nineteenth century. Several provisions in the constitution of India, either as fundamental rights or as directive principles of state policy are utilized to promote ECCE services in the country. As a sequel to the adoption of the National Policy for Children (1974), the Government of India evolved the Integrated Child Development Services Scheme, popularly abbreviated as ICDS. Over a period of time, this centrally sponsored scheme of ICDS, which came into existence in 1975 in 33 selected community development blocks of the country, has come out as one of the innovative programmes of its kind and the largest public initiative in the world to offer the early childhood education and care services in an integrated way (Working Group on Development of Children for the Eleventh Five-Year Plan, 2007). The basic premise of this centrally sponsored and state administered nation-wide program, revolves around the common consensus among educationists, researchers, and practitioners that early childhood education and care are inseparable issues and must be considered as one. Based upon this fundamental assumption, the functioning of the program has been designed in such an integrated way so as to meet early childhood education and care needs on a continuum basis adopting a holistic approach (Working Group, 2007).

Sunbeam's Location

Sunbeam *anganwadi* is an ICDS program located about 40 kilometres from a large city in the state of Gujarat, in small town called 'Vallabh Vidyanagar.' The anganwadi is surrounded by a community comprized of working class families. The term anganwadi indicates a courtyard garden. Courtyards are a characteristic of a majority of Indian homes. In line with the non-formal approach of the ICDS, the preschools are named anganwadis, indicating a place where young children normally play. Typically, each anganwadi has its own single-storied building made of cement and bricks. A small portion of the room, usually at the back, is used as a storage area for food, resources for children, and supplements for pregnant women and lactating mothers, and iron-folate tablets for adolescent girls.

Sunbeam anganwadi functions in a vacant house owned by the preschool teacher's family. While the teacher's family live independently in a separate house, they use this house as a mode of service to the community. The preschool caters to children residing within 1,000 households in the vicinity. The majority of the people in the community are Hindus and belong to a scheduled caste (SC). Most families in the community had three to four children on average. The women earned a living by working as maids, while the men worked as office helpers in educational institutes or in the *panchayat* (local government). Some men in the community were unemployed.

Typically, the preschool education component of the ICDS caters to children in the age range of 3 to 6 years. The majority of the children attending Sunbeam were between 3 and 6 years, however, most days saw a mixed group including infants, older siblings, and toddlers. Most of the children were from local families, while a few were children of migrants who had moved there from neighbouring states.

The house consisted of a small veranda where the teacher and the children removed their footwear. Adjoining the veranda was a small rectangular room, filled with displays of growth charts for children, a weigh scale, and a clock. The room often served as a waiting area for parents and visitors. A tiny window overlooking the community was located on one of its walls. Children often used to peak through the window onto the road or play with the sunbeams that entered through the slits. Adjacent to this room was the kitchen, where food for the children was prepared by the anganwadi helper. The kitchen also had containers which could stock grains like wheat, rice, and pulses for up to a year.

Major activities of the preschool program were carried out in the biggest room of the house, situated just opposite the veranda. It had a fan and a tube light, a daily 'time table' for the children, colourful mobiles and posters related to animals, birds, vaccinations, and nutrition. The room had a window, consistently kept closed to avoid distractions for children. As a result, the room often would be suffocatingly hot, especially during summers and power failures. The room opened up to an adjoining sanitary facility, consisting of a separate bathroom and a toilet.

On arrival at the anganwadi, children were made to sit cross-legged on the floor. Most of the days, children sat on the floor mats facing the teacher. During action songs, children would stand up and form circles or semi-circles. It was only when the children were left on their own (during meal/arrival time) that they sat according to their wish: either in groups or alone.

The teacher-child ratio was 1:30 with 12 boys and 18 girls registered in the 3 to 6 year-old age group. Children younger than 3 years of age participate in the program accompanied by their mother, grandmother, or siblings. The adults or older siblings would often stay at the back of the room for the entire duration of the program, or leave part-way through. The helper would take care of the basic physiological needs of the children, by ensuring the children drank enough water, took breaks for toileting, and washed hands. Children were taught and encouraged to use the toilet in the anganwadi. The anganwadi had no defined play space. The indoor play area was the same room where the children would sit close together and do the activities directed by the anganwadi.

There were few play materials: a cloth ball and cloth elephant made by the anganwadi worker seemed to be the children's favourites.

A Typical Day at Sunbeam

The day began around 10:45 a.m., with the helper fetching a few children from nearby houses. With the anganwadi lying in the absolute vicinity of the community, no specific routines were observed regarding who brought the children to the preschool. Mothers, grandparents, older siblings, fathers, and sometimes even the neighbours were found to be a part of the morning drop off.

The anganwadi teacher welcomed the children at the doorstep, instructing them to remove their slippers before helping them settle down in the room for the morning ritual of prayers and attendance. This was accompanied by free flowing conversations about yesterday's events, breakfast at home, inquiry about hygiene (bath, nails, combed hair), and so on. Classroom activity consisted of an action song or repetition of names of vegetables, fruits, animals, and colours from the display charts. A short break for water and toileting followed the free play session, after which the meals were served. Every meal began with prayers followed by instructions from the teacher to not soil the floor with food, to eat carefully, and how food would help them become physically strong.

The ICDS scheme has a provision to provide one mid-day meal for each child. Children attending Sunbeam anganwadi often carried light snacks packed by their mothers, who used to leave early for their own work. As a result, mothers often instructed children to eat it once they reach the anganwadi. The anganwadi teacher was aware of the practice and did not discourage children from eating their snacks. However, she ensured the snacks were eaten early in the program schedule, to ensure children did not miss the regular mid-day meal. On various occasions children were served the meals in the tiffin boxes they carried from home. Thus, if a child was unable to finish his/her meal, it could be taken back home.

The post-meal session would generally be a quiet time, in which the teacher would tell a story and ask children questions pertaining to the main characters. A few children would run out through the main door towards their homes, right after the meal. The teacher would sometimes restrain them, but mostly remain unperturbed at the snag in the routine. However, the promise of a story or a song would ensure most of the children remained until the very end of the program.

The departure would typically consist of the teacher at the door bidding goodbye to everyone, asking children to arrive on time the next day. Daily informal talks invariably ensued with most mothers fetching their children, as they asked the teacher about the day. The preschool typically followed an 11:00 a.m. to 2:00 p.m. schedule, changing to 9:00 a.m. to 12:00 p.m. during summer. The lengths of the program components were flexible, as decided upon by the anganwadi.

Table 3. Sample Schedule at Sunbeam

Time	Activity
10:30 a.m.	Staff arrival
10:45	Arrival of children
11:00	Prayer, attendance, general discussions with children
11:30	Classroom activity (music, chart reading, number concepts)
12:45	Free play
1:00	Meals
1:30-2:00	Quiet time consisting of stories and discussions followed by departure

Teaching in the Anganwadi

A variety of curricular guidelines for ECCE are available in India. However, a large gap exists between what is prescribed and what is practiced. Activities of preschool education under the ICDS are usually conducted for a period ranging from 45 minutes to two hours duration daily, with minimal play and learning material support (Working Group on Development of Children for the Eleventh Five Year Plan, 2007-2012).

The program at Sunbeam did not have a focus or requirement on learning to read or write. Children usually encountered a non-formal environment. Stories, songs, conversations, and free play found a wide berth in most of the program even while they may not have been transacted in the recommended format.

The program assumed a teacher-dominated format with active participation on her behalf. Teacher direction was evident in the learning of concepts, where children would unfailingly repeat after her the names of vegetables, fruits, animals, and colours and follow instructions of proper posture and eating at meal times. Children anticipated that the anganwadi would control and direct their physical movement. The anganwadi and the helper were frequently observed to be involved in manually lifting children, arranging them in lines, correcting their postures and generally deciding the boundaries of their movement. The concepts taught were linked with the home or local community, which is more in line with the preschool education scheme of the ICDS.

Children interacted with each other whenever there was an opportunity, usually when the teacher was busy with administrative tasks. Outdoor play was minimal but not absent. The teacher considered it an important part of the program, but not essential. Play materials were not available in quantity and neither were they readily accessible to children, save for a small throw ball or a rag doll. All anganwadi centres are equipped with toy kits/resources for children. However, the anganwadi worker did not always allow children to handle them, fearing the toys would break.

Teacher Qualifications

The anganwadi workers, supervisors, and Child Development Project Officers (CDPOs) of the ICDS programmes are provided with induction and in-service training programs. The National Institute of Public Cooperation and Child Development (NIPCCD) coordinates training of ICDS functionaries. Training for the grassroots functionaries is provided in partnership between the government and non-government sectors. This operates through the Anganwadi Workers Training Centre (AWC) and Middle Level Training Centre (MLTC) for CDPOs and supervisors. There is some training backlog of ICDS functionaries at all levels in the country. Das (2003) reports an evaluation of ICDS scheme by the National Council of Applied Economic Research found 84% of the functionaries to be trained, but most of the training is pre-service and in-service training remains an unmet need.

The National Council of Teacher Education (NCTE) as a statutory body has the mandate to provide the norms and standards for preschool teacher programs. Changes in the ECCE workers and teachers can be expected once the norms laid down by NCTE are enforced.

The Nature of Teaching at Sunbeam

The National Council of Educational Research and Training's (NCERT) *Minimum Specifications for Pre-schools*, published in 1996, sets out basic norms and specifications for ECE centres. However, the document guidelines do not restrict program implementers from designing their own interventions, independent of these guidelines, as was the case at Sunbeam.

Sunbeam anganwadi differs from other anganwadi centres in terms of infrastructure. A typical anganwadi in an ICDS setup is an independent one-room building located in the community or near the local primary school. Sunbeam functions in a residential built-up area, located in the midst of a housing colony. It contains a separate kitchen, a program room and attached sanitary facilities. Children attending Sunbeam thus encounter spaces not very different from their own homes.

The teacher-parent interaction was observed to be functional, related to the health, hygiene, and attendance of the child. The scope for child-child interaction seemed minimal due to the overall teacher-directedness of the program; however, interactions were evident during meals, free play, or when the anganwadi was busy with administrative work. The child-material interactions usually took place during meal times (children played with tiffin boxes). A single picture book used by the teacher to display pictures of various birds, animals, and fruits was much sought after, long after the book had been closed.

The anganwadi worker at Sunbeam considered taking care of young children as 'god's work' and maintained cordial relations with the people in the community. Both the anganwadi worker and the helper approached their work with sincerity and tried to incorporate the learnings from their in-service training in the program.

What Does the Future Hold?

The Working Group on Development of Children for the Eleventh Five Year Plan (2007-2012) reports on the 'ICDS in the Eleventh Five-Year Plan' and states that stimulation at the early childhood stage involves efforts to activate the child's early development. Thus promoting early stimulation activities through home-based models or an institutional setup would be an important aspect for all the interventions of ICDS. The execution of the program would include delivery of an integrated package of basic services—health care, nutritional nourishment, and early childhood educational nurturance to children—so as to reach a multitude of objectives including development of school readiness competencies and various others psycho-social domains.

NOTES

[1]   The term genocide did not exist prior to the Holocaust, but the practice did. It is defined by the 1948 UN Convention as "an act intended to destroy a national, ethnic, racial or religious group by killing, causing bodily or mental harm, deliberately inflicting conditions of life designed to bring about physical destruction, preventing births, forcibly transferring children to another group" (Fein,1993).

[2]   The Quiet Revolution in Quebec refers to the period of time from the early 1960s through the late 1970s that focused on the role of French in Quebec society and on the power relations between the then dominant English-speaking numerical minority and the French-speaking numerical majority. Several bills and laws were passed reinforcing and thus protecting the French language and culture with Bill 101 in 1977 affirming French as the official language of schooling in Quebec. The small English-speaking minority were granted historical rights to English language schooling for their children.

[3]   In this project the video-taping day was taken as a main source of information about what constituted 'a typical' day in each centre, with the data corroborated by observations on many other days, as well as through discussions with teachers and observations in several other preschools.

[4]   In South Africa, Grade R refers to the reception year which is the equivalent of the North American kindergarten.

[5]   March 2, 2005 Address by the Minister of Education, South Africa, Naledi Pandor, MP, at the Early Childhood Development Conference, Birchwood Conference Centre, Johannesburg.

[6]   Some readers may recall that this British nursery rhyme goes on to say, "have you any wool? Yes sir, yes sir, three bags full. One for my master, one for my dame, and one for the little boy who lives in the lane."

[7]   This information stems from interviews with the former principal of Tshwane Preschool, as well as video footage.

CHAPTER 3

EARLY CHILDHOOD POLICY AND CURRICULUM LANDSCAPES

This chapter describes the policy context of the three preschools with particular reference to curriculum. An official curriculum, issued by a government agency, describes how and what is to be taught, as a vehicle for achieving national goals and aims. While curricula at the preschool level tend to be less specific with regard to particular subjects to be taught, the objectives, as expressed in policy documents, are no less tied to the kind of citizen and society that is envisioned.

CANADA

Aboriginal Head Start

Aboriginal Head Start (AHS) is an early childhood intervention program designed to enhance child development and school readiness for Aboriginal preschool-aged children. It is administered by federal government health agencies in two divisions according to children's place of residence: Aboriginal Head Start Urban and Northern Communities (AHSUNC) for First Nation, Métis, and Inuit (FNMI) children living off-reserve in urban and larger northern communities, and Aboriginal Head Start On Reserve (AHSOR). The two versions of what is essentially the same program is an artefact of the colonial relationship between the government of Canada and Aboriginal peoples. AHSOR has recently been called First Nations Head Start in some federal government publications, and is called BC First Nations Head Start in British Columbia (Terbasket & Greenwood, 2007). In addition to the two AHS programs, other government-funded early childhood programs for FNMI children include the First Nations and Inuit Child Care Initiative (administered by the Department of Human Resources and Skills Development Canada), the Department of Indian and Northern Affairs Kindergarten program, and other child care and kindergarten programs at the national and provincial levels.

The number of government-supported programs for young FNMI children has increased dramatically over the past 15 years (Greenwood, de Leeuw, & Ngaroimata Fraser, 2007). Up to the 1990s the major initiatives in preschool education over two centuries in Canada largely excluded FNMI children (Prochner, 2004, 2009a). A scattering of compensatory programs were established in the 1960s along the lines of the U.S. Head Start preschools. An example is a preschool centre in Moosonee, Ontario, that opened in late 1965 for young First Nation's children and their mothers. The program is described in a newspaper report from the time:

> The preschoolers will be taught English in that period of childhood when the mind is most receptive to a new language, and will therefore enter formal

33

school equipped to proceed as rapidly as their schoolmates of another race. ("A most hopeful experiment," 1965, p. 06)

This school readiness program, as well as others in Canada, were intended to replace First Nations languages with English, and were modelled after Project Head Start in the United States.

A program for Indigenous children called American Indian Head Start was part of the original Head Start Initiative in 1965; Alaska Native Head Start (ANHS) was developed in the 1990s. The Special Field Projects branch of the Office of Equal Opportunity administered AIHS along with Head Start programs in Puerto Rico, the U.S. Virgin Islands, and the U.S. Trust Territory of the Pacific Islands (Small, 1979). The history of the development of Head Start for Indigenous children is related by Jessen (1974) and Niles and Byers (2008). In the late 1960s, Head Start worked with the local communities and the Bureau of Indian Affairs (BIA) to incorporate and extend the existing BIA kindergartens and to develop staff training, notably through the Bank Street College of Education. In 2003, the AIHS program was serving relatively few children—approximately 20,000 children in 180 settings (including 40 Early Head Start). This was a small increase from 1986, when there were 106 programs with no Early Head Start (Washington & Oyemade, 1987). Few reviews of the history of Project Head Start include any reference to AIHS and little research has been undertaken (Marks & Graham, 2004). There is, in general, a paucity of research on early education and intervention programs for Aboriginal children in the United States, as noted by Niles, Byers, and Krueger (2007), who found in their review that "Indigenous children are absent from formal early childhood research studies and programs ... [and are] systematically excluded in even the best-known early childhood program in the US," with the result that "no longitudinal research in the literature relates to the success of Indigenous children" (p. 113). This situation has not stopped intervention programs developed for other populations from being applied to Indigenous children.

The neglected status of AIHS was described at a Senate Committee Hearing on Head Start Reauthorization in 1994, at which time, seven "Indian issues" were identified: the proposed decentralization of federal administrative functions for serving Indian children; the family income requirement; restrictions related to tribal membership and members living off-reserve; a need for prenatal and infant-toddler programs; physical facilities; funds for training and staff; and the expansion of the program. Linda Kills Crow, then President of the National Indian Head Start Directors Association, stated at the hearing: "In our communities ... the early childhood program [is] often ... the only game in town. If we didn't have Indian Head Start, our children would have nothing" (Senate Committee Hearing, 1994, p. 9).

Project Head Start is a program where participation is restricted to low-income families. AIHS/ANHS are grounded in a social welfare ideology which holds that the primary risk factor for child development and school success is poverty, and that poverty is the result of environmental factors. Insofar as children's early experience at home and in their communities does not prepare them for the skills, language, and behaviours required for success in formal schooling contexts

(Freeman & Hatch, 1989), they are considered to be unready for school. Head Start programs, and other similar initiatives, are designed to make up or compensate for these perceived deficits, which are assumed to have their origins in the children's culture, community, or family.

Though Project Head Start did not pay explicit attention to culture, parents judged the majority of programs to be responsive to family diversity (Weststat, Xtria, & the CDM Group, 2003), and the curriculum of most programs had some cultural component (Marks & Graham, 2004). In the case of AIHS, pressure from parents and the community in the early years of the program ensured that culture was included as a program component (Jipson, 1991). Children's wellbeing therefore included cultural survival—where children were seen to be at risk due to post-colonial cultural disintegration—as well as inadequate physical care and preparation for schooling. Miskimmin (2007) argued that a similar situation was true of AHS in Canada, where Health Canada, the program sponsor, regarded children as being at risk on multiple dimensions by virtue of their Aboriginality.

Aboriginal Head Start began as a Canadian version of U.S. Head Start in 1995 (Budgell, 1998). The aims of the Canadian and United States' programs for Indigenous children are outlined in Table 4. The research basis for AHS was drawn from Project Head Start studies in the United States with non-Aboriginal children, as described in a document compiled for project operators (Sheila Clark & Associates, n.d.). However, there was a strong emphasis on community participation in curriculum development and program management in the Canadian case. There is evidence that the program operators were in contact with their U.S. counterparts while developing the programs in Canada. The Calgary Native Head Start Program was established in 1994 prior to the start-up of AHS, as a service of the Calgary Native Women's Shelter Society. Staff members from the Blackfeet Tribe Head Start Program in Montana provided initial training, and U.S. Head Start Bureau policy handbooks were used as the basis for the Calgary program's handbook (Weasel Traveller, 1995). Formal contact between the Canadian and U.S. programs continued with the Canadian director attending the annual National Indian Head

Table 4. Mandates of Aboriginal Head Start (Canada) and American Indian Head Start (USA) (Public Health Agency of Canada, 2004a; U.S. Department of Health & Human Service, n.d.)

Aboriginal Head Start	American Indian Head Start
The primary goal of the AHS Initiative is to demonstrate that locally controlled and designed early intervention strategies can provide Aboriginal preschool children in urban and northern settings with a positive sense of themselves, a desire for learning and opportunities to develop fully and successfully as young people	Provides American Indian and Alaska Native children and families nationally with comprehensive health, educational, nutritional, socialization and other developmental services promoting school readiness. These services are directed primarily toward economically disadvantaged preschool children (ages 3 to 5) and infants and toddlers (birth through age 3).

Start Directors Association meetings in the United States (Public Health Agency of Canada, 1999). Intervention programs for young Aboriginal children in Canada have followed other international models in addition to Project Head Start; for example, the Home Instruction for Parents of Preschool Youngsters (HIPPY) program has been implemented as Aboriginal Hippy in British Columbia (Beatch, 2004). HIPPY was developed in Israel in 1968, and aims to support children's school readiness by modifying the parenting practices of 'at risk' parents (Powell, 2007; Rich, n.d.). In this case, 'at risk' refers to parents who were living in poverty.

Aboriginal Head Start (Canada) was not specifically designed as a poverty program and has no mandated economic criterion for enrolment. However, some AHS sites have established their own guidelines that now may include economic criteria. The design of AHS, reached through community consultation, includes six integrated components, with the first being Aboriginal culture and language. The other components are education and school readiness; parental involvement; health promotion; nutrition, and social support. Thus while AHS shares a general framework with AIHS as a comprehensive community-based program administered within a government division of health, it differs in its explicit aim to be a site and stimulus for cultural education.

In 2004, at the start of our field research, there were approximately 130 AHS sites located off-reserve (Urban and Northern), serving over 4,000 children (8% of the 3 to5 year-old Aboriginal children living off-reserve) (Public Health Agency of Canada, 2004b). In the same period, there were 354 programs on reserve serving approximately 9,000 children (Health Canada, 2003a). Most programs are half-day, and operate following the school calendar from September to June. The majority are centre- or school-based. Alternative program delivery options are outreach and home-based, or some combination of the two.

There have been no independent studies on the AHS program and the results from a government evaluation—the Aboriginal Head Start Urban and Northern Communities National Impact Evaluation, 2002-2005—have never been released to the public. The following information is drawn from government-issued summary reports and AHS annual reports and newsletters (Public Health Agency of Canada, 1999, 2000, 2002; Health Canada, 2001, 2004). One half of the children served in AHS off-reserve programs were First Nations children, and the remainder were Métis and Inuit. About 17% were classified with special needs (language delays were the highest category, and other high categories were Fetal Alcohol Syndrome/ Effects or developmental delays).

Key cultural activities across all projects were those encouraging the use of the mother tongue in the individual community. In 2000, 15% of children attending AHSUNC programs spoke an Aboriginal language fluently, the majority were Inuit. In 2001, this figure was reported to be 28%, suggesting a doubling of fluent Aboriginal language speakers in one year. The increase is not commented upon in the report. In 2001, it was reported that the number of Inuit children in AHS had gone down 11%, and it was noted in 1999 that most of the children who were fluent speakers of an Aboriginal language were Inuit. The primary language used for instruction in the programs overall was English, along with one or more Aboriginal languages, most commonly Cree. In Alberta, the AHSOR program reported that 85% of their projects incorporated components that involved speaking to children in their First Nation language on a daily basis, and 72% of the projects had adults telling children stories in their First Nations language at least once a week.

About one third of the AHSUNC staff had some ECCE training, and most staff members were Aboriginal, including almost all teachers. Non-Aboriginal staff members most often held positions as "special needs aides, speech pathologists, and psycho-educators" (Health Canada, 2001, p 15). In a variety of regions, AHSOR programs reported the continued need for staff development and training as employing certified staff continued to be a challenge for many.

A collection of stories by AHSUNC parents, community members, teachers, and directors, focused on the impact of the program on children's self esteem, their perception of school as an enjoyable place to be, and their readiness for academic learning. A grandmother related: "When this program started, children learned their alphabet, colours, shapes, and numbers. When children go into kindergarten, they get a head start in school, which is very good for them" (Health Canada, 2002, p. 39). The program's logo, included on its publications and posters, is a set of alphabet blocks with the letters A, H, and S.

There is no single pedagogical approach, curriculum, or curriculum framework that must be used in the AHS programs. Some programs use the High/Scope approach that was endorsed as an "optional training approach" by the AHS Resource Review Committee in 1997 (Health Canada, 2000). As explained by Jeela Allurut, director of the Igloolik AHS, the High/Scope approach was comprehensive, supporting a range of teaching and learning activities:

> The children learn to plan, experiment, play with materials, toys, make their own things and use a lot of the language. They also learn to share and follow routines. We do small teacher-directed activities and large group activities. The children learn traditional games, songs and stories. (Health Canada, 2002, p. 74)

AHS newsletters provided regular updates on the spread of the High/Scope model. In 1999-2000, training and certification in the High/Scope approach to early childhood care and education was "delivered" to 64 Aboriginal Head Start staff (Health Canada, 2001, p. 5). The High/Scope preschool approach was originally developed for use with at-risk children, but now has proven to be effective with a full range of children. For AHSUNC, High/Scope training was reported to have been adapted to the needs, circumstances, and cultural approaches of Aboriginal communities. An Aboriginal Elder was present at every training session to ensure that the methodology was consistent with Aboriginal values. In addition to High/Scope, training in the Work Sampling System—a child observation tool—has taken place in approximately 20 sites. Over 100 sites sent delegates to the National Training Workshop in Ottawa in 2002 (Human Resources Development Canada, et al., 2003, p. 50).

High/Scope was developed in the United States as a compensatory program for preschool-aged African-American children living in urban communities. It was described by a founder as "an open framework of educational ideas and practices based on the natural development of young children" (Weikart & Schweinhart, 2005, p. 235). Learning within the framework is organized around 10 key experiences (creative representation, language and literacy, initiative and social relations, movement, music, classification, seriation, number, space, and time). Child development ideas are drawn from the theory of Jean Piaget, and in particular the notion that children are active learners. Teachers listen to children and use "open-ended" questions to lead them to think in more complex ways about their plans and actions. Learning activities take place in a plan-do-review cycle that encourages children to determine future goals, assess their own progress, and modify their plan accordingly. Research conducted by the High/Scope Educational Foundation indicates long-term social benefits stemming from program features that include "empower[ing] children by enabling them to initiate and carry out their own learning activities and make independent decisions" (Weikart & Schweinhart, p. 289).

In a survey conducted in 2000, the two dominant curriculum packages used in Head Start programs in the United States were the Creative Curriculum and High/Scope, which accounted for 36% and 22% of all programs that identified a main curriculum. This was a significant change from 1998, when the numbers were almost in reverse: High/Scope at 36%; Creative Curriculum at 18%. In the competitive marketplace of early childhood curriculum packages, the research-oriented High/Scope Education Research Foundation issued a press release highlighting those findings in the report that pointed to benefits of High/Scope as opposed to the Creative Curriculum (Weststat, Xtria, & CDM Group, 2003). We note that the extent of the use of Creative Curriculum in AIHS or AHS programs is unknown.

However, the child development assumptions built into the High/Scope approach, with its theoretical roots in Piaget, may not be consistent with Aboriginal views of children and childhood. Moreover, the export of programs such as Head Start from non-indigenous to indigenous cultures, whether commercially packaged or not, creates a need for trained teachers (Johnson & Gaiyabu, 2001) that can lead to a gulf between traditional and western scientific understandings of how children grow and learn.

The goal of the AHSUNC National Impact Evaluation was to demonstrate and describe effects of program participation on AHS children, families, and communities in the six program component areas, including children's readiness to learn. Many sites (42%) were already assessing children formally. The *Guide for Applicants* (Health Canada, 1995) to the AHS program suggested that all programs include "preschool and child development activities that are appropriate for children in the two years before they enter school" (p. 5). The criteria for what is appropriate were not stated. However, the emphasis on the cultural relevance of programs is strong, suggesting cultural relevance as the primary program element. There are no statements, as are common in early learning curriculum frameworks, indicating that learning should be achieved through play. The Calgary Native Head Start schedule below reflects the aims in compensatory programs in the United States, as identified by Lubeck (1985), to include a mix of social service and educational activities, limited free choice (just 15 minutes), and extended group time.

Table 5. Calgary Native Head Start Schedule (Weasel Traveller, 1995, p. 110)

Three hour morning program	
8:30 a.m.	Hot breakfast
8:45	Circle time (using lesson plan)
9:15	Art centre
9:45	Sand and water centres
10:00	Free choice of centres
10:15	Library centre (story time)
10:30	Nutritional snack
10:45	Gross motor centre (active games)
11:00	Fine motor centre (manipulative skills)
11:15-11:30	Free play (until picked up by parent)

SOUTH AFRICA

When the apartheid system ended in 1994, South Africa's newly elected government sought to break free of the influence of apartheid at all levels of the society. The government thus formulated many new policies in order to restructure the society and implement new programs in all sectors, especially those that had been historically disadvantaged. The main issues addressed through most of the new policies, including education, were issues of equity, redress, and social justice.

In South Africa, the central state is "responsible for policy development, planning and coordination, setting standards, norms, quality guidelines and information systems". The provinces are "responsible for implementing policy, developing delivery systems and managing resources" and the local authorities are responsible for ensuring that community centres and facilities are made available for ECCE programmes (DoE, 2001b, p. 28). Children are considered to be the country's key to economic growth and success, underpinning the nation's entry to the world stage. The government considers health, education, culture, and respect to be the foundational elements intended to foster the development of children and, subsequently, the development and growth of the nation.

Since the end of apartheid and the establishment of the Constitution of the Republic of South Africa in 1996, there has been a plethora of reports and documents relating to the provision of education services for all, including young children. Act 108 of the Constitution contains the Bill of Rights for children from 0 to 9 years of age. It states that children have a right to a name and nationality from birth, to family, parental, or alternative care, to basic nutrition, to shelter, to health care and social services, to protection from maltreatment, neglect, abuse and degradation, and to basic education in the official language or languages of their choice (Republic of South Africa, 1996).

What follows are thumbnail sketches of a few of many key policy documents that concern ECCE in particular.

The 1995 White Paper on Education and Training states that the Department of Education is responsible "to develop national policy frameworks for the education of the young children, including the structure of provisioning, determination of financial systems and establishing national norms and standards for ECD curricula and training curricula" (DoE, 2001b, p. 33).

The White Paper for Social Welfare (1997) stipulates that of the 0 to 9 age group, disadvantaged children under the age of 5 are prioritized because they are the least serviced and most vulnerable, while urgent attention is given to children aged 0 to 3, and the disabled (DOE, 2001b, p. 32).

The White Paper on Local Government (1998) elaborates the constitutional role of local governments in child care, which is to "provide child care facilities and may provide grants to associations for this in terms of the Child Care Act of 1983" (DoE, 2001b, p. 28).

The 2001 Report on National ECD Policies and Programmes outlines the language in education policy. An additive multilingualism approach is advocated that aims to promote and develop all the official languages and to support teaching and learning other languages as required by learners or that are used within South Africa's communities. The aim is to reinstate the status of previously marginalized African languages in the schools (DoE, 2001b, p. 38).

Pre-Primary Education

In South Africa, pre-primary education refers to pre-grade 1 education for learners 0 to 6 years of age (UNESCO, 2006). Pre-primary programs are of two types: Grade R (reception year) which refers to the school preparation year for 5 and 6-year-olds and pre-Grade R programs that cater for children 0 to 4 or 5 years of age.

Early child development (ECD) is governed by the 1983 Child Care Act 74. The Department of Education (DoE) draws on the 2001 White Paper 5 to guide the implementation of ECE and ECD programs. The DoE aims to phase Grade R into the public system, providing access for all. Until very recently, Grade R was included in ECE and ECD programs, about 15% of which were school-based, and the remainder community- or home-based. There was, and remains, a huge range of quality and of content in preschool programs, particularly with regard to the school preparation year. As Grade R is now being incorporated into the formal education system, teachers are being trained and the DoE is further developing, in conjunction with the Department of Health and Social Development, an integrated service for vulnerable children with special needs—the disabled, the poor, and those affected or orphaned by HIV/AIDS.

South Africa's Policy of Outcomes-Based Education

As part of South Africa's rebirth, the government looked to the West for ways to change the education system. It needed a better skilled workforce that would be able to compete on the international stage. South Africa thus borrowed, adapted, and adopted outcomes-based education (OBE) as its national standard for all levels of formal schooling. As the reader will see, this policy is important for our analysis of Tshwane preschool because of the transitional status and nature of Grade R, and in light of the content of the curriculum, then known as C2005. As mentioned, until very recently, most Grade Rs were housed in ECED centres; they are currently being moved to public schools in order to provide a year of preparation for primary schooling for all 5 and 6-year-olds. By 2008, C2005 had been further revised and renamed the National Curriculum of South Africa.

The new curriculum policy is the result of two competing tensions. The first was the "need to break from the past and embrace the global system" which was done by "adopting international models and world-class standards" from countries such as the United States, Australia, New Zealand, and Canada. The second tension was the "need for the transitional government and an emerging democracy to establish legitimacy and ownership of the policy process and educational transformation" (Spreen, 2001, p. 237). Because education had become the key to economic growth, economic considerations influenced the new educational policies. The three key goals of transformation through OBE were: 1) to achieve equity and redistribution, 2) to make South Africa internationally competitive by developing the human resources of the country, and 3) to integrate education and training as a means of achieving the first two goals (Spreen, 2001, pp. 239-240). South Africa now has a hybrid form of OBE which includes both international and local influences. While the process of policy borrowing and establishing a sense of ownership over policy is described by Steiner-Khamsi (2004), suffice to say here that in due course OBE acquired a South African identity and evolved into an apparent panacea for the country's educational transformation (Spreen, 2001). The resulting main features of the curriculum are an "egalitarian political message, anti-rote learning, critical thinking, learner-centred approach to teaching, teachers as curriculum developers, group work rather than directive teaching and community participation" (Spreen, p. 241).

The National Curriculum and Grade R

Grade R was a recommendation contained in The White Paper on Education and Training (1995), and evolved out of the "National Early Childhood Development Project", implemented as a 3-year pilot project starting in 1995. It was recognized from the start that "the long history of discriminatory provision in this sector delivers a set of conditions that make it difficult to provide a quick-fix solution" (DoE, 1997, p. 2).

Policy statements for the Grade R to Grade 9 curriculum find their way into policy statements for Early Childhood Centres due to the history of most Grade Rs being housed in EC centres. Both the Constitution and the national curriculum provide the policy framework for the education of all South Africans from birth, for lifelong learning.

41

The Grade R curriculum "aims to develop the full potential of each learner as a citizen of a democratic South Africa. It seeks to create a lifelong learner who is confident, literate, multi-skilled, with the ability to participate in society as an active citizen (UNESCO, 2006, p. 7). The focus of the curriculum is on literacy, numeracy and life skills. The curriculum reflects the tenets of the 1996 constitution—social justice, healthy environment, human rights, and inclusion.

South Africa is a multilingual, multicultural country now with 11 official languages (Afrikaans, English and nine African languages). The policy calls for the mother tongue to predominate in the early years of schooling with slow and well-planned introduction of the First Additional Language from the start (this is increasingly English, though in some regions Afrikaans predominates). The emphasis at first is on listening skills, using formulaic language (greetings), repeating frequently used words and phrases, responding to simple questions with one or two word answers, singing simple songs, and performing action rhymes. A high level of proficiency in at least two languages is expected. The language policy for the foundation phase (Grade R to Grade 3) notes that by Grade 4 a reading vocabulary of several thousand words in the additional language (as noted above, this is increasingly English) is expected. Clearly, the policy focus is a bilingual one with the aim of competency in the language of instruction (LoI)—the first additional language. In light of the increasing use of English as the LoI, one South African teacher noted astutely that "it may be necessary for learners to use their home language when discussing how a story makes them feel."

The curriculum spells out the OBE learning outcomes for listening, speaking, writing, reading and viewing, thinking and reasoning, language structure and use. "If learners are to achieve similar levels of competence in their home and additional languages by the end of Grade 9, vocabulary development must be a priority from Grade R onwards" (DoE, 2008, p. 13). Assessment standards for each learning outcome as outlined in the curriculum document appear to be reasonable; however, since the word 'play' is not mentioned in relation to Grade R, it is evident that play is not considered part of a child-centred curriculum once formal schooling has begun. It is of note that Grade R teachers tend to be hired from the pool of Grade 1 teachers who have been trained for primary school teaching, not for ECCE.

At the start of 2009, the situation continues to change quickly. The curriculum for the 0 to5 age group is evolving. Although Grade R is meant to be the link between ECCE and primary school, such organizational changes have serious implications for preschools that are left without a Grade R. In such cases, the 4 to 5 year age cohort then implicitly becomes the group to be prepared for school. Thus we saw pressure to lower the age of formal school preparation, with the 4 to 5-year-olds taking the place in EC centres of the previous Grade R 5 to 6-year-olds. In turn, we expect (and saw the evidence) that 3-year-olds will also be increasingly involved in school readiness activities. The extent to which this will result in earlier and earlier introduction to the First Additional Language, due in part to pressure from parents to have their children taught in English, remains to be seen, as is the case with the status of the government's policy to promote a bilingual or multilingual school system that gives space to the nine official African languages, in addition to English and Afrikaans.

INDIA

Integrated Child Development Services

Children's services in India are often described in the context of numbers. India has the largest child population in the world. According to the 2001 census, there are 170 million children between ages 0 to 6, many of whom live in poverty. The wellbeing of children has been an integral part of India's developmental planning—expressed as successive national five-year economic plans—beginning from its post-independence period since 1951. However, until the Third Five-Year Plan, ECCE continued to be in the purview of the voluntary and private sectors. The Fifth Five-Year Plan saw a clear shift in approach from child welfare to child development. This shift culminated in the declaration of the National Policy for Children in 1974. Subsequent Five-Year Plans have reaffirmed the priority to develop early childhood services as an investment in human resource development.

There are several provisions in the Constitution of India, either as a Fundamental Right or as a Directive Principle of State Policy, that have been used to promote ECCE services in the country. As a Fundamental Right, Article 15(3) of the Constitution of India empowers the State to practice positive discrimination favouring economically and educationally weaker groups. This allows for special provisions for children in difficult situations, children of disadvantaged groups, and girls. ECCE has now been included as a constitutional provision, but not a justifiable right, for every child through Article 45 which outlines that the State will attempt to provide ECCE services for all children under the age of seven. The various schemes and programs of government clearly reflect the influence of, and adherence to, global trends. All key principles a good ECCE, ranging from developmentally appropriate curriculum, to a play-based pedagogy and a rights-based perspective are reflected in government policies and programs. It is significant to observe that right from its independence in 1947, the Indian constitution stated its perspective on young children and their education. Pre-school education is still considered crucial. It is hoped that enhanced levels of school readiness will eventually translate into lower drop-out rates and lower grade repetition rates.

Public, government-sponsored programs are largely directed towards the disadvantaged community, particularly those residing in rural and marginalized areas. Some of the major programs in the public sector include Sarva Shiksha Abhiyan, aimed at universalizing elementary education, and Integrated Child Development Services (ICDS), for children aged birth to school-age. The ECCE services being provided by voluntary and non-governmental organizations play a vital role in providing education for all ages in socially and economically marginalised areas. These organizations primarily work with special communities in difficult circumstances like tribal people, migrant labourers, and rural children in specific contexts. They run creches (child care centres) and ECCE centres by mobilizing local resources. Some NGOs run mobile creches and accompany the labourers as they shift construction sites. The effectiveness of these programs requires further systematic evaluation; however, children who attend them are more likely to move on to primary schools and parents have generally reported positive outcomes (Swaminathan, 1998).

Private initiatives usually encompass the fee-charging, profit-making initiatives in ECCE. In India, as elsewhere, ECCE falls in a dual-track mode (Swaminathan, 1993). While the public sponsored ICDS caters to children from disadvantaged communities, private initiatives target children from families that have greater economic stability. These initiatives impart preschool education through nurseries, kindergarten, and pre-primary classes in private schools. Though exact figures are not available, it was estimated in 1998 that about 10 million children receive ECCE from privately-owned programs (Sharma, 1998). This type of preschooling is oversubscribed and the competition for spaces in the lead schools is intense, with as many as 300 children competing for a single opening (Prochner, 2002). Essentially, ECCE in private sectors is a profit-making enterprise and caters to those who can afford them. The private initiatives range from moderate to high fee-charging centres. Thus, there is a clear difference between public and NGO sectors on one side and the private sector on the other.

The 1974 National Policy for Children included measures related to child and maternal health, nutrition, and informal education for preschool children, all of which were combined in the national ICDS program, which was launched the next year. The focal point for the delivery of its services is the anganwadi centre (AWC) (courtyard garden), a term borrowed from the simple child care centre which could be run in the courtyard of any village home. The anganwadi worker (AWW), usually a local woman, is the key worker and first paraprofessional in the child care service. Considered as a community worker, she earns a small honorarium for the services she renders to the community. A helper (AWH), again a local woman, assists the teacher at the centre and is responsible for fetching children from their homes, earning her the title of *teragar* (the one who fetches).

The ICDS is centrally sponsored with administration within each state. The basic premise of the program is that early childhood education and care are inseparable issues and must be considered as one. Based upon this assumption, the program was designed in an integrated manner. The major aim is to meet the early childhood education and care needs from a common platform of AWC.

The initiative started with 33 projects reaching about 150,000 young children. Today, it has expanded to nearly 700,000 AWCs located in almost every region. Currently, it is estimated that the program reaches over 34 million children (under the age of 6) from disadvantaged groups. Of these, about one half (between the ages of 3 to 6), participate in centre-based preschool learning activities. However, barely one fourth of these children are covered under the supplementary nutrition component of the program. The program concentrates on urban slums, tribal areas, and the more remote and rural regions of the country.

The Tenth Five-Year Plan (2002-2007) focused on a rights-based approach to the development of children, with major strategies envisaged to reach out to every young child in the country, to ensure survival, protection, and development. There are several government initiatives that aim to promote ECCE as a critical element of Education for All, including attempts to introduce holistic curricula, trained teachers, and several other indicators. The current Five-Year Plan (2007-2012) continues to stress a rights-based approach to child development "to ensure that children do not lose their childhood because of work, disease, and despair" (Planning Commission, 2008, p. 185).

The ICDS program holds a prominent place in achieving child development goals. However, the Government of India acknowledges that there is a significant gap between policy statements and the working of actual programs. The Eleventh Five-Year Plan includes a review of the mostly dismal state of ICDS centres, with the program in the state of Tamil Nadu a notable exception for its strong preschool curriculum, as described next.

> In Tarana village of Madhya Pradesh, the AWC is a *kutchcha* house with slush outside. Foodgrains are stored in the house of the AWW who states that, 'There are rats at the centre. So I can't leave food there.' Meanwhile villagers complain that their children fall ill if they eat at the AWC. In Gohilaon in Bhadohi District of Uttar Pradesh, the AWC runs from an empty room with broken furniture in the primary school premises. The registers are missing, AWW is seldom present and grain is stored in the helper's house next door. Gokarnapur ICDS centre in Ganjam district of Orissa has been running from the AWW's house for over five years now. A handful of rice and dal provides meal to 30 children. Immunization, weighing scales, growth charts, preschool education, etcetera are all unheard of here. In Barmer district of Rajasthan, ICDS workers are illiterate. Some, like the AWC at village Rawatsar can't even fill growth registers. In Chizami village of Phek district in Nagaland, the centre runs from a dank and cold building. Children receive two glucose biscuits as SNP [supplementary nutrition program]. And six AWCs with 150 children run from a single verandah in Maalab village of Mewat in Haryana. In Jehangirpuri, in Delhi, ICDS centres do not have weighing scales and they have not received deworming capsules and iron folic acid tablets for 10 years. In states like Himachal, Kerala, and Tamil Nadu, the ICDS program is doing better. In Chamba in Himachal, toilets are being built at AWCs. In Tamil Nadu, there is a proper preschool curriculum followed by the AWW. Children are well fed and stay at the AWC for almost six hours. They have sleeping mats, toys, even mirrors to comb their hair and stay clean. In Chamarkundi village of Ganjam district of Orissa, women's SHG supplement the Anganwadi food with eggs and vegetables. (Planning Commission, 2008, p. 204)

The program as it currently operates cannot meet its stated child development goals, and it is now undergoing evaluation and restructuring. The aim is to universalize a high-quality version of the program, the result of a Supreme Court Order in 2001, but still unrealized (Nayak, 2006). This will require raising the quality of preschool education, identified as "the weakest link of the ICDS" (Planning Commission, 2008, p. 114). Suggestions for improving the preschool education component of the ICDS program include collaboration with Sarva Shiksha Abhiyan, further training for AWWs, and reducing their workload, or training adolescent girls to assist the AWWs.

DISCUSSION

Early childhood policy across the three countries reflects global concerns. In India and South Africa, ECCE policy has been stimulated by the Education for All movement which includes the very young child and emphasizes community participation and non-formal learning. However, recent policy is embedded in a long history of ECCE services in both countries that has seen various EC models imported from Europe starting from the 1820s (Kaur, 2009; Prochner & Kabiru, 2008; Prochner, May, & Kaur, 2009; Prochner, 2009a). For much of the history, ECCE programs were segregated by social class and race, with very few programs available for poor Indigenous children. A similar situation existed in Canada, where there are very few examples of ECCE programs especially for young Aboriginal children prior to the 1960s. The first common element in EC policy then, is that it is meant to fill a gap and provide services for children who were previously not accommodated within programs, or who were offered a sub-standard program in earlier times. ICDS, AHS, and Grade R are all government-run and organized by the central state, replacing services that may have been provided by churches, charities, or NGOs in the past. As part of government policy, ECCE is valorized as a means of social reform and nation building, and touted for its ability to change the trajectory of individual lives (Cleghorn & Prochner, 1997; Prochner, 1992). A key difference between Grade R in South Africa and the ICDS and AHS, is that the latter two target specific populations (the most vulnerable in India, and Aboriginals in Canada), whereas Grade R is a universal program, accepting all children who meet the age requirement. Grade R was established, however, to meet the needs of previously underserved black children, since quality programs have long been available for others.

The second common element is that in all three countries, EC policy was initially borrowed from examples in the minority world. The Grade R curriculum was drawn from international sources, as described in this chapter. In terms of its education program, AHS policy has left the approach to curriculum and pedagogy open to community choice, while at the same time endorsing the High/Scope approach as an option without mentioning others. In India, playway is officially recommended in the ICDS. Playway was initially a borrowed pedagogy. Despite the fact that it has become indigenized to the extent that it is often critiqued by both Indian and foreign ECE experts as too formal in its execution (Prochner, 2009b), it remains popular with anganwadi workers and parents.

ICDS and AHS were established two decades apart, in 1975 and 1995 respectively. Both were inspired by the early childhood intervention model of Project Head Start in the United States, which was aimed at poverty reduction. This has had long-lasting consequences, for example, in the development of a system of employing paraprofessionals as key workers. The ICDS program adopted elements of U.S. Head Start, such as parent participation, and including the involvement of parents or other community members as teachers or teaching assistants. Community participation in the program in India has been criticized as lacking in many instances, and the use of minimally-trained community members as key workers has contributed to its inability to meet its goals for preschool education in particular. In the United States, Head Start teachers currently require a Child Development Associate (CDA) credential, a basic-level training developed for Head Start and child care workers in the early 1970s. A critic of the CDA program at the time of its introduction called it an 'honorary credential'. ICDS anganwadi workers in India are still provided with an honorarium and classed as volunteers. In Canada, AHS teachers require the provincial standard for training. This generally involves a two-year diploma in early childhood education or for staff to be in the process of undertaking coursework. As with U.S. Head Start, community participation is seen as an essential element of the preschools, and this sometimes means involving parents as volunteer teachers with little or no prior training. In any case, as Miskimmin (2007) points out, participation of this sort sometimes "simply means 'education' with a goal to correct assumed deficiencies of mothers" (p. 121). Indeed, policy borrowing is a complex matter when the policy in question guides a compensatory program freighted down with deficit ideas about poor parents and children, and assumptions about Aboriginal parents and their children as being "at risk" (Miskimmin, 2007).

An element common to the programs in India, South Africa, and Canada is that there is a strong emphasis on preschool education without the oversight of an educational body. In South Africa at the time of our study, the Grade R was being incorporated into the MoE/DoE via the new national curriculum and the plan to move all Grade Rs into public schools. In India, the ICDS program is situated within the Ministry of Women, Development, and Child Welfare. The AHS program, like U.S. Head Start, is administered by a public health service. In McElhinny's (2007) analysis of the situation in Canada, this reflects the colonial history.

> The very fact that an educational program is situated under a health and medical rubric is evidence of historical and continuing colonial interventions into Aboriginal practices a kind of 'racial uplift,' with certain linguistic, medical and hygienic practices being closely linked to integration. (p. 12)

CHAPTER 4

SOCIAL RELATIONS: PARTICIPANTS IN EACH SETTING

In this chapter we take a close look at the participants in each setting, the children, teachers, parents, and other adults. The interest here is on the structural and other influences affecting how they relate to one another in the variety of situations and contexts that occur throughout a typical day. That is, this chapter examines the people in the case study preschools as both structural and process elements of the programs, including such matters as the adult-child ratios, the roles and training of teachers and child care workers, and relations with parents and the surrounding communities.

"Structural quality is a characteristic of the environment that is independent of human interaction between individuals" (Cassidy, et al., 2005, p. 551), whereas "process quality requires human interaction among individuals" (p. 510). Although structure and process are often studied with regard to indicators of child care quality, assessing quality is not our purpose; our interest is in how structure and process factors play out differently or in similar ways in these three very different preschools—Sunbeam in India, Little Lake in a First Nations community in Canada, and Tshwane in South Africa.

In the sections below the people in each setting are first introduced. Then we give the various accounts of how the children get to, and into, the preschools. From there the chapter moves on to how the children are grouped in their classrooms and the issue of positioning—teachers in relation to children. Finally, the chapter focuses on the extent to which the preschool settings are familiar to the children in terms of the organization of space, cultural norms and the like, more or less reflecting what they experience at home. The chapter concludes with an analysis of the foregoing, framing the discussion in terms of the concept of border crossing: we ask to what extent the three settings require preschool children to cross linguistic, cultural, and/or conceptual borders as they traverse from home to preschool and back home again.

PARTICIPANTS

There are considerable similarities, as well as stark differences, with regard to the people one finds at Sunbeam, Little Lake and Tshwane preschools. All schools have an onsite supervisor, lead teacher, or principal, all of whom are female. All have a cook on staff. All teachers are members of the local community; however, that is defined quite differently in terms of the geography of what constitutes community. For example, in the India setting the teachers live within view of the

49

preschool and in very close proximity to the children's homes. In South Africa, the teachers are from the same general community as the children, however the catchment area of the preschool is over 100 square kilometres in size. The community of Little Lake in Canada is the largest in geographical area at 402 square kilometres, but a small and close community in another sense due to the fact that the population is relatively small (about 2000) and the residents—teachers and parents—are from the same or neighbouring band (First Nations group) and thus well-known to each other.

Sunbeam served 30 children aged 3 to 6 years, though some were as young as 18 months. Little Lake's children numbered between 6 and 12, ages 4 to 6, while Tshwane served 131 children (infants to 6 to 7 years). Sunbeam and Tshwane thus include children from a wide age range, but only Tshwane cares for infants and babies under the age of 2. Attendance was found to fluctuate the most at Little Lake, while attendance was more stable at Sunbeam and Tshwane. The mixed-age Sunbeam program operates for a few hours each morning. Little Lake holds two sessions per day, one in the morning, the other in the afternoon. At Tshwane children are grouped by age and organized into classrooms, very much in a western type of school-like structure. Officially, Tshwane runs from 7 in the morning until 1:00 in the afternoon.

The number of boys and girls was about equal at Tshwane. At Sunbeam, there were more girls than boys, by a ratio of three to two. The situation was different at Little Lake, where the morning class was comprised of four girls and two boys, with two girls and six boys attending in the afternoon.

One matter that varied greatly between the preschools was the adult-child ratio. At Sunbeam the ratio was 2 adults to 30 children, or 1 to 30 when the helper was not in the program room. The ratio at Little Lake was the lowest with 3 adults to between 6 and 12 children. At Tshwane, the adult-child ratio was quite similar for the Grade R's 5 to 6-year-olds, the 4 to 5-year-old group, and the 3 to 4-year-olds, at about 1:25 to 30 children. The ratio for the infant group was generally around 1:18. These ratios were reduced from time to time as the principal visited the four different classrooms to help out by giving individual attention to small groups or individual children.

Little Lake

On the day of the video-recording there were six children attending. The regular adult participants are the program co-ordinator, a classroom aide, a mini-bus driver, and a cook. All are women. The co-ordinator is a trained health care worker and is completing a diploma in early childhood development. She has been in her position with the preschool since its founding in the late 1990s. The classroom aide has worked at the preschool for several years, and has also taken college courses in early childhood development. The driver remains in the preschool during the morning, having similar duties with the children as the classroom aide. The cook spends less time in the preschool, but she also participates in activities such as crafts in the few minutes before serving breakfast and lunch. Other members of the community, such as Elders and parents, participate periodically to share specialized knowledge and in particular their knowledge of the indigenous culture and language. There are no fees for parents to pay.

The afternoon session was attended by children who had been recommended by the kindergarten teacher at the nearby band school. While this points to a close connection between the preschool and the regular school, it remains that many Little Lake children, mostly boys, were reported to have behavioural or social adjustment problems in kindergarten and were considered to be in need of preparation for regular school, as can be provided by Little Lake preschool. In one instance, this included a boy suspended from the band kindergarten due to what was perceived to be his unruly behaviour. Although the practice of suspending children from preschool and kindergarten has rarely been addressed in the research (Gilliam and Shahar, 2006), the fact that it occurred in this small setting raises questions about the possible lack of cultural congruence between home, preschool and regular school. Current academic discourse implies that indigenizing schooling practices and curricula will increase school readiness and reduce school adjustment problems (Semali & Kincheloe, 1999).

Tshwane

The regular participants of Tshwane preschool are the principal, 4 teachers, and 131 children—70 girls and 61 boys. The Grade R has an enrolment of about 30. One teacher is assigned to each classroom. There is a male cook who works exclusively in the kitchen. Children come from quite far to this preschool because of its good reputation. Some travel a distance of 10 to 15 kilometres on mini-buses at their parents' expense. Thus we see that at the organizational level, Tshwane operates much more along the lines of an educational institution than a community preschool or day-care centre; however, relations within Tshwane exhibited a strong sense of community and care.

Tshwane has a reputation for accepting children with special needs or from difficult circumstances. The principal has established a close relationship with the children's families. She reported that the centre enrols three children with Down syndrome (two were observed during different visits). About 10% of the children are orphaned and being cared for by grandmothers. These children are exempt from the tuition fee of 170 Rand per month. Many of the parents are unemployed younger women who are on social grants (i.e. welfare). If parents cannot pay the fee, the principal subsidizes the child from other sources, such as donations from her church. Some of the poorest parents who cannot pay volunteer on their own initiative to clean the grounds, wash the windows, and look after the vegetable garden.

The schedule of the centre also reflects its community service approach. As mentioned earlier, though the official hours are 7:00 a.m. to 1:00 p.m., it remains open later according to the needs of the children's families. The principal reported that she arrived by 6 a.m. most mornings due to the need of a few parents to leave their children early as they went into the city to work. She gave these children their breakfast.

Sunbeam

Thirty children are registered, though 24 to 26 typically attend. The 2 adult participants are the female teacher whose formal designation is anganwadi worker, (AWW) and her female assistant, the anganwadi helper (AWH). Both are members of the local community. The AWW leads the children's program, maintains health and attendance records, liaises with public health workers, conducts home visits with mothers of preschool-aged children, and supervises the AWH. The AWH prepares and serves the meal, cleans up after the meal, serves water to children, cleans the program room, supervises the children's group visits to the toilet, and participates in disciplining the children and in some activities. Except for the time she is in the kitchen, the AWH spends all her time in the program room or assisting with toileting. Teachers, helpers, parents, and children all use the same local language. There were no costs or fees for parents to pay.

TRANSITION FROM HOME TO SCHOOL

There are some marked differences as well as a few similarities in the process of children moving from the home and into the preschools. For example, all children at Sunbeam walk to school, accompanied by a parent or caregiver. All children at Little Lake arrive by mini-bus or car. Some children at Tshwane walk with a parent or older sibling, while most arrive by mini-bus. In all three preschools, children arrive with belongings (backpacks, coats, shoes, food containers) which they store in a designated location. Entry in all three cases was routinized but marked by a minimum of ritual. Self-help in taking off shoes, putting away coats, and jackets was most evident at Tshwane and Little Lake.

Little Lake

Little Lake AHS is situated across a road from the band administration buildings and a distance of about a kilometre from the band school. All children live on the reserve, but many homes are distant from one another. All of the children arrive by vehicles, most in the small AHS van, with the remainder brought by parents or a family member. The transition from home to preschool for most thus occurs when children board the school bus where they are expected to abide by established rules under the supervision of the driver who also works as classroom aide. Children who arrive by private car with a parent are brought into the preschool individually, allowing parents and teachers to exchange greetings and share information, as in the following example in which the coordinator asks whether a child will be at the preschool next week. This exchange indicates familiarity in the nature of the connection between the preschool and a child's home.

Coordinator to mother: *You phone me anyway.*

Mother at doorway, kneeling, with hand on child's arm: *Yeah, I'll give you a call.* She sets his shoes in front of him. She opens his shoes. He places his hand on her shoulder for balance, and steps into shoes.

Coordinator: *You phone me if he's coming next week.*

Mother: *I don't think so.*

Most children arrive in a group, escorted from the bus by the female driver and walk together the short distance from the parking area. The preschool is entered through a door separate from the main entrance to an adjacent administration building. The entrance is designed as a gateway with cubbies on either side, in which children transfer from outdoors to indoors, changing shoes or clothing as required. Opening the door triggers a buzzer, which was installed for security reasons. Once open, an adult or a child holds the door open for the others. What children do upon entry depends on the season. In the winter or in wet weather, they remove their coats, hats, mittens, and boots, in which case most remain in stocking feet for the morning. In warmer weather, children remove their coats, but most leave on their shoes.

Children disperse from the entrance area individually when they are ready, going to play in the easily accessible learning centres until breakfast is announced.

Tshwane

The preschool is located in a semi-rural area, a former township, about 30 kilometres from the centre of a major city. The fenced compound is large with a play area and some climbing equipment at the rear. Almost all the children arrive between 7 and 8 a.m. and leave between 1 and 3 p.m.; some stay for "after care" until 5 or 6 p.m. The transfer over of children from parent to preschool takes place at the gate to the compound or at the main entrance to the preschool as children arrive by mini-bus, car, or walk in the company of a parent or older sibling. One father was observed to playfully run into the preschool with his two small children balanced on his shoulders. Then they find their way through the hallway of the preschool to the Grade R classroom, often having been greeted at the entry by one of the teachers or principal. The principal arrives by 6 a.m., to receive the few children who are dropped off early because their parents work in the city. She gives these children breakfast. She also stays most days until 6 p.m., thus providing after-hours day care.

The researchers arrived on one of the observation days just as two mini-bus loads of children came through the gate. As we entered the school looking for the principal, the little girl with Down syndrome and very dwarfed, greeted us and helped us to find her. Having never 'graduated' from the preschool this child seemed to know the routines very well, following along with the various activities with considerable competence.

According to the posted schedule, children were to play independently until 9 a.m. breakfast time, but this schedule was followed loosely. Breakfast consisted of a bowl of maize or cassava porridge which the children fetched in a disciplined way: all were led to the kitchen, and after waiting in line for their food bowl, returned with it one by one to the classroom.

Sunbeam

At Sunbeam the transition to the preschool space occurs at the door. The AWW and AWH greet parents as they arrive with their children. Most children live in the houses nearby, and could easily be observed by the parent from the doorway of the home. Some parents enter with their children, while other children enter themselves, stepping over the high sill. Some are lifted over the sill by the AWW. When children are new to the program or very young, mothers or grandmothers frequently stay with them for at least part of the morning. Children leave their shoes in a row against the wall outside as they do at home. Some of the mothers assist children with removing their shoes and children enter the preschool barefoot. Once inside, children hand their food container brought from home to the AWH, who places it in a large metal pot. They then enter an interior room which is the main program space, where they sit on the floor and talk until the formal start of the program. Some children might ask for their respective food containers and eat the light snack packed from home.

GROUPING

Grouping students, when used as a teaching strategy, "involves taking decisions about how and when to bring children together to assist their learning" (Mac Naughton & Williams, 2005, p. 104). A basic consideration in grouping is group size. While didactic teaching methods can be used with groups of any size, large groupings are usually associated with direct instruction, and small groups with experiential learning and more informal teaching. Grouping in early childhood classrooms is believed to foster relationships among children and between the children and teacher, allowing more or less individual attention. While most western experts favour small group teaching, it is not common practice everywhere. As Weikart (2003) highlighted in his summary of the IEA Preprimary Project research involving 15 countries, "dependence on a whole group organization in early childhood care and education settings is international" (p. 245).

Some general observations in each setting reveal the following differences and similarities. Children at Sunbeam are grouped as one for all activities, whereas children at Little Lake and Tshwane are grouped according to the nature of the activity. Teachers in all preschools use movement exercises to gain children's attention or as cues for activity changes. Children in all three preschools are arranged on carpets or mats as an organizing strategy for whole group time: in rows at Sunbeam, and in a cluster, lines, or a circle at Little Lake and Tshwane. At Sunbeam the teacher sits on the floor as do the children, cross-legged and in rows or in a circle. The circle arrangements are used for less formal times, such as eating or games. At Little Lake and Tshwane, furnishings and equipment play a role in dictating arrangements and groupings, thus tables, shelving, etcetera, are strategically placed. At whole group time at Little Lake and Tshwane, children sit on the floor while the teacher sits on a chair facing them. Circle or whole group time at Little Lake and Tshwane is a time for direct teaching. At Little Lake and Tshwane, children select their own groupings during free play. During free play at Little Lake, children often play with one other child, alone, or under the watchful supervision of a teacher. There was minimal free play time at Sunbeam. These observations point to important differences between the settings in the conception of the role that play has, or does not have, in learning, as well as its role in the lives of children.

Little Lake

The indoor space is a single large room, with smaller areas for specific activities separated by the arrangement of tables, low shelving units, or carpets. A playground is located at the rear of the building with climbing equipment, a slide, and a sandbox. Children go outside as a group, under the supervision of adults. Inside, the children are grouped according to the schedule, the dictates of furnishings and equipment, and their own choice. All children are involved in the same activity at circle time, group work time, and meal time, representing about 40% of program time. A schedule is included in the parent handbook and is posted in the centre.

At circle time children gather on a carpet, facing the corner with the wall of windows to the left and posters of teaching materials and other decorations on the wall to the right. The coordinator sits at the junction or corner of the two walls on a child-sized chair, with her back to the wall. Children sit in a cluster, with the requirement that they do not block another child's view. Prior to whole group times, the coordinator uses transition strategies to gain the children's attention by managing their bodies, directing them in movement routines (hands in the air, hands on your head, etcetera), or asking them to "fix their legs." In group-work time, in which the teacher introduces academic tasks, memory games, etcetera, children sit on the carpet or on chairs at small tables facing the teacher who sits close to one or another of the children.

In the larger portion of the program children choose how they group themselves, with the exception of required craft activities that are completed under teacher direction at a table with one or two other children. In the video examples, children are most often paired with a teacher at a required activity, or play with or beside one other child. Children frequently play alone. While teachers do not encourage solitary play, they also do not encourage peer play.

In many instances, furnishings and equipment influence groupings of children. Some tables are equipped with a set number of chairs in order to regulate the number of participants. Other activities had limits that were made known to the children as rules: the small water table could be accessed by three children. At meal times, children sat at their assigned places. Owing in part to their small numbers, children are often situated near an adult. In the playground, for example, there were two groupings consisting of two children and one adult. Each group used the same materials but in parallel tasks with no communication between them. At these times, the adult assumed the role of a patient and more knowledgeable playmate, though on occasion she stepped out of this role to reinforce rules ('don't throw sand') or to comfort a hurt child.

Tshwane

Children are grouped in classrooms by age. The 25 to 30 children in Grade R are sometimes grouped as one on the carpeted area, and at other times in small groups of four to six around small, rectangular brightly-coloured plastic tables. During the scheduled free play time, children access the toys and the playhouse corner in pairs or small groups. Free play did not appear to present occasions for teachers to seize on learning opportunities. If the children were busy and relatively quiet the teacher did not involve herself. At one time three boys were very busy trying to fit the operating handle to the drive mechanism of a home-made wire truck. They cooperated easily and with evident interest. According to one of the South African researchers, they learn this kind of cooperation from their siblings at home and do not expect intervention from an adult during such play. Similarly, the teacher did not direct children to the book corner during free play, nor were they observed to gravitate to it. Books were mainly used in teacher directed activities such as story telling and the teaching of English vocabulary.

On the wall was a commercially produced poster with a daily schedule given to the preschool by an NGO. The teacher explained that she did not really follow it. Partially hidden underneath it on a larger handmade poster was the schedule that she said suited her better and was the one she followed more closely (see chapter 2).

The teacher's shyness about admitting that she did not really follow the NGO schedule was a good example of a teacher's confidence being undermined by experts who use more formal language and may not spend long enough with the teacher to come to a meeting of the minds. In fact, the NGO schedule was not that different—it was just more formal and academic in terminology.

Whole group time is structured by the teacher who emphasizes school readiness skills. One whole group activity, a version of 'pig in the middle,' was conducted in the children's home language. The game involved turn-taking. The teacher joined in and there was much laughter. The teacher noticed one boy who was not participating and in the L1 reminded him to pay attention. He did so for a moment but then his attention wandered again, as did that of several other children, as the game appeared to go on too long. When the game stopped the teacher switched to English and told the children to go to their places at the tables. She quickly changed her mind and called them back to the carpet area for a pre-reading story, *My Sister's Wedding*. This was a big book with the English pasted over with the children's home language. The teacher pointed to certain words saying them with emphasis, and the children repeating the pronunciation a couple of times with her. With the book closed the teacher posed some comprehension questions in L1 to the children. Individual children were asked and stood up to shyly give answers, clearly in preparation for the behaviours that would be expected of them in regular school the following year.

Sunbeam

As mentioned earlier, the indoor space at Sunbeam is small, permitting about one square metre of space per child. The room is dark, with only a small amount of light coming in through the door or the tiny window. While sunlight would be beneficial for health reasons, there is no need for additional lighting for the activities which take place. Children participate in the program as a group, with the major exception being trips to the toilet or for a drink of water. For most of the morning, children sit on the floor cross-legged, some on burlap sacks or on long and narrow multicoloured carpets called *pattas*. There are five rows of four or five children in each, with the child in the rear of each row having his or her back against the wall, and the rows on each side lined with shoulders against the walls. The seating is arranged by the AWW, though she also physically shifts children in reaction to their behaviour during the course of the morning. Younger children generally sit at the front of a row, occasionally moving to sit beside the AWW and facing the group.

During some activities such as physical exercises, children stand in their place as directed by the AWW. During games such as 'duck-duck goose,' or 'drop the hanky' children are organized in a circle of the whole group against the walls of the program room. Children also sit in a circle for mealtime. There are set times for having a drink of water and going to the toilet. However, as the need arises, individual children will ask permission and leave the room to go to the kitchen for a drink or into the next room to the toilet.

POSITIONING

In this section we ask where the teacher or teachers are located in relation to the children, and if and how this changes during the course of the day. Positioning as a teaching strategy "is the process of placing oneself near other individuals, groups or objects in ways that support children's learning and that maintain children's safety" (Mac Naughton & Williams, 2005, p. 135). Some general observations follow next, pointing to important differences and similarities.

At whole group time at Little Lake and Tshwane, the teacher faces the children, who sit as a group on the floor. The teacher at Tshwane, and the lead teacher at Little Lake, each sit in a chair, placing themselves higher than the children. The other teachers at Little Lake sit on the floor behind the children, participating with them. The teacher at Sunbeam often stands while the children sit on the floor, creating a significant difference in height between them. Positioning of teachers at Little Lake and Tshwane is more variable than at Sunbeam: during free play time, the teachers at Little Lake and Tshwane circulate in the room; at Little Lake, teachers at free play generally join the children, sitting beside them and offering instruction, modelling play strategies, or asking questions. Teachers at Little Lake were more likely to move down to the children's level than the teacher at Tshwane. All participants at Little Lake and Tshwane have freedom of movement in the classroom for large periods of time in the program schedule; at Sunbeam, only the adult participants have freedom of movement. Teachers at Little Lake and Tshwane use verbal commands and requests to position children. The teacher at Sunbeam uses verbal commands and physical interventions.

Little Lake

During free-choice time, teachers are generally positioned at or near tables with the children, sitting or standing, making themselves available to give directions or offer assistance. Children are situated throughout the room, and the coordinator frequently moves about as a way of keeping check on their activity, or organizing and gathering materials on their behalf. During group work time, the coordinator situated herself at the front of the group of children either standing or seated on a small chair. The other adults sat on the floor with the children at the back of the group, or stood behind them. Teachers frequently used hand over hand guidance during work time to demonstrate letters, etcetera. During these observations it was noted that this kind of guidance or instruction was often coupled with friendly conversation, as in the following example.

> Teacher: (smiling at little boy) *Where is your pencil? Are you eating it? You were that hungry? I thought you were going to eat snack?*
>
> Child: (Hiding something behind his back, suddenly and laughingly brings out the pencil as if to surprise the teacher) *I found it!*
>
> Teacher: *There it is. You're tricking me!*

The physical space, with its many low barriers that defined the learning centres, would allow children to place themselves at a distance and out of sight from their playmates. This was not normally the case however, and children generally placed themselves in proximity to one another during free choice time. This did not mean that they played actively with one another or engaged in a task with a shared purpose; they were often engaged in separate activities in close physical proximity. The absence of intense interaction between the children in this small group was notable, reflecting quite markedly the indigenous interaction patterns of native peoples who are reported to communicate effectively in quiet, often non-verbal ways (Lipka, 2002; Mohatt & Erickson, 1981).

Tshwane

The teacher's position changes in accordance with the schedule and groupings, with the teacher in front of all the children at story and pre-reading time, and circulating during small group activities. When the teacher is in front of the whole group there is very little child-to-child interaction, though there is some occasional fiddling or poking. This is met with mild admonishment by the teacher and a reminder to pay attention. During small group time, when the children are seated at the tables, there is some interaction between the children; however, the level of noise is low. During independent activity time, the children go to the interest areas of their choice. Children play and work together without anyone telling them to cooperate. Over a four-year period of visiting this preschool there were no observed instances of extremely difficult behaviour or children fighting seriously.

It seems that interaction is controlled more by the teacher than by the organization of space. However, the space allows for certain kinds of interaction and indigenous culture appears to persist in subtle ways. During the independent activity, for example, children relate to each other in a very cooperative way. They have access to the kitchen and perform tasks like serving others, which is reported to be similar to what is expected of them at home.

Sunbeam

The AWW sits on the floor with her back to the wall, facing the children, at about the midpoint of the long side of this small, rather darkened room. When the AWH is in the program room, she mostly sits beside the AWW to the left and near the kitchen. When leading exercises or games, singing songs or reading a story, the AWW stands, moving back and forth in the narrow space at the front of the room. The AWW frequently also moves between the rows of children and between children within rows, to quiet them and keep them from moving about or from their space. As the AWW stands, whether she is disciplining the children or telling a story, the children are looking up, craning their necks, while the teacher is looking down upon them.

The greatest change in interactions occurs with changes in grouping during meal time, when children freely talk amongst one another, and when the AWW leaves the children unsupervised, even briefly. Then there can be an uproar, the children become boisterous, followed by a quick and firm rebuke from the AWW. This pattern was observed often: the children shifted, seemingly on cue, between tight control and spontaneous release and back again. Bhattacharjee (1999) used the word *dhammaal* to mean uproar in the context of disobedience at school. In her study of a municipal primary school in Gujarat, the children "carried out little subversions within their immediate environments, without getting out of their 'places'" (p. 346). This involved talking, teasing, hitting, and playing. Bhattacharjee described the teacher's discipline strategy as "mob control" supported by the "ideology of the stick" kept visible at the front of the classroom (p. 338). At Sunbeam there was also a stick on display. We doubt that the application of the idea of resistance is applicable in the situation of the anganwadi. Certainly the children did not subvert authority. Rather, they brought on stern measures: the stick or a slap, and tears. As well, it would be necessary for a deeper analysis to consider the issue of gender here, as it was boys, those primarily involved in *dhammaal*, who worked to disrupt the female-led classroom.

The small size of the room, the large number of children in relation to the space, and the absence of materials, all contribute to the group's focus on the activity at hand. Arranging children in rows is used as a means to focus children's attention on the teacher, and precisely, to diminish the possibility for play or child to child interaction. Conversely, the circle formation encourages their social interaction, and allows all children to see each other. Structuring the children in rows with the teacher formally located at the front also creates a hierarchy of distance between teacher and pupil, even if the physical space is not great. A further means to create distance, as suggested by Thirumalai (2003) in his analysis of Edward Hall's (1966) proxemics, is the use of a loud voice, much louder than required in the small space.

The consistent presence of structure within a classroom space is typical in Indian preschool and school classrooms. Structures are thought to *induce* discipline. This pattern of structure is thus encountered by children beginning with preschools, followed up by primary schools, and extends well up to the high school. Art activities emphasize colouring within the lines and selection of appropriate colours as the correct way of learning art. Schools typically begin morning assemblies with children standing in rows of straight lines, reciting morning prayers in unison, with acts of breaking lines or fidgeting looked down upon. Sitting upright with folded arms and a finger on the lips indicates a child who is properly disciplined, in accordance with Indian norms.

Another private preschool near Sunbeam was also observed by the research team. There, while learning to write, children were taught to create 'equivalent' spaces between two words. This was accomplished by asking children to place one end of a vertically placed eraser on completion of a word, and begin a new word on the other end of the eraser. The teacher would erase a word if the spaces were not equal, and remind the child that the teachers in first grade would not wait for the child while writing on the board. Interviews with parents revealed a trust on the parents' part regarding the methods teachers use with their children, as well as the parents' stance of non-interference. The parents would actually reinforce these structures at home by telling their children to do as the teacher says. Transitions to these structures from preschool to higher grades are swift and experienced unquestioningly.

PRESCHOOL – HOME CONNECTIONS

In this section, we ask to what extent the preschools resemble the children's homes in terms of organization of space, norms governing relations between adults and children, activities, behavioural expectations, and the like. In what ways and through what mechanisms are there similarities between the preschools and the homes? A few general observations will follow in relation to each setting. In chapter 5 more will be said about decor and the use and display of materials in the preschool spaces.

At Sunbeam and Little Lake the adult-child relationships were found to be reflective of those established in the home, and were clearly familiar to the children. That is, there was little or no discontinuity in the norms governing adult-child relations between the home and the school. Children and adults met one another's expectations for appropriate behaviour. The situation at Tshwane was more mixed, with the school organized and its activities patterned on a western schooling model, yet within that context there remained much that was familiar to the children: the manner in which the teacher addressed (or admonished) them, the saying of grace before snack or lunch time, the ease with which children fetched their own maize meal porridge bowls from the kitchen, bringing them back to the small tables in the classroom. In contrast, at Little Lake, teachers consciously managed social interactions in ways that promoted and supported indigenous cultural values; for example, the sweet grass ceremony as a prayer to start the day and the giving of thanks to the Creator for all.

All three preschools, in their physical set-up as teaching and learning spaces, were modelled on local ideas of a school. In the cases of Sunbeam and Little Lake, however, social interaction was influenced by culturally established norms governing adult-child relations. At Little Lake, children are not grouped in large numbers of same-aged peers within the home setting; at home they may be cared for by other adults in the community who have a collective responsibility for their wellbeing. Thus the social dimension of Little Lake's preschool space, as defined by the adult-child relationships, was familiar to the children; adults referred to themselves as grandma and aunty, underlining the presence of an affective relationship to the children and pointing to an important cultural value. In some cases the children also had an actual kinship relation with a staff member.

An important opportunity for parent-teacher connection is when, or if, the parent brings the child to the preschool and hands him or her over to the teacher. When this occurs, communication can be specific and to the point. In contrast, the children at Tshwane are bussed to school, and communication between parent and teacher is more formal: notes are sent home, or telephone calls are made. Such information would be shared at Little Lake with the bus driver, who also works at the school, so she is an important point of contact.

Little Lake

The social dimension of the preschool space defined by the adult-child relationships would be familiar to the children from home. However, the preschool was also very much a place for children to be prepared for real school, on the reserve, where a hybrid mix of western and Aboriginal cultures prevailed and where the school was engaged in the community's effort to reinforce the native culture and develop the children's local identities within the larger Canadian context.

Tshwane

On the surface, there would seem to be little relationship between home and school in the preschool's formal activities: the setting in question here is clearly modelled after an idealized vision of a western type of school with the exception of the babies' room, that has some mats for children to sleep on, one crib, and very few toys—a small ball, a doll, and 3 to 4 pieces of a large LEGO-like toy. In this space with one caregiver, the 18 to 24 month old toddlers mostly wander about. Nevertheless, there are many ways in which the school reflects the kind of social relations of the community and home. The preschool has played an important but informal community outreach role. The principal knows all the children, their families, what they need, who is orphaned, who is HIV positive, and so on. For example, one child with unruly hair was reported to be looked after by "a very old granny." The principal was going to take her to have her hair plaited (braided) that afternoon, pointing to the deeply rooted possibly pan-African belief that children are the responsibility of the community, not only of the immediate family (Nsamenang, 2004).

In relation to local cultural expressions reflected in the school space, there is a poster of duties at the preschool, indicated by colour code. Children know which colour team they are in—cleaning up, serving lunch, etcetera. There is no such poster of duties in homes of course, but this is an instance of how values, conceptions of childhood and child-rearing, including a responsibility to perform tasks, are related to the family or household. Responsibility is taught early with tasks being assigned according to African conceptions of child development and intelligence (Serpell, 1993).

Sunbeam

Although it may be too broad a generalization, traditionally in India the authority of adults over children is unquestioned in the home, and this authority is transferred to the AWW and AWH in the preschool (Gupta, 2008). It would appear that the home-preschool correspondence at Sunbeam was close to absolute in terms of behavioural expectations, teachers' authority, and parents' and teachers' conceptions about what the function and activities of the preschool should be. Teachers were members of the community and thus subject to close scrutiny should they deviate from parental expectations of behaviour towards the children, including the use of corporal punishment. Home-preschool differences lay mainly in the fact that children would not be in the presence of so many same-age peers in situations outside of the preschool, nor would their homes be occupied by a large group of unrelated people.

DISCUSSION

At the outset of this chapter, it was noted that structural qualities of the environment are independent of human interaction, while process qualities require human interaction. What is clear, however, is how the two are so often interrelated. Let us look, for example, at the issue of adult-to-child ratios.

A simple count of the numbers of children and adults provides a quick and easy means of comparison. In many western countries this aspect of preschool service is carefully regulated according to legislation. The ratio 'rule of thumb' in settings in Canada and the United States is that as the age of children goes down, the number of caregivers should rise, with about one adult for three or four infants considered acceptable in many cases. Younger children, it is believed, need more individual attention for optimal development. Older children are more oriented to peers and in western thought considered more self-directed in their learning; however, they are also thought to continue to require close individual attention from an adult caregiver. One adult is judged able to care for about eight children aged 4 or 5.

Child-to-adult ratios provide a quick view into local beliefs concerning children, learning, and teaching as these are embedded in a culture. As Tobin (2005, p. 422) observes with regard to Japan, a high adult-to-child ratio does not universally lead to problems in learning. And, as Moss (2005) notes in his essay on the construct of quality, "ideas about pedagogical work are inherently perspectival, each perspective is inscribed with its own understandings, traditions, and values" (p. 412). Thus, from a western point of view, the ratio of children to adults and the sheer numbers of children in the preschool classrooms in India and South Africa appear too high to support good learning outcomes. From an Indian and South African perspective, the issue is much more complex.

How did the issue of ratio play out in the case study preschools? The highest adult-to-child ratio was at Tshwane preschool (1:25 to 30 children); the lowest at Little Lake (3 or 4:6 to 12 children), and in between was Sunbeam (2:30 children). In other words, the greatest number of adults was in the preschool with the least number of children, a situation that would have been true even with full attendance. At Little Lake and Sunbeam, non-teaching staff helped improve the ratio, as did the manner in which the principal at Tshwane circulated from classroom to classroom. The cook at Little Lake, while having no specific duties related to the educational program assigned to her, engaged with the children for about an hour each day. Her involvement went beyond preparing the meal and serving it to the children, as in this example:

> The cook and a child are sitting at an art table, making hand prints on paper. The child is painting her right hand with red paint, using a brush held in her left. The cook is pressing the palm of her own right hand that is covered with red paint onto a large piece of green paper.

> Cook to child: *This is how I make it, look* (presses hand).

> Child: *A red hand?*

> Cook: *This, look.*

> Child: *Oh, that's a red hand.* Continues to paint her hand.

> Cook fills in handprint with brush. Child opens and closes her hands, gets up from table and walks off.

Again from a western point of view, the amount of physical space per child might be an even greater concern in two of the settings. The European Commission Childcare Network recommends four square metres per child for 3 to 6 year-olds (Beach & Friendly, 2005, p. 3). In this study, Sunbeam anganwadi, having one of the largest numbers of children, had the smallest program space at just over one square metre per child. Little Lake had by far the largest amount of space per child with a rough estimate of 5 square metres per child, while Tshwane was somewhat in between at approximately 3 square metres per child. In each case we have seen how ratio, as well as size of space per child, are intimately tied to the forms of interaction that prevailed, underlining the points that Strong-Wilson and Ellis (2007) make with regard to Reggio Emilia's conception of the environment as third teacher, though in a different manner from that intended by the exponents of the approach.

Another structural/process element related to ratio is group size. In educational settings such as school-based kindergartens, where there is typically one teacher per classroom, ratio is more often discussed in terms of class size. The matter of class size is a highly charged political issue in the West, very much part of the discussion of educational reforms. The importance of small class size is in the West a belief strongly held by parents as well as by teachers themselves (Snider & Roehl, 2007), though research on its benefits are inconclusive (Milesi & Gamoran, 2006; Yan & Lin, 2005). Moreover, reductions in class size do not necessarily bring on a change in the way teachers teach (Graue, Hatch, Rao, & Oen, 2007).

With regard to the variety of ways in which children were grouped, it is thought that being a member of a large group can lead to a negative perception of crowding. Much of the research on crowding has been done from within the disciplines psychology and design, and few have focused on the situation in preschools. An oft-cited study by Evans and Lepore (1993) suggested that large numbers of children in a small space is highly stimulating for children and may lead to withdrawal, evidenced, for example, by a child turning to face the wall. Studies by Liddell and Kruger (1987, 1989) found that crowding had only a moderate influence on children's play behaviour at preschool, making the largest difference—more onlooker behaviour—for children who experienced crowding at home and at school. It may also be the case that teachers, unawares, benefit from the emotional dampening effect of crowding on children (withdrawal) as they undertake whole-class teaching in a small space such as that of Sunbeam described above. Indeed, children would occasionally fall asleep. Loo (1972) found less aggression among children in a crowded classroom condition, and that "children isolated themselves by interacting with fewer other children ... Thus a spatially crowded condition seemed to create physical and psychological restraints on children, as demonstrated by fewer social behaviours" (p. 379). It might also simply be the case in which teachers are "geared up to handle large numbers of children in the classroom" as expressed by Joshi (2009, p. 295), due to the perceived inevitability of the situation.

While physical and psychological *tolerance* for crowding has been found to be similar across cultures (Evans, Lepore, & Allen, 2000), *perceptions* of crowding differ amongst cultures and within socio-economic class. Collectivist, non-contact cultures (Hall, 1966) living in high density conditions such as in Japan, are more likely to experience crowding as a stress, and to use strategies to increase social isolation in crowded situations, such as reading on the subway (Iwata, 1992). However, in a collectivist contact culture such as India, child socialization supports a positive perception of crowds. As expressed by a leading Indian scholar in ECCE to one of the authors, "our children like to be in groups." In this case, the environment at Sunbeam with its relatively large grouping within a small space dovetails with cultural aims for childhood socialization. In a study carried out in another collectivist contact culture, Kenyan children were observed to choose to be in close physical contact with each other and to crowd three to a desk even when there was space for this not to occur (Cleghorn, Merritt, & Abagi, 1989). At Little Lake, within a collectivist, non-contact First Nations culture, the partitioned environment provided a means of structural isolation, although the numbers of children were few. The partitions at Little Lake may also have served indigenous cultural patterns of teaching and learning; learning by observing is encouraged over learning from verbal instructions. A question remains about the influence of the visual boundaries. Citing a study by Legendre, Schneider (1993) noted, "In preschools where there were many visual boundaries, children generally spent more time in close proximity to adults" (p. 96), desiring to keep them in view.

In each of this study's three preschools, class size was mitigated differently. At Sunbeam, the additional staff member had the official designation of Helper. The Helper, having less training, was more likely to use harsh discipline strategies and she played a role in keeping children's behaviour in check. Her official duties centred on feeding and cleaning. (See chapter 6 for a discussion of care and pedagogical dimensions.) However, the two mealtimes occupied 30% of the morning's activities, and she was present in the program room for long periods at a time. She also assisted children during the toileting routine. The AWW did not enter this room, allowing her to be mostly attentive to the children remaining in the program room. This was unlike the situation at Tshwane where the lone teacher was fully responsible for her class of thirty children for the duration of the program, with the exception of the few moments in a day or during a week that the principal would visit.

Though there were few children attending the morning class at Little Lake on the day of the video-observation, this was not an unusual occurrence. The afternoon class for older children from the kindergarten at the band school had eight attending on the same day. This situation allowed for more diffuse adult attention than at Sunbeam, where the AWW did not generally move from her position at the front of the class except to discipline or rearrange children. At Little Lake, the coordinator frequently moved throughout the room, pinning a child's painting on the drying line, writing a child's name on her drawing, and at one point, stopping to mop up around the water table. During outdoor play, she remained indoors, cleaning the room after free play, and preparing for group-work time. At Tshwane the teacher moved quite seamlessly from whole group to small group activities along with the children, with a minimum of disruption during the shifts.

These three preschools throw considerable light on the topic of home/school continuities and discontinuities. These can be seen from a theoretical vantage point in terms of border crossing. Border crossing was defined in chapter 1 as the ability to shift cognitively as well as culturally, and when possible or when necessary linguistically, between different taken-for-granted ways of looking and understanding the world as represented, for example, by the home and the school (Aikenhead & Jegede, 1999; Nsamenang, 2004; Serpell, 1993). Thus it is important to consider the extent to which the children in these three preschools were required to cross such borders as they moved from home to preschool and back again.

CHAPTER 4

Firstly, Sunbeam is located within sight of the children's homes and in fact is located in a building that is much the same as the homes nearby. Thus the children cross very little ground or physical distance to get to the preschool. Secondly, despite the fact that the children could take themselves to the preschool (with the mother watching from her own doorstep), they are held by the hand, usually by a parent, as they are brought to the preschool. Thirdly, the staff (the AWW and AWH) that the children find at the preschool are members of the immediate community and well known to the parents and to the children, outside the preschool. Next, the language spoken at the preschool is the same language as is spoken at home. In sum, the transition appears almost seamless, however what goes on in the anganwadi is clearly designed to prepare children for the kind of experience they will have in regular school, quite a drastic shift from the routines and activities of the home.

In contrast, the children who attend Little Lake are bussed to the preschool, located as it is in a community institution a few kilometres from their homes. The building and the layout within does not resemble the children's homes. Nevertheless, the teachers and helpers are indeed like parents in the quiet, warm manner in which they interact with the children, calling themselves Auntie or Grandma. Thus we might say that from an affective point of view, there is no border to be crossed. Although most of the children use English at home, both English and the indigenous language are used in the preschool, the intention being to develop the children's knowledge of their heritage language and culture and thus to nurture personal identities that will ensure them a secure place within the larger Canadian multicultural setting. Further, although the activities of the preschool differ from those of the home, the manner in which teaching takes place is not unlike the way that children are socialized at home: with little verbal instruction children are expected to learn when they are ready, mostly by observing older children and adults. This is reflected in the situation observed in an urban AHS centre by Miskimmin (2007), in which an Aboriginal teacher preparing her group for a field trip was challenged by her colleague for taking on what she believed was an alien style of relating to children.

> Before setting out, the teacher first laid down the ground rules of the walk (children to hold hands, not run off, look both ways before crossing the street, etcetera). Immediately two children became rambunctious and the teacher attempted to rein in their behaviour. The assistant teacher, an AHS mother who had had the job for a few months, said to the teacher, half facetiously, "…, you sound like a white mother!" (p. 122)

Accounts of this type of teasing were shared with the researchers by several Aboriginal teachers, in relation to comments to their own children. Children judged to be talking and asking too many questions were teased, "You sound just like a little white girl/boy." These anecdotes point to the fact that cultural identity is clearly in the consciousness of these adults, suggesting that it is part of the surface culture as described in many accounts of racial awareness when different racial groups are in contact and experience a history of conflict (Guerrero & Enesco, 2008; Hirschfeld, 1993).

At Tshwane we see the issue of border crossing played out differently again. Many of the children travel over large distances by minibus or car to arrive at the preschool. Once there, they find a building that is unlike any of the homes. Most of the homes are small bungalows built of cement block or bricks, with tin roofs. The preschool is a large, well-built single story red brick building with a red tile roof. The grounds of the preschool are large and fenced with play and climbing equipment. As you will read in chapter 5, the hallways of the preschool are decorated with posters, six of which contain messages about HIV/AIDS, one with Mickey Mouse, another with edifying sayings about going to school. Once inside the classroom, the children find one side set up with child-sized tables that seat four to six, another side is carpeted and ready for circle time, songs, dancing, or group reading readiness. Another corner is organized with interest areas—a small kitchen, a doll corner, some books. The walls are decorated with pictures of numbers and letters as well as some of the children's art work. Thus the boundary crossed from home to preschool in this regard is large. Beyond that, however, the children find much that is familiar: the teacher uses a language most of them know well and generally speak at home. The teacher also uses English, especially when formally teaching, since this will be the language of instruction when the children go to regular school. So here we find the teacher engaging in cultural transmission, taking the children from the language and culture of the home to the language and culture of western or post-colonial schooling. In an interesting way however, as noted in the discussion of policy in chapter 3, the aim here is also to foster a secure identity, in this case one that softens age-old racial and ethnic differences between groups within a post-apartheid South Africa where everyone is deemed to be equal. The extent to which these boundary crossings are more than linguistic and cultural, amounting to fundamental cognitive shifts, remains unanswered for now.

MATERIAL CULTURE AND SPATIAL CONSIDERATIONS

This chapter examines the way preschool space is constructed and used in the three settings with reference to pedagogical materials. A basic assumption in our study was that the arrangement of the preschools as learning spaces, including the selection and placement of materials, is purposeful and holds some significance for understanding approaches to learning and teaching and conceptions of children and childhood. Materials are described as an element of the spatiality of preschool, their meaning constructed from the interaction between physical and social forces. In this view, "the way space is organized in schools *produces* particular social relations ... and space is made *through* the social—it is enacted and so continually created and recreated" (McGregor, 2004, p. 2). Importantly, global and local influences are not separate forces acting on early childhood practice in this view, but "they are intimately bound together." Global processes "operate in particular local areas, thus shaping that area, but also themselves [are] remade in the process" (Holloway & Valentine, 2000, p. 767).

We ask if there are elements in the organization of materials within the given spaces that point to western conceptions and theory regarding ECCE, and if so, do these elements support or conflict with local goals and conditions? What lessons can we take from the design and use of space in three culturally diverse preschool settings? In what ways can the materials be seen to reflect local concerns and priorities for young children? What is the meaning of materials to children and to adults in these settings? Together, the three preschool settings tell us much about what communities believe is the correct way to work with children, as well as the dual influences of local (indigenous) cultural practices on the one hand and the trend towards globalization in ECCE on the other. We suggest that the ways in which preschool environments are arranged point to important differences in conceptions of childhood and ECCE. Even when materially impoverished, the organization and use of space directs attention to what a community considers to be important for its children. This includes the design of the building, its location in the community, and the people, materials, and furnishings within it. There lies deeper meaning in *space,* however, when it takes on social meaning as *place.*

Place is constructed, interpreted, conceived, or imagined through the ways in which people inhabit space, through routine physical interactions and lived experiences (Ashcroft, 2001; Brey, 1998; Tuan, 1977). A physical locality becomes place when human consciousness creates and attaches meaning to it. As one gradually experiences a space, certain meanings and values are endowed upon it (Relph, 1976). The sociological perspective assigns prominence to symbolic meanings, such as describing place as school or as a site for work versus play. These meanings are structured socially or are learned interpretations of objects, events, or places (Giddens, 1991). The socio-cultural perspective values built or natural environments as places that people become attached to not simply for practical reasons but because they may hold emotional, symbolic, and spiritual meaning. This was particularly important in the preschools examined in the present study which were located in communities undergoing rapid social change.

The importance of place is also central to the concept of "developmental niche." Super and Harkness (1986) describe developmental niche as "a theoretical framework for studying the cultural regulation of the micro-environment of the child" (p. 552). The framework explains the interaction of three subsystems involved in the process of developing culture: "the physical and social settings in which the child lives; culturally regulated customs of child care and child-rearing; and the psychology of the caretakers" (p. 552). The framework applies as well to preschool, as a "niche" for development.

Preschool settings as spaces for the care and education of children are created and used with intent, which may be clearly articulated in the form of policy or legislation, or rest unexamined within cultural practices or historical traditions. Western (minority world) taken-for-granted discourse on ECCE emphasizes the importance of flexible space arrangements for ECCE programs in order to be deemed of quality. In the West, established tradition in preschool education, what Bennett, Wood, and Rogers (1997) call the "nursery inheritance," has included a belief in the value of learning through the hands-on manipulation of materials, in particular, and through self-directed play. Typical settings therefore include structures such as learning centres: designated space such as block corners, book corners, and so on. The environment is organized so children can choose materials and actively learn through play with blocks, construction kits, puzzles, and dress-up with miniature home equipment. In centre-based ECCE programs, one finds the adult's role involves a significant amount of observing children and talking to them as they handle these materials. According to Fleer (2003), in these arrangements we (in the West) position children in an artificial, child-centred world geared to their needs, with environments or spaces intended to produce predetermined outcomes (Dahlberg & Moss, 2005; Moss & Petrie, 2002). That is to say, the learning space is constructed as a "social technology" (Lawn, 1999, p. 77), with some definite purpose in mind. Our study prompted us to ask if and how this is the case elsewhere such as in the three international settings.

The vision of an early childhood classroom in the minority world is of a single, multi-purpose room, stocked with materials freely accessible to children, arranged according to themed activity centres. Tables are mainly for using small manipulative materials, crafts, writing, or eating. Larger materials are used on the floor. An open area is used for whole-class meetings led by the teacher, often referred to as circle time. The organization of space thus presumably supports the educational purpose of the program. In free play, small tables and play spaces reinforce the importance given to children working in small groups in collaborative learning. Room for larger gatherings is limited: the meeting area where children gather for teacher-led activities called circle time, often doubles as the block or the book corner. Frequent whole group activities are viewed as a sign of lower quality early childhood settings (Montie, Xiang, & Schweinhart, 2006). There are also likely to be few private play spaces, since a child playing alone is considered by some to be a worrying sign. Solitary play, as established in Parten's (1933) classic study, is considered less mature than social play, an idea that persists in early childhood discourse to this day. Children playing alone are often encouraged to pair up with a buddy. The private space that is available, in a reading corner, for example, is generally planned to permit adult supervision or monitoring. Although there is now research indicating that solitary play can be beneficial to children's development (Lloyd & Howe, 2003), the bias toward small group play persists and influences the materials and the organization of space available to children in preschools. The large blocks designed for social play in the early twentieth century by Patty Smith Hill and Caroline Pratt were purposefully created to be too large for children to manage on their own, thus pointing to a hidden curriculum within the materials themselves, in this case to promote cooperation.

Much recognition for new ways of thinking about early childhood settings has taken place in recent years, stemming in part from perspectives gained from Reggio Emilia (Ceppi & Zini, 1998; Strong-Wilson & Ellis, 2007). Firstly, as Loris Malaguzzi (1993) claims in his notion of a pedagogy of relationships, the pedagogical relationship is what makes a setting a learning place—knowledge is co-constructed in relationship between the teacher and children or between the children. This is similar to Helfenbein's (2006) assertion that place "must be seen possible only in its interactions" (p. 112) Secondly, the boundary of the learning environment extends into the community, ideally if not actually. Today we think differently than in the past about preschool and home connections, about the involvement of parents, and about parent education. The equipment and materials available to children are often real tools, art supplies, etcetera, representing what is available in the adult world and often reflecting the diversity of cultures (Fleer 2003). Thirdly, we think positively now about sharing space with children as equal participants. In this sense, a children's space is a "discursive space for differing perspectives and forms of expression, where there is room for dialogue, confrontation (in the sense of exchanging differing experience and views), deliberation and critical thinking, where children and others can speak and be heard" (Dahlberg & Moss, 2005, pp. 28-29). This does not mean that the space has no fixed features. As described by Wien and her colleagues (2005) who experimented with Reggio Emilia principles in a preschool in eastern Canada, children and adults can be creative and full participants within a design which is "fixed and stable" (p. 24). Thus we see in current western ECCE discourse a persistence of the tension between fostering cultural diversity on the one hand and creating uniformity of policy and practice, with its quest for consensus on definitions of quality, on the other (Myers, 1992; 2007; Tobin, 2005).

THE MATERIALS AND SPACE IN EACH SETTING

Little Lake

There was an abundance of materials and furnishings at Little Lake, making the space appear crowded. Cabinets often had a dual use as storage and dividers for learning centres. Learning centres consisted of a designated space for a specialized activity. The centres included (1) the materials related to the activity, (2) storage for the materials, and (3) room for several children to play or work within the boundary of the centre. Not all centres were designated as 'open' all the time. In one observation, 13 of 15 centres were open for the 9 children then in attendance: puzzles, logs (construction toy), animal centre (small plastic figures), writing (matching cards), house, reading, craft, paint, blocks, scissors, Cheerios® Play Book, writing centre, Marble Works® (toy), computer (closed), and play dough (closed). Most materials were open access, available to all children during free play or prior to the first all-group meeting of the day. Materials associated with a learning centre, which includes most materials, were used within the boundary of the learning centre. A large storage room containing other play materials and teaching supplies was for adult-access only.

Indigenous imagery was dominant on the walls, which had an abundance of child- and adult-oriented displays. Symbols of a wolf, a buffalo, and a feather were painted in a circle in a full-wall mural near the entrance to the toilet. A poster describing indigenous teachings was placed high up on the same wall out of the children's line of vision. The preschool mission statement was printed on a large poster beside the bulletin board. In contrast to the visual displays, there was little evidence of indigenous play materials. Some indigenous materials had religious significance or were associated with indigenous ownership protocol that prevents their use in the preschool space or other space accessible to non-native peoples. Indigenous materials were used in connection with a visit from an Elder, or in carefully arranged situations such as the smudging ceremony that marked the official start of the day's program at the morning circle. The children's playthings, however, did not include indigenous materials. Nor did they include many items from the natural environment. One exception was sand brought indoors from the playground, in which children traced letters with their fingers.

Tshwane

In the Tshwane preschool, the walls outside of the Grade R classroom were decorated with many posters. Six posters were about HIV/AIDS, one of which included an image of Mickey Mouse. As mentioned in chapter 2, in the entrance hall featured a fresco-type painting, which measured about 1.2 by 1.8 metres and depicted the history of the preschool from its days in thatch-roofed huts in the southern part of Botswana, to its magnificently tiled roof of today, which was donated by a church organization.

The Grade R classroom was arranged according to interest areas designated with carpeted space on the floor, and relevant materials. During free play time the children had access to all the materials that were set out. The crayons and paper were kept in a cupboard and taken out by the teacher during small group work at the child-sized tables. Interest areas included a block corner and a music corner. The low table pushed against a wall was covered in a cloth with an African print, and on it was set several musical instruments and toys. Taped to the wall above the table was a small label with the word 'MUSIC.' In addition, there was an area for playing with dolls and playing house. The one doll was white. The classroom was decorated with many posters, curriculum lists, etcetera. Some of the posters depicted white people or racially ambiguous people.

There were also didactic posters on the walls, the labels of which were written in English. However, in one of the observations, a poster was being used to teach the parts of the body. Although the parts of the body were labelled in English, the lesson was in Setswana, the home or first language (L1) of most of the children. The children were called one at a time to point to the different parts of the body, spoken in Setswana by the teacher. Thus we saw quite explicit attention to the local first language in the context of imported, foreign curriculum content (Nsamenang 2004).

There was a book corner in the Grade R classroom with about 10 books, none of which were in Afrikaans or any of the other official South African languages. Included were several booklets about AIDS, one titled *HIV and AIDS Affects all Children*, published by the Soul City Institute in Johannesburg. Some of the books could be considered culturally inappropriate, continuing the influence of the colonial era. For example, the cover of *My Bedtime Story* depicted a white mother and father reading to their children. This is the image of 'early literacy promotion' so often seen in newspaper articles in the West on the importance of reading to children at home. Elsewhere, literacy researchers such as Barton and Hamilton (1998) note that the image typifies the culture of the white middle class, while reading to preschoolers at bedtime is simply not a social class or cultural universal. Oral story telling may in fact be more widespread. Other books included: *It Takes a Village, Donald Duck and the Witch Next Door, My Book of Shapes, Itsy-Bitsy Spider, My First Action Rhymes, Hattie and the Fox*, and a Big Book version of Eric Carle's *The Very Hungry Caterpillar*. One of the large books used for L1 reading (*My Sister's Wedding*) had the Setswana translation pasted over the English text. The South African researchers explained that such translations are sometimes a too simplified version of the English; because of a lack of equivalent vocabulary the Setswana translation of an English sentence might be descriptive and thus three times as long.

There was a locked cabinet in the principal's office with about 30 to 50 additional children's books which the principal referred to as the library. Most were in English but a few were in Setswana and a few in Afrikaans. There was one series of encyclopaedia-type children's books—"to know about all sorts of things," reported the principal. These books were to be loaned out to teachers and parents. This limited access suggests again that children's books are not yet an integral part of the preschool culture. A year later, the books that had been donated to the school were prominently displayed in the Grade R room, though children were not observed to gravitate to the book corner to look at the books on their own.

The preschool's outreach to the community was evident by the above-mentioned informational HIV/AIDS posters that adorned its walls. The disease was being taken very seriously—children, teachers, parents could not fail to notice the materials. Even children not directly affected by AIDS could explain, up to a point, what it was.

Sunbeam

The material environment of the Sunbeam anganwadi was spare. There were no furnishings, and the few teaching materials that were in frequent use were placed on a small wooden shelf high on the wall in a corner of the program room. These were, in total, a ball, a cloth elephant, a tambourine, two plants in pots, and a small plastic container. Other play and teaching resources were stored out of sight of the children, and were not used during the period of observation by the researchers. The teacher did not have a desk or separate storage area for her own supplies, but she did carry a briefcase to the preschool. The case, which sat on the floor beside her, held her materials: a pen, one copy of a child's workbook, a cloth doll, and program record books. Materials were all accessed by the teacher only, used for the activity, and afterward were immediately returned to storage on the shelf, a hook on the wall, or the teacher's briefcase.

The walls were covered with a variety of visual learning materials. Posters, placed high, were about health, religion and education, including the warning signs of leprosy. There were several pictures of religious deities, and posters that depicted local imagery. Some of the educational posters included English. One poster for example, listed the names of the birds in three languages underneath each specimen: English, the local language, and Hindi. There were also several story strips hung on hooks, and a teacher-made mobile hung from the ceiling. There did not seem to be any deliberate attempt to place the posters within the view of children, or even the easy view of adults (their placement high on the wall did protect them from being destroyed by rodents).

Positioning Materials

Mac Naughton and Williams (2004) define positioning of equipment and materials in ECCE settings as "the process of placing objects in relation to each other or in relation to people … in ways that safely support and enhance children's learning" (p. 14). The view from western ECCE on how best to do this is quite specific. Research in western contexts indicates that "more space, more toys and equipment, and a partitioned environment rather than a large open space per child are indicators of higher quality programs" (Essa & Burnham, 2001, p. 70). Even the teacher is identified as an "educational material" in a textbook for beginning teachers (White & Coleman, 2000, p. 297). The variety and number of materials in a preschool has been established by Montie, Xiang, & Schweinhart, (2006) as "positively related to children's cognitive performance" (p. 327). In their 10-country study, which included several non-western nations (Finland, Greece, Hong Kong,

Indonesia, Ireland, Italy, Poland, Spain, Thailand, United States), and used data from the IEA Pre-primary Project, they found that the average number of materials per setting was 49, with a range of 1 to 80. With these ideas in mind, we can consider the preschools in our study, starting with Sunbeam Preschool, the one most at odds with the western notion of quality described above.

As an ICDS centre, Sunbeam was planned as a teaching and learning environment in addition to its paediatric (care) functions (LeVine et al., 1994) as described in more detail in chapter 6. Its paediatric functions were well supported, although the community served by the preschool was not impoverished. None of the children required supplementary nutrition. Many children brought a snack from home in a plastic container or tiffin, and ate this in addition to the ICDS supplement. Nevertheless, feeding remained a major activity in the centre. At another ICDS centre, we observed children coming to school with plastic bags for the same purpose. The children used their bags to clean their slates, the slates a forbidden academic-type teaching material in ICDS programs, before the bags were filled with a snack at the end of the day for the children to eat on their way home.

The shelves were mostly bare at Sunbeam despite the availability through the ICDS project at low cost of "story cards, charts, indoor and outdoor play material, colour concept, puzzles, school readiness kits, and activity kits" (Government of India, 2004). Even some well-resourced preschools in India visited by the researchers were spartan by western standards. Though the popularity of what is called the playway approach in India suggests the adoption of a western child-centred pedagogy with its focus on materials, the emphasis at Sunbeam remains on the relationship between teacher and pupils without the mediation of objects (Prochner, 2002).

Positioning materials to support learning, where there are few materials and when there is no intent that they be used on children's initiative, was mainly a matter of storage at Sunbeam. The high open shelf placed within the classroom put on display the modest teaching resources. Along with the wall displays of educational posters, the materials were an important visual element in the room, adding to its overall aesthetic, and helping to identify it as a preschool, just as the chalkboard does in Indian primary classrooms (Alexander, 2000).

The inclination from a western standpoint is to look at the Sunbeam anganwadi as impoverished in its lack of materials, a situation in need of greater resources. It is consistent, however, with provisions of objects for children's play at home. As with Mayan homes in a study by Gaskins (1996), where there were "few objects available to children for play, and virtually none that are intended to be supportive of or suggestive for play" (p. 359), there are few toys in the homes of the children attending Sunbeam. This may reflect a cultural value that emphasizes the importance of people over things (Messerschmidt, et al., 2009).

At Little Lake and Tshwane preschools there were many more materials in keeping with the conventions of western ECCE, in which more materials are associated with higher quality programs (Packer, 2000). The materials were sometimes arranged as collections according to a common theme and called learning or interest centres. Some of these displays were subject specific. Others focused on skills, such as the scissors centre, with the supposed purpose to aid small motor development and build pre-writing skills. The music centre at Tshwane was an example of a subject-specific learning centre. Arranging materials in this way, according to subject, skill, or theme, is intended to help children make sense of the preschool environment, which provides a wealth of choices. Warner and Sower (2005) describe "centres of interest" as "designed to pique children's curiosity" (p. 215); Beaty (2004) highlights their ability to support brain development by classifying knowledge for children. Learning centres are also a curriculum organizer with a long tradition in the ECCE field (Kuschner, 2001).

Beaty states that "many [preschools] follow a rule of thumb that counts four to six children to a large learning centre" (2004, p. 68). A question remains: how large does a learning centre needs to be? The relation between child behaviour, density, and resources was the topic of a study by Kantrowitz and Evans (2002). The researchers varied the number of children in the classroom while keeping the number of learning centres that were available the same, finding that the non-play time (off-task or unoccupied behaviour) increased along with the number of children per learning centre. However, the type of play (solitary, parallel, etcetera, using Parten's scale and functional, constructive, etcetera, drawing on Piaget), did not change, with the exception of a "marginal increase" in constructive play in lower density learning centres.

Learning centres influence social interaction as well as the curriculum by the way in which the centres group children and adults within the preschool space. The general idea in western preschool practice, is that the centres should encourage children's self-guided play. Moore (1986), looking at the influence of well-defined versus poorly defined learning centres, found "significantly fewer adults involved in activity pockets when they are well-defined and resource rich" (pp. 224-25). At the same time, in early childhood environments with well-defined learning centres, teachers' interaction with children was more active and classed as "co-action and encouragement" (p. 225). At Little Lake, the placement of items with high appeal throughout learning centres supported children in their apparent choice to scatter and play individually or in pairs. There were many more learning centres available than children to play within them. In this situation, two children who played a metre apart were sometimes separated by a shelving unit placed as a barrier between learning centres. Nor did teachers spend much time facilitating children's cooperative play. The greater focus was on developing skills perceived as important for school, as revealed in the coordinator's encouragement to children as they left from group time: "So away you go, and while you're playing, practice your colours, your shapes, and your numbers." The coordinator had clear academic goals for the children, which could be more ably accomplished through exploring materials with an adult 'expert,' (echoing a Vygotskian approach), than in peer play.

It may also be the case that greater numbers of materials leads to more object play and less social play. This was a finding in a study of children's play before and after the introduction of a set of enrichment toys by Liddell (1995) in South Africa. Even when these toys were minimal, as they were in Liddell's study, it was found that after enrichment there was an increase in solitary play and a decrease in language use by children. Caregivers in rural centres also used less language with children, explaining to the researcher that the enrichment toys "kept children occupied and permitted them to attend to other duties, such as food preparation" (p. 65). Western practice aims to develop children as self-directed learners who also engage in cooperative play with their peers. However, there is, at the least, an expectation that teachers remain involved by observing and guiding the play. This suggests a need for in-service or pre-service teacher education regarding the meaning and potential pedagogical use of such materials, if, that is, the aim is to promote a materials-based western model of preschool education.

This follows Gaskin's (1996) finding that Mayan mothers accepted children's play as a way to keep them busy while they were "get[ting] their work done" (p. 358). In Liddell's (1995) study, the positive impacts on the children's play were noted to be their greater attention to the objects, and their more mature object play. This is consistent with an earlier finding by Smith and Connelly (1980), who reported that solitary and small group play increased along with greater resources. In home situations in the West, toys such as children's picture books, paper and crayons are specifically marketed for their ability to amuse children while their parents or caregivers are otherwise occupied. Objects, in this case, are used as substitutes for social relationships. It is important to emphasize that more materials does not have the same impact in all situations, either across cultures or at home and in school. In Gupta's (2004) observation of the situation in private schools in New Delhi, fewer materials meant more group play, which in turn eased supervision of large numbers of children by a single teacher.

Along with the quantity of materials, partitioning the environment, or choosing not to do so, was seen to influence the nature of social relationships in our study. Learning centres are both a space for play with materials and a place for storing them. Large numbers of materials require careful thought to their storage (Bunnett & Kroll, 2000). If it is desirable for children to access them freely, the shelving and cupboards need to be low to the floor. This is also a safety consideration. One result, as at Little Lake, was a large number of storage units with each containing a small number of materials, making little use of the vertical space. However, while the child's line of vision is blocked by the shelving, the vertical space above was open to adults who use it to supervise children covertly. This contrasted with the situation at Sunbeam, where the absence of materials and furnishings facilitated intensive and constant engagement amongst the children and between the children and their teacher. Partitioning at Little Lake and Tshwane also had an influence on the teachers' movement, who needed to move throughout the room in order to interact with children. In this way, they dispersed their attention amongst the children. In contrast, at Sunbeam, the teacher could remain in place at the front of the room and concentrate her attention on the group.

It is general practice in western ECCE to require, or at least request, that children clean up at the end of play sessions. This is rationalized as a lesson in responsibility, citizenship, and a useful problem-solving task as they seek to find the proper place for everything (Cartwright, 2004). Clean-up time marks the end of one activity and serves as a transition to the next. Cleaning up after each free play session means that each day is self-contained, each new day a fresh start. At Little Lake, the main reminders of past accomplishments were crafts displayed on walls. The few children's drawings, which were primarily semi-permanent classroom decorations, served a similar function at Tshwane. In the case of Sunbeam anganwadi, teaching materials were simply returned to the shelf by the teacher or left by her on the floor beside her briefcase. Time was spent between activities repositioning bodies—aligning children into rows, moving them into a circle formation—and not materials; again, the focus is on people, not objects.

Accessing Materials

Providing children free access to educational materials within an environment structured by adults and with consideration for grouping and the schedule is a hallmark of the western ECCE tradition. This is most common in periods of 'free play.' Free play is an activity carried out over a protracted period of time in which children choose the activity and their playmates. A particularly important part of this is socio-dramatic play, using props, dress-up materials and furnishings with other children as a means to develop higher-level thinking skills, foster social relationships, and aid emotional growth. Free play is seen as the mark of a mature idea of early childhood education, as explained by Dudek (2000).

> In order to allow more relaxed kindergarten systems to emerge, not only must the environment and the space support free learning activities, but the staff and, to a degree, the children's parents, must understand kindergarten culture and be in tune with its traditions. When the staff are secure and mature as a profession (and the kindergarten environment is fully supportive), they are more open to the authentic needs of modern children's culture. (p. 24)

In reality, at least in the West, the teacher's surveillance during free play limits choice, and play is permitted according to constraints such as the number of children in the centre, the available materials, and the time allotted for play. Dudek's view, however, is that the least mature system is one in which the preschool includes direct teaching and school-like activities with little or no play. Phrased in another way, the most mature preschool system (high emphasis on play) is the one least like elementary school (with its low emphasis on play).

The free play sessions at Tshwane and Little Lake took a different course, being more whole group oriented at Tshwane, and including more direct teaching at Little Lake, than in the mature approach described by Dudek. At Tshwane, children remained together, collaborating at one learning centre before moving off to another, again as a small group. Children preferred to be in contact even if there was space for independent play. One result was that while some children manipulated materials, others observed. During the free play period at Little Lake, children selected materials and used them for sustained periods within learning centres, mainly alone or in dyads with other children or adults. One boy spent considerable time watching other children play. The bias in western ECCE is toward learning by doing. While observation is a technique used by teachers as a means to gain knowledge about child behaviour, it is not generally supported as a children's learning strategy. Indeed, it is classed as non-social play (onlooker/unoccupied behaviour) in stage theories of social play development (Parten, 1933). Children evidencing such behaviour on an ongoing basis are considered developmentally immature, and are supported by teachers in their bids to join in the play with their peers. At Little Lake no such attempt was made. The child's behaviour was neither encouraged nor discouraged; he was simply left to be. Their approach in this case may have reflected Aboriginal child-rearing patterns, where in the community and home children learn through observation and imitation (Kaulback, 1984). It is noteworthy that children at Little Lake used observational learning despite the physical barriers created by the many learning centres. Moore (1986) found that one outcome of well-defined learning centres was that children displayed "considerably more engaged or immersed behaviours with little or no time spent watching other activities or being interrupted" in their play. While this was reported by Moore as a benefit, it may be that for the children at Little Lake the use of learning centres does not support informal social and observational learning. Here the concept of surface versus deep culture may be relevant, in the latter's possible persistence into the otherwise western school-like setting. Deep culture refers to entrenched culturally-specific patterns of behaviour and thought that are taken-for-granted by the members of a group; that is, they lie outside the realm of self-awareness and are not generally conscious in nature.

The materials children selected when given free access at Little Lake included some surprising choices. Socio-dramatic play was minimal and sustained for only for a few minutes at a time, though solitary fantasy play was more frequently engaged in. Alternatively, school-like activities involving counting and crafts were extremely popular. This runs counter to research in international contexts indicating that when children are allowed free choice of activities, they rarely select pre-academic tasks (Lockhart, Xiang, & Montie, 2003). In many instances at Little Lake, children engaged in these activities alongside an adult. To varying degrees, all three preschools were less readiness programs for first grade, than they were a version of a school themselves. The fit between preschool and actual primary school was closest at Sunbeam, with its didactic teaching practices, minimal resources, and values emphasizing literacy, discipline, cleanliness, obedience, and patriotism (Alexander 2000). The fit was least evident at Little Lake, with its participatory teaching practices (Nsamenang 2006), plentiful and freely accessed resources, and values stressing spirituality, cultural allegiance, communalism, as well as literacy and numeracy. McElhinny (2007) observes that "Aboriginal Head Start programs have the dual, and perhaps contradictory, aims of preparing Native students for participation in mainstream schools and educating them in Aboriginal heritage" (p. 12). The staff at Little Lake, however, believed that children with a strong cultural identity were more capable learners in all situations.

Indigenous Materials

In western ECCE the matter of employing cultural materials—those associated with the non-dominant culture—is mainly considered within a discourse on diversity, which takes place in non-Aboriginal communities in Canada in line with the ideology of multiculturalism. The use of cultural materials at Little Lake is done for reasons of cultural survival in the context of systemic racism, a history of state-organized assimilation efforts, and inferior and inappropriate educational interventions.

As mentioned in the Parent Handbook, Little Lake aimed to provide "a holistic early learning environment that reflects First Nations cultural values and teachings into daily programming". The preschool takes a bicultural approach to education, whereby children are encouraged to retain their home culture through schooling and also be competent in the dominant culture (Pacini-Ketchabaw, 2007). This is accomplished in a number of ways, including the provision of standard school materials and toys and indigenous materials. In some cases there is a blending of material cultures. For example, the yardstick used as a pointer at the morning circle was given an indigenous meaning as a talking stick.

In general, at Little Lake materials with strong cultural meaning are not used as playthings. Bringing material associated with traditional and cultural knowledge into preschool has the potential to change its meaning. Moreover, it may breach cultural protocol. The coordinator was cautioned by Elders not to use drums in the preschool, as one example. The morning smudging ceremony using sweet grass, was done by the children under supervision and with the assistance of the coordinator. Smudging, or what the coordinator called "spirit-cleansing," is quite commonly used at the start of circle time in First Nations preschools, as well as some school kindergartens.

The few materials in use at Sunbeam anganwadi were indigenous, being locally made and having meaning within the local culture. The cloth doll used by the teacher during a song was similar to that which a child may have at home. The tambourine, an indigenous musical instrument, was used by the teacher as a device for keeping time in a game of hot potato.

At Tshwane, there were few materials other than a drum that suggested African culture and these were kept randomly along with other materials, with no apparent separation, again suggesting a kind of cultural hybridization. Although the preschool setting is very school-like, during independent activity time the children play and work together in the same manner they do at home with siblings, helping each other, and so on. Thus in terms of interaction patterns, the preschool would be quite familiar, again suggesting that deep or indigenous cultural patterns find their way into a setting that, on the surface, is physically organized along western preschool lines.

DISCUSSION

Western preschools typically have an abundance of materials organized into categories suggesting curriculum areas or type of play. This arrangement of materials was evident at Little Lake and Tshwane, but not at Sunbeam. The basic materials at Sunbeam were discussed in this chapter in terms of the importance given to teacher-child interaction rather than children's play or interaction with objects. All three preschools were designed to have a role in preparing children for school.

As a Grade R classroom, this was most highly formalized at Tshwane, where readiness for later grades and for useful participation in society was part of the official curriculum. Educational policy in the post-apartheid era has borrowed from a western model of outcomes-based education (OBE). This is reflected in Grade R "assessment standards" where learners (children) are expected to "differentiate between play and useful tasks at home," and "participate in creative activities that will stimulate entrepreneurial thinking (e.g. drawing, cutting, singing, playing, talking)" (DoE, 2008).

However, none of the preschools were merely an adjunct to primary school: each possessed a distinct preschool material culture in its own right. Third space theory and hybridity theory (Bhabha, 1994; Soja, 1996) is helpful as a means to understand this. The preschools, as seen in their use of materials in the present analysis, were neither school nor home but hybrid learning environments, the "space between home and school discourses" (Levy, 2008, p. 48). The preschool culture and the role of materials varied in part according to different home/school discourses, but they were also shaped by political, historical and social influences. The meanings attached to preschool, as a *space between*, are thus contested and the various discourses sometimes conflict, leading to the sort of disabling and "disorganizing hybridism" described by Nsamenang (2004, p. 10) as common in majority world preschools. Overall however, the preschools were seen to support indigenous culture, values, and beliefs, in their role of preparing children for formal schooling in their local communities.

CHAPTER 6

PAEDIATRIC AND PEDAGOGICAL DIMENSIONS

The out-of-home care and education of young children has historically been provided in separate institutions, each with its own practices, and grounded in different ideologies (Prochner, 1996, 2009a). In Europe, the crèche model of child care for children under the age of 3 had an overriding social mission "to lower the child mortality rates; to educate, normalize and civilize the mothers (including in a moral sense); and to assure the nation's strong race" (Vandenbroeck, 2006, p. 368). Infant schools and *salle d'asile* (asylum or refuge) for preschool-aged children had definite educational aims. However, due to the age of their charges, they also made provisions for feeding, sleeping, etcetera, and for the children's moral and social protection. The institutions were an alternative to play on the streets under the influence of older youth. In the twentieth century, the "'welfare' nursery school" (Aubrey, et al., 2000, p. 67) model emerged under the influence of Montessori in Italy and Margaret McMillan in England, with its focus on health promotion and skills development for working class children, and concern for their readiness for school. Contemporary programs, such as Head Start, evolved from this model and share the same concerns.

A trend in child care policy in Canada and other western nations is the recognition of child care as a site for early learning as well as care, while kindergarten and preschool programs are more likely to stress their educational purpose. Nevertheless, some elements of care are included within the typical kindergarten and preschool curriculum. Examples are physical development, part of movement and physical education (Krogh & Morehouse, 2008), and "nutrition and food experiences" which are a "significant aspect of personal and social development" as described by Eliason and Jenkins (2003, p. 207). The latter is considered to be particularly important in that families are eating "fewer meals together and they are eating more fast foods and snack items" (p. 208). Teachers thus have a role in shaping children's "eating habits" to minimize their nutritional risk and meet needs for social and emotional development (Murray, 2000).

In general, child development policy includes care and education as essential parts of the whole, along with community development and health and education supports for families. The policies under discussion in the three case study countries fit this vision. Aboriginal Head Start (AHS) guidelines in Canada list health promotion and nutrition, along with school readiness and goals for developing culture, language, parental involvement, and social supports. The Integrated Child Development Services (ICDS) program in India incorporates health promotion for mothers and their young children, as well as preschool education. Grade R programming in South Africa is now planned as a part of the formal education system; as noted earlier, an integrated service is planned for vulnerable 0 to 4 year olds, as well as those affected by HIV/AIDS. A government funded feeding program is provided for previously disadvantaged black children. In this chapter, we examine the components of care and education in turn, and in relation to one another, to shed light on the care and education dynamic, and the way policy unfolds in the day-to-day life of children and their teachers in community preschools.

Two Models of Child Care

As a framework for thinking about care and education we look to the work of LeVine et al. (1994). Their comparative study of child-rearing amongst the Gusii people of Kenya and white middle-class families in the United States provides insight into non-western and western visions of childhood via two distinct models of child care, the paediatric and the pedagogical. Although these models refer, in particular, to the characteristics of infant childcare, they include behavioural patterns and attitudes that persist through the early socialization of children into later teaching-learning situations, whether formalized or not. We have found that the respective values inherent in each of these models are found in various combinations in the EC programs in non-western settings with which we are familiar. It is to be noted, however, that the paediatric and pedagogical models are ideal types in the sociological sense; that is, seemingly dichotomized conceptual models made up of essential characteristics that are used in the social sciences for the purposes of analysing and understanding social phenomena (Weber, 1925/1946, as cited by Babbie, 2002). We acknowledge that the LeVine et al. models were developed from research in only two cultures—one African and the other North American; however, we have found them helpful for looking at and understanding a variety of EC settings. They are also useful because they bring attention to the shifts in EC practice that tend to coincide with economic development, such as: increased rural to urban migration, decreased child mortality, increased access to preschool and regular schooling, increased western curriculum content, and increased formal training of EC educators and teachers. Table 6 summarizes the characteristics of the models of childcare and their equivalents in EC programs.

To elaborate, the paediatric-pedagogical models are sometimes discussed in terms of a society's value on interpersonal relatedness versus independence, emotional interdependence versus autonomy, material interdependence versus material emancipation, and collective versus individualistic identity (Kağitçibaşi, 2007). Each model is well adapted to a group's needs for survival: the paediatric model to an agricultural subsistence economy and the pedagogical model to the highly complex and differentiated economy of urban North America, for instance. More specifically, when the home environment is relatively non-literate and non-western, as in rural South Africa and India, the model of childcare that prevails may be viewed as closer to the 'paediatric' than to the 'pedagogical' model (LeVine et al., 1994). That is, parental concerns are likely to emphasize health and survival, and the teaching of moral values may occur through oral story telling, but there is typically little use of language between adults and children for encouraging

Table 6. Adaptation of Paediatric and Pedagogical Models of Early Child Care and their Relation to Schooling (Source: LeVine et al., 1994; Kağitçibaşi, 2007)

	Paediatric model	*Pedagogical model*
Early maternal attention		
Emphasis/goal	Protection, health, survival	Active engagement, social exchange
Means	Soothing, responds to distress	Stimulation, proto-conversation, responds to babble
Cultural script for responsiveness	Modulates excitement, commands	Elicits excitement, praises
Time/care distribution first 30 months	Decreases (with evidence of survival)	Increases (with pre-verbal development)
Societal values		
Interpersonal/ emotional relatedness	Interdependence	Individualistic
Identity	Collective	Individualistic
Adaptation to group's need for survival		
Economy	Subsistence/still-developing/poverty	Complex, highly differentiated/ 'developed'
Physical environment	Precarious Need for group safety, cooperation	Controlled – safe Need for achievement, competition
Social organization to be maintained	Hierarchical	Egalitarian/ 'democratic'
Home/community-school link		
Language and social organization	Oral story telling, mixed age groupings of children, child-child interaction	Storybook reading, verbal interaction, questioning parent to child; same age groupings (e.g. day care)
Acquisitions of academic skills	Mastery of skills through observation and imitation	Early emphasis on pre-literacy (drawing, number, letter, shape recognition)
Home school borders to be crossed	School not a familiar place with cultural, linguistic, conceptual, borders to be crossed	School a familiar place due to style of interaction in home, TV, etc., minimal borders to be crossed

or answering questions, reading stories, vocabulary building, or conceptualization, as one observes in many educated middle class families in North America. Rather, value is placed on the child's ability to master specific skills through observation and imitation. This model is thus well suited to raising children in a precarious environment where survival depends on a shared communal orientation, on co-operation, and obedience to the commands of a knowledgeable Elder, and where sharing of communal tasks and of food is essential to group survival. This model of childcare also suggests a culturally-shared vision of the adult-to-be as one who can function within an hierarchical, communal society, where the authority of a parent or other adult (such as a teacher) is not to be questioned (Shumba, 1999). For children beyond infancy, the paediatric model shifts to what LeVine et al. (1994) call the respect-obedience model.

In contrast, the pedagogical model of childcare and early socialization is well adapted to the social and economic structure of the minority world where the majority of individuals complete secondary school, and a large percentage receive post-secondary education. Then, the vision of the adult-to-be may be of a person who values individual competition and achievement and is ideologically oriented to democratic ways of doing things—within families as well as in school and in society at large. Middle class parents, and especially mothers, dovetail their childcare methods to the kinds of interaction patterns that the child will encounter in school. These patterns are now found in schools across the world, due to the globalization of western schooling, as discussed in chapter 1. The patterns include the extensive use of language for listening, speaking, reasoning, explaining, asking, answering, comparing, labelling, computing, and eventually reading and writing. In preparation for the world of school, the mother is expected to take on a teaching role, in contrast to the paediatric model, in which children are often cared for by older siblings once they can walk and are no longer being nursed. In the pedagogical model the mother's attention to the child increases as the child gets older, with more and more attention being given to school-like activities and patterns of language use. Thus children are spoken to and even asked questions long before they can speak; many are read to years before they are expected to read; questions are encouraged, explanations are freely offered. Children's pre-reading and pre-writing play are especially encouraged and praised in home environments that are highly literate. In rural South African homes, it is not uncommon to find only one book: the bible. In urban North American middle-class homes, one might easily find dozens of books, and a child under the age of 2 might have a collection of 50 or more baby picture books. As a result, the middle-class child raised in the minority world is likely to find the interaction routines, as well as the materials in school, very familiar. The linguistic, cultural, and conceptual transitions from home to school are minimal.

As discussed in this chapter's introduction, ECCE programs in the West have inherited features of both the paediatric and pedagogical orientations. Since the 1960s, childcare and early education programs have conflated to some extent, with childcare in particular taking on a greater pedagogical role, as more and more children spend their preschool years in childcare centres. On the other hand, school-based programs such as kindergartens have largely retained their pedagogical orientation as a preparatory stage of formal schooling with minimal attention to paediatric concerns. Important exceptions are meal programs in schools for children deemed at-risk. In the United States, 60% of children in school are provided with lunch through the National School Lunch Program (LeVine, 2008).

To recapitulate, the paediatric orientation to child-rearing involves provision of food and shelter in the early years, and intellectual stimulation is a minor concern. In terms of EC programs, it is a social welfare program, sometimes called custodial, that minds children in the absence of their parents. Beyond food and shelter and medical care, this service generally adds moral training in social skills and teaches values such as listening to teachers and getting along with friends. Concern for health often extends to the family as a whole, and the mother in particular; joining with the mother—or instructing her—in raising a healthy child through clinics, feeding programs, and vaccination campaigns. The focus of the pedagogical orientation to child-rearing is mental and moral training, although physical well-being exists as a background concern. Indeed, the two orientations are not situated at opposite ends of a continuum, but represent distinct dimensions in the design of EC programs. Individual EC programs can be identified as having a high or low pedagogical orientation, and a high or low paediatric orientation. Programs with a high pedagogical/low paediatric orientation are mainly concerned with academics and preparation for later schooling; whereas those with a high paediatric/low pedagogical orientation focus on child welfare and survival. In the discussion of the case study preschools which follows, paediatric/pedagogical orientations will be considered in relation to the curriculum, the schedule, and the arrangement of the classroom environment.

CARE AND EDUCATION IN THE THREE SETTINGS

Little Lake

Care. Care activities centred on physical development are most evident in the breakfast and lunch programs at Little Lake. The dining area is adjacent to the kitchen, and the tables for eating are not normally used for teaching or play activities. The space is clearly distinguished as a 'dining space,' with wall displays and place settings for diners. Adults eat at the same time as the children, but do not always sit with them at their tables. Wall displays in the dining area include posters related to nutrition—*Canada's Food Guide, First Nations, Inuit, and Métis*—and materials related to national health awareness campaigns, such as Heart Month in February.

Children wash their hands in a well established routine before sitting down to their breakfast and lunch: they line up at the sink, and when it is their turn, wash their hands under close supervision of staff. The water is turned on by the teacher who sets the temperature, and it is left running from the faucet for all children. Children stand on a plastic step stool to reach the sink. They dry their hands with a paper towel which is handed to them by the teacher, and discard it in a garbage can beside the sink. This activity illustrates a key element of care at Little Lake, with its abundance of direct adult supervision.

The children's toilet is located near the library area. There is a single toilet for boys and girls. A toilet for staff and visitors is available in an adjoining building, accessible through a common hallway. Children use the toilet on a 'need to go' basis and do not ask permission. Similarly, drinking water is available to the children at anytime. Although drinking water supplies are contaminated on many reserves (Indian and Northern Affairs Canada, 2003), water was judged safe to drink from the tap at Little Lake.

Caring for children's cultural identity by promoting and protecting culture and language is tied to caring for children's physical health. An example is the preparation and serving of traditional foods. The cook prepares two meals: a light breakfast when the children arrive, and a lunch at noon just before they depart. The breakfast and lunch menus are posted each week for parents to view, both for their information and as a form of parent education. Lunch, including a hot item such as soup or stew, is made on site, accompanied by a starch such as bannock, potatoes, or cheese buns. The "knowledge and preparation of traditional foods" such as bannock and wild meat stews is a specific requirement for the position of cook, as stated in the *First Nations Head Start Standards Guide* (Health Canada, 2005, p. 22).

A further example of caring for culture is the attention to children's spiritual development through the daily ritual of smudging, the sweetgrass ceremony at Little Lake which emphasized the "interconnected relationship between health and spirituality," as in Gerlach's (2008, p. 22) description of her research with members of the Lil'wat Nation in British Columbia.

Schedule. Little Lake is a part-time program, operating three mornings per week (see chapter 2 for the detailed schedules of the three preschools). A kindergarten program and parent groups, also organized by the AHS, are scheduled at other times. Every Friday is reserved for program planning. The preschool space is not greatly altered by its multiple uses. The materials and furnishings are shared, though the afternoon class with older children has a different schedule, including more individual 'seat work.' The room contains additional furnishings required for adult meetings, with stacks of chairs lined against the wall in the dining area, along with one adult sized table.

The defined learning centres such as blocks, house area, and computer, remain in place throughout the program day and from one day to the next. The greatest change in space across time occurs with the rearrangement of tables and chairs. During the free play period, for example, a craft was set out on a round table with four chairs. Afterward, while the children were outdoors, the coordinator moved a rectangular table next to the round one, placing chairs on one side of the tables. This was used for a 'group work' activity, with the children facing the coordinator during a lesson on the alphabet.

The schedule is planned by the coordinator and follows a set routine each morning. The coordinator also manages the flow of time from one activity to another. After breakfast, she tells the children what happens next, although they have followed the same routine for ten months: "We need to just finish up our snack, and drink up our juice, and then go to circle."

The coordinator sets the pace and establishes the sequence within activities. During the circle, she moves the children from one sub-routine to another: "Okay now, let's go do the weather." Near the end of the circle time, she tells the children, "We are going to do our story really quick." Though the other adults work with her as a team, the coordinator is the ultimate governor of time. In the playground, the teacher announced to the children: "Come. Let's gather our stuff. Grandma wants us to go inside."

Curriculum. The curriculum at Little Lake is organized around broad subject areas: the arts, literacy, math, health, social skills, and cultural knowledge. Group time, held on the carpet, is focused on literacy, receptive language, and cultural knowledge. Teaching strategies at group time are mainly telling, describing, demonstrating, and modelling (Mac Naughton & Williams, 2005). Since one of the aims of the program is to re-root children to their cultural origins, the indigenous language, though no longer spoken in the children's homes where English predominates, is used in a limited way at group time, mainly as individual vocabulary words, informally, and on rare occasions, in the normal course of the program. Elders are invited to the program to share their knowledge with the children, and they use the indigenous language in story telling and in songs. Health and nutrition information is included as part of the two mealtimes in the dining area, where new foods are introduced and children are also encouraged to develop social manners and take responsibility for cleaning up. Child to child and child to teacher talk is not explicitly encouraged in either the formal (group time on carpet) or informal (dining area) preschool spaces.

The traditional academic work of preschool—learning shapes, colours, numbers, and the alphabet—crosses over into all areas of the preschool. The coordinator dismissed the children from group time to go to free play, saying: "So away you go, and while you're playing, practice your colours, your shapes, and your numbers."

Outdoor play is planned around concept formation and skill development. As children made sand moulds, for example, teachers offered instruction on digging down to the damp sand, demonstrating the proper technique. Motor skills were developed incidentally in using the climber, but this was not a focus for the teachers, and their climbing was neither encouraged nor discouraged. A game of tag organized by a teacher at the very end of one outdoor play period lasted only a few minutes.

The various indoor 'learning centres' are set up as discrete areas for developing specific concepts and skills. However, the actual subject matter they are associated with is sometimes ambiguous. The library corner is focused on literacy, but what is the aim of 'water play'? For the children it seems mainly a sensory activity. A child was observed for several minutes to submerge his hands in the soapy water, lift them out, and repeatedly opening and closing his hands, presumably enjoying the experience. The coordinator, however, imagined water play as an opportunity to develop math skills and practise fine motor skills in pouring, etcetera, as in the following example. The children played silently and in parallel (Parten, 1933), and the director did not encourage their interaction.

The teacher is at the water table with two children, with her hands in the water with the children. She places the funnel in a plastic container.

Teacher: to child: *OK. Go ahead pour it in.*

The child pours a smaller container of water into the funnel.

Teacher: *That's three.*

The child walks to an adjacent table, looking away.

Teacher: pours the next container full in herself, saying. *That's four.*

Teacher to child: *It's not full yet, we still have to fill it up.*

Tshwane

Care. Although the organization of space at Tshwane preschool is very school-like, its use lends itself quite regularly to care activities. The children are given a morning bowl of porridge, either maize meal or cassava meal. They fetch it themselves from the kitchen in a very orderly fashion, sitting down at the tables for four, the same tables that are used for learning activities, such as cutting and pasting or colouring. The children needed no direction during this time; they carried the bowls competently, as if this kind of responsible behaviour had been well established at home. Children did not start to eat until grace had been said. The children did not regularly wash hands before this meal. When they did so, several children at a time washed their hands in a plastic tub on the veranda. The teacher assisted them, drying their hands and washing their faces with a common cloth.

There is a bathroom with about eight small toilets and a sink. Toilets are in separate cubicles with no doors. The children are encouraged to go before going outside to play, but they are also free to get up and go as needed after letting the teacher know their intent. Boys and girls share the same bathroom. There is another toilet near the principal's office for the teaching staff.

The care dimension at Tshwane is most evident in the principal's concern with the children's health and general well-being. When children are in need of medical attention or have colds, she takes them to a nearby clinic and pays out of her own pocket. Children with special needs such as the little girl who is dwarfed and has Down syndrome are treated with love and protection and concern for their future. Next to the principal's office is a room which she uses to isolate children who are clearly infectious.

The care dimension extends beyond the preschool to the community since about 8 to10% of the children are HIV positive and several have been orphaned. The walls of the preschool thus have six posters about HIV/AIDS, evidently for the information of visiting parents and the staff. Near the end of the research project, when the

Grade R class was destined to be moved to a regular school (the previous year's teacher had already been transferred), the principal thought that she might use the Grade R space in the future for a drop-in centre for people with AIDS. A member of the research project team wondered if the parents of the preschool children would object to having AIDS patients in such close proximity to the children. The principal did not see this as a problem.

Schedule. The daily schedule of activities was posted on the wall of the Grade R classroom. It was a standard western-type of schedule, and was donated by an NGO. It showed the times of arrival, free play, morning snack, reading readiness, outdoor play, lunch, rest, and so on. Underneath this commercial, rather glossy poster, was a hand-made one. As mentioned earlier, this was the schedule that the teacher shyly said she actually followed; it was of her own making, less formal, and, as she indicated, subject to variation "depending on the weather." Starting at 7 a.m., it included arrival time, independent activity until breakfast at 9 a.m., story telling, music or movement at 10 a.m., and pre-reading, pre-writing, and number concepts at 11:30 a.m., followed by lunch and departures. In practice, the schedule was followed loosely, with outdoor play often added into the otherwise fairly regular routine from one day to another. There was a definite lack of rigidity to the flow of activity, as well as in the shifts from one activity to the next, which created an ethos of informality within the fairly formal organizational structure of the centre.

Curriculum. The Grade R at Tshwane preschool was influenced by the national curriculum. The curriculum represents South Africa's aim to "break from the past and embrace the global system" (Spreen, 2001, p. 237) by borrowing, adapting, and adopting outcomes-based education as its national standard for all levels of formal schooling, including Grade R. At Tshwane however, Grade R was in a state of transition; it was slated to be moved the year after our research project ended, out of the preschool and into a nearby regular school. However, it was also very much part of Tshwane preschool. Thus, in the minds of the Grade R teacher and Tshwane's principal, the purpose of the Grade R curriculum was both to socialize children in age-appropriate ways and to prepare them for formal schooling.

South Africa's national curriculum includes the Grade R. It aims to develop the full potential of each learner as a citizen of a democratic South Africa, a lifelong learner who is confident, literate, and multi-skilled, with the ability to participate in society as an active citizen. The curriculum reflects the tenets of the 1996 constitution—social justice, healthy environment, human rights, and inclusion. The eight learning areas pertain to all grades (language, mathematics, life skills, technology, arts and culture, social science, natural science, economic and management sciences), however the recommended emphasis for Grade R is on literacy (40%), numeracy (35%), and life skills (25%) (Republic of South Africa, 2005; UNESCO, 2006, p. 7).

The curriculum for 0 to 4 year olds is still being finalized; however, as indicated earlier, it takes an integrated approach with the emphasis on care, addressing in particular the needs of children most at risk from poverty and disease.

Sunbeam

Care. Care for children at Sunbeam occurs in the preschool and in the community. The AWW is responsible for conducting a household survey of all participating families, and she visits them in their home. The focus of this activity is child and maternal health. Anganwadi workers are also sometimes recruited for public health initiatives such as the nation-wide polio vaccination campaign in 2008. They are thus associated in the community with their role as basic health workers: many are provided with a supply of medicines which they distribute to families. In addition to feeding, the AWW places great importance on children's cleanliness and health habits. Each morning begins with a health check in which she asks children 'daily activity questions.'

Have you all taken a bath?

Did you all brush you teeth?

What did your mother make [for breakfast] this morning?

Physical exercise is an important aspect of the program, and is conducted as a teaching strategy and for health reasons. As a teaching strategy, it is believed to focus children's attention and eases transitions between activities. As a health activity, it likely has minimal value. In a typical exercise, the AWW demonstrates a movement or series of movements for the children to follow as a group, for example, while seated with hands on her hips, she twists her torso from side to side.

The AWW shows concern for children's tidy presentation, and takes care to straighten their clothing, fasten their buttons, and help them to remove or put on sweaters, etcetera. This hands-on help—despite the large numbers of children—is an aspect of care that the children expect. There is no focus on developing self-help skills. While most teaching was to the group, the AWW gave children individual attention by scolding or comforting them. A crying child was attended to immediately. Because the AWW led all aspects of the program, her attention to an individual child brought the program to a halt.

Eating takes place within the main program room. The space is reorganized, however, with children in a circle arrangement to create a more informal social experience for eating, though conversation is minimal. Eating is preceded by a prayer. The AWW and AWH do not eat with the children. The *nashta* (meal) includes carefully portioned food supplements for some children. At each meal, children sit in their place while the food is distributed to them by the anganwadi staff. Children do not wash their hands before eating, nor does the AWH before preparing food. Hand washing before eating, preparing food, or after defecation is not the norm within some sectors in India.[1] Following ICDS standards, all children are weighed once per month; a few children are weighed each day. The procedure is well practised and the children are cooperative: the AWW calls a child forward and places her in a harness, after which the AWH lifts her, suspending the harness on a hook attached to the doorway to the toilet.

Drinking water is located in a container in the kitchen. There is a designated time for children to have a drink of water. At other times, they can ask permission to have a drink of water, and are served by the AWH, drinking from a common tumbler. The use of a single tumbler, while perhaps unsanitary, indicates the absence of caste distinction in the preschool.

Food is prepared on site by the AWH in a small kitchen where foodstuffs are also stored. This is not common in all anganwadi centres. In an urban centre visited by one member of the research team, the food supplement was brought by a man on a motor scooter every day at the appointed hour. Children do not enter the kitchen. The AWH prepares one meal each morning. It includes a cooked item. The meal is served just prior to departure. Most children will eat again when they return home. As well as cooked meal at the AW, almost all children bring snacks from home prepared by their mothers. This is of variable quality and quantity. In some anganwadi centres, government-issued food rations intended for children, or as supplements for pregnant women, have been used improperly for trade or barter or for cattle feed, though this was not the case at Sunbeam. Evidence of corruption in AWs is generally in relation to foodstuffs, the only item of value.

A single toilet is located in a room at the back of the anganwadi. Children are meant to use the toilet at the designated toilet time but are free to go at other times after asking permission. At the group toilet time, children are assisted with their clothing, etcetera by the AWH, who locates herself near the facility with children around her waiting. When individual children use the toilet at other times, the AWW keeps an eye on them through the doorway as she continues with the program.

The preschool is located in a home given over to the preschool, and the rooms are unused at other times. The same space is used for all the preschool activities: games, exercises, songs, stories, and eating. The change in the space during the morning occurs through the arrangement of children's bodies in the space. For some games and for eating, children sit in a circle. For other activities, they sit or stand in rows. There is no regularly scheduled outdoor playtime.

Schedule. The schedule is set by the AWW, and she also manages the flow and pacing of activities. Progression from one activity to another is generally made by the AWW, who directs the group of children to move their bodies in some way. At the start of a song, the AWW says, "Okay, everyone, lift your hands up." She then physically arranges children in two lines, one against the wall, and a second in front, with arms stretched high above their heads. The process takes time, and as children tire, most put their hands down. The AWW claps to regain the children's attention, and hands shoot up again. When children are judged to be ready and in their places, she commences a song or story. The timing of the program also depends on the preparation of the nashta by the AWH, and the AWW extends activities until it is ready to be served.

Curriculum. The subject categories in the curriculum at Sunbeam are oral literacy (as contrasted to the introduction to print literacy), health, nutrition, and physical education. The space designated as the program room is used for teaching all subjects and for all activities. Rather than moving to a new area for the various subjects, the AWW organizes children within the space differently for mealtime as opposed to exercise, for example. All activities are undertaken by the children as a group under the direction of the AWW. The AWH interacts with the children when she is not cooking, cleaning, or assisting with toileting, mainly as a disciplinarian. The AWW's teaching strategies are telling, demonstrating, and modelling, with a limited use of questions posed to the group, meant to elicit a group response (Mac Naughton & Williams, 2005). Child to child talk is discouraged by the teacher and would be difficult anyway due to the children's arrangement in strict rows. Nevertheless, there is an almost constant undercurrent of chatter in the classroom at all times. Informal child to teacher talk is rare. The AWW addresses individual children mainly to comfort or scold.

Activities were often done while singing or chanting under the lead of the teacher. Games were generally played indoors, and were held about three times per week. A boisterous game of hot potato lasting twenty minutes was played to the accompaniment of a tambourine. Because it is a game of elimination, the first children out were left to wait for a long period, standing against the wall. Two of the oldest children were left playing at the end, but because the AWW was in charge of determining the winner by stopping the tambourine, there was no element of real competition.

The use of workbooks or slates is common in urban anganwadi centres, though it is discouraged in ICDS policy. At Sunbeam, a workbook was sometimes given to an older child while the class was waiting for lunch. Younger children would gather around her while she worked.

DISCUSSION

The AHS and ICDS programs target children deemed to be at risk, including risk of school failure, but also poverty, racism, or developmental or family circumstances. What counts as care varies in accord with the circumstances of risk. In situations where racist policy or beliefs have worked to marginalise cultural knowledge, as at Little Lake, traditional knowledge and language are deemed 'at risk,' along with the health of the children.

In contrast, due to the legacy of the apartheid era, South Africa aims to reduce the meaning of racial and other differences so that the society becomes truly democratic, with equal rights for all. In this vein, nine African languages are given official status, on par with Afrikaans and English. The notion of risk is associated with persistent poverty in some parts of the country, and the assumed correlation of poverty with health matters. The new curriculum makes scarce mention of traditional knowledge.

The programs at Little Lake and Sunbeam resemble Head Start programs, and include attention to children's health and physical development and in the case of Sunbeam, maternal health as well. Joint attention to care and education is an aim of the Aboriginal Head Start program, which is administered by the Public Health Agency of Canada. Care and education are also explicit aims of the Government of

India's Integrated Chid Development Services, which is administered by the Ministry of Women and Child Development as a child welfare scheme. There was a definite recognition of the need for early intervention to ensure the development of young children's body, mind and intellect to its maximum potential. The ICDS programme is thus formulated to enhance the health, nutrition and learning opportunities of infants, young children and their mothers, and is especially targeted for the poor and deprived. The AWW is responsible for monitoring child and maternal health, and she reports on the health of the preschool participants in six different record books: the 'Anganwadi Survey Register,' 'Supplementary Nutrition and Preschool Education Register,' 'Immunization Register,' 'Services for Pregnant and Lactating Mothers Registers,' 'Mortality Register,' and the 'Daily Diary.' These activities are detailed in the document, "Monitoring in ICDS" (Ministry of Women and Child Development, n.d.).

The AWW has 21 distinct responsibilities, and most of these related to care in some way. When anganwadi workers occasionally press the government for greater remuneration or to be recognized officially as employees of the government, they have protested by refusing to perform some of these record-keeping tasks. Anganwadi workers were originally classed as volunteers within the ICDS scheme, receiving a small honorarium rather than a salary. Since the launching of the ICDS scheme in 1975-76, the AWW and the AWH were recruited as 'honorary workers.' At inception, the then AW teacher received a monthly honorarium of INR 125 (about $3.00), and the helper INR 50. The passing decades saw subsequent changes in the honorarium, though the changes followed no clear rationale. Recently, the government of Gujarat increased the honorarium of the AW teacher and helper by INR 500, thus since the 2008 fiscal year, an AW Teacher in Gujarat gets a monthly honorarium of INR 2000, while the helper receives INR 1000. The union of AW workers have insisted upon a change in their profile by demanding that the status of a IVth Class employee of the government and subsequent pay package be recognized as a 'salaried employee.' However, the government is yet to address the demand. Workers have protested on occasion with marches, work stoppages, and other protests (*dharna*). In Karnataka in January 2009, AWW and AWH pressed for benefits, including a pension after 30 years service and a salary increase to INR 1500 for AWWs and INR 750 for helpers. The form of their dharna was to refuse to submit "any details such as quarterly report of self-help groups to the department concerned" ("Anganwadi workers," 2009).

Cross-Curricular Activities

In the west, even in an early childhood program lasting a few hours, children are generally provided with a snack. This may be served to the group as a whole at a single sitting, or made available to children on a self-serve basis. Snack preparation is a popular free-choice activity, involving children in slicing fruit for a fruit salad, for example. Sometimes food preparation or eating is viewed as a cross-curricular activity, enhancing math skills through counting, patterning, or shape recognition, for example (Meriwether, 1997). Roberts (2003) points to the "practical side" of curriculum integration as a time saver.

In this "two for one" lesson, both snack time and mathematics time occupied the same space in the daily routine. With the increased demands of the curriculum, she was constantly searching for ways to integrate topics and maximize the minutes in the busy kindergarten day. (p. 258)

On one occasion at Little Lake, a child was observed to spontaneously link math with snack, as related below:

Child to Teacher: She has taken a bite from her bannock, and holds it up to Teacher, saying: *Look'it mine, a rectangle.*

Teacher: *Oh you did make a rectangle. Yeah, we're going to change our squares into different shapes.*

Food items were also used purposefully as counters in a math exercise in the Cheerios® workbooks. The children were not observed eating the Cheerios® until their task was completed. For the most part, however, eating at Little Lake is organized as a dining experience, with placemats serving to "define 'personal' space," to "provide visual cues to assist in organization," and to "focus [the] child's attention" (Eliason & Jenkins, 2003, p. 209).

Food has a value for some First Nations people as a symbol of generosity, shown practically through sharing with visitors and guests. As a guest at the centre, the researcher was always offered food and a beverage upon arrival. Dining was used as a time to develop relationships amongst children and adults, and although the children ate communally, there was minimal interaction with peers. As well, there was emphasis on developing nutritional knowledge through conversations about new or unfamiliar foods, food charts on walls, and field trips to a grocery store off-reserve to shop for food supplies.

There was no evidence of cross-curricular content during mealtimes at Sunbeam. Snack time was marked by more relaxed behaviour as children, the AWW, and AWH all sat in a circular arrangement. It is notable, however, that the children frequently played with their tiffin boxes after eating, by stacking the lids of the plastic containers, for example. The focus, however, was on eating and not conversation or play. The approach was in keeping with the ICDS program's history as a feeding centre, but it also reflects child-rearing values which do not emphasize a role for adults in facilitating peer relationships amongst preschoolers.

Similarly at Tshwane, there was little or no evidence of cross-curricular content during snack or lunch time. Children were well-behaved, did not play with their food, nor did they waste it.

Self help – Fostering Independence / Dependence

There is a lot of 'hands on' help given to children by adults at Little Lake and Sunbeam. This runs counter to the western view that stresses the development of children's self-help skills. Bainer and Hale (2007) describe the teacher's goal for children in their "model early childhood program" as "self-sufficiency, not efficiency, so they [the teacher] resist the short-term efficiency of having teachers unzip, remove, and hang up the toddlers' jackets" (p. 86). Helping a child is therefore negatively portrayed as a choice made for reasons of efficiency, not care. Alternatively, at Little Lake and Sunbeam, where children's dependence was a goal, teachers often moved to help or 'do for' children. At Tshwane preschool children appeared to require little help with jackets or shoes.

The goal of dependence in First Nations child-rearing is described by Light (1985), cited in the Native Council of Canada document, *Circle of Care.*

> As opposed to contemporary white culture's pressure on children to become independent, assertive, and competitive at an early age, the child must first have opportunities to be dependent, learn to respect and value Elders, and be taught to obey through explanations for desired behaviour. (Native Council of Canada, 1990, p. 25)

At Little Lake First Nation, as a culture in transition, the AHS presents a cultural model of child-rearing believed by the director to be disappearing. This re-creation is not the same as the historical model, but it consciously adapts aspects considered to be important for cultural survival and communal identity. An important part of this is evident in the metaphor of 'circle of care' in which teachers relate with children and parents as members of a family. The situation at Little Lake is complicated by the disrupted family life experienced by some community members in their own childhoods while at residential school.

Unless a situation was dangerous, teachers at Little Lake were more likely to take a 'hands-off' approach in relation to unwanted behaviour. An example was the director's request to a group of children kneeling precariously on a table containing the fish tank, to stand on the floor. As described in field notes:

> The children have been on the table all along, and only when tipping the tank was imminent, did the director step in with a mild warning, that started with "excuse me" and ended with "thank you."

In this example, the director guided the children with a gentle reminder befitting her identity as grandmother in the classroom, and reflecting the concepts of non-interference in the choices made by others and the valuing of autonomy (Glover, 2001). Although she was aware of the situation, she addressed their behaviour only when an accident seemed about to happen. Identifying herself as grandmother was also an act of caring in the context of some children's families, in which biological grandmothers were reported by research participants to be less involved in their grandchildren's lives.

At Sunbeam, on the very few occasions when children could help themselves, for example, at mealtime or in adjusting their clothing after toileting, adults took charge. This follows cultural expectations for young children's continued dependence upon adults (Kakar, 1978a, 1978b; Sinha, 1988). At Sunbeam, it was the children's responsibility to submit to the care of adults, as it was for the adults to care for the child, and in many instances this involved considerable physical contact. Sunbeam anganwadi is decidedly not a "no touch" zone, as described by Johnson (2000) of the situation in the west, where it is claimed that teachers are fearful of contact with children's bodies. The children at Sunbeam were frequently shifted in their place or carried about by the workers, who often lifted them by their arms a few inches off the floor to move them about.

Again in contrast, the dependence-independence situation at Tshwane was somewhere in between that of Sunbeam and Little Lake. As such, it might be said that they were in transition from the communal, mutually dependent preschool culture of the home environment to the individualistic western culture of formal schooling.

Orientations Towards Time: Influence on Scheduling

At its most basic, the dimension of time in schooling is associated with the scheduling of educational and care-giving activities designed to maximize learning and healthy development. In scheduling, decisions are made on the length of the overall school day, the division of lessons within it, and the sequence of one activity to the next. In many cases, scheduling is organized around a perceived need for efficiency. If "time is the currency of teaching— what teachers have to spend to buy learning" (Hunter, 2004, 116), it must be used wisely. This is particularly true in the case of preschool education, where time is short and children's minds are ripe for learning, as indicated by brain research. It therefore behoves educators to make the most of children's learning time. In western practice, this is accomplished by organizing the preschool day into periods of large and small group learning activities, outdoor play, punctuated with care activities such as toileting, eating, and rest. While there is flexibility in the schedule, it tends to follow the clock, as Leavitt (1994) found in the schedule at a child care centre in the United States, which included 14 distinct time divisions. The schedule at the Child Development Laboratory School (2009) at Iowa State University has 16 divisions including 5 minutes in the morning for group toothbrushing. Micro-divisions of time have also been observed in majority-world preschools, as in a program observed by the researchers in Zimbabwe, which had 16 time blocks in an 8-hour day (Cleghorn & Prochner, 2008).

Wien (1996) called an orientation to the clock evidence of a "rigid production schedule" (p. 386), similar to a factory. While claiming to have "open schedules that follow children's interests and needs" (Wien & Kirby-Smith, 1998, p. 8), teachers, like factory managers, send children to their work stations to busy themselves in their tasks, and afterward, to tidy-up their materials. The development of a clock-based time perspective was also a colonizing strategy used with indigenous peoples: "life was lived by the clock" (Miller, 1996, p. 426) in residential schools in Canada. "The colonial desire to order [Aboriginal] domestic space" (Raibmon, 2003, p. 69) and to treat it as "spectacle" (p. 71) is evident in the photograph of a model Indian family at home included in an early Department of Indian Affairs annual report: a clock is prominent in the background, as seen in figure 1. The caption noted that Ben Stone Child was formerly a student in the File Hills Boarding School in Saskatchewan.

Figure 1. Interior of Ben Stone Child's house with clock in corner. Source: Dominion of Canada. (1904). Annual Report of the Department of Indian Affairs for the year ended, June 30, 1904 (Ottawa: S.E. Dawson), frontispiece.

In a novel experiment, Wien and Kirby-Smith (1998) observed the impact of removing clocks and watches from a preschool while retaining the existing sequence of activities to maintain the "children's sense of security" (p. 9). Released from the confines of a lockstep preschool production schedule, the children were observed to engage in more creative and extended play. However, what Alexander (2000) calls a teacher's or pupil's pedagogical clock is also culturally influenced, with clocks not necessary for time regulation. In Alexander's international study of primary education, lessons in primary schools in the United States are more flexible in length than what seems to be the case in preschools, and we might expect a similar situation in Canada. In his comparison of pedagogy, Alexander classed schedules—or at least the timing of lessons—as either elastic or fixed. This varied across his case study countries, where schools in India have lessons that were of "regular and predicable" length (p. 298), and those in the United States of variable length. Alexander referred to teachers in Russia and India, where lessons have a fixed duration, as having "developed internal 'pedagogical clocks' governing lesson periodicity almost as an extension of the way biological clocks governed their circadian rhythms" (p. 299). At Sunbeam anganwadi, the AWW regularly shifted the children from one activity to the next, the timing of which was sometimes with the help of the clock. In Alexander's analysis of lessons in the United States and England, lessons were more elastic in terms of their timing. In these settings, "teachers were both more anxious about time and less able to control it" (p. 298).

At Little Lake, the director sometimes showed a concern about time. Children at group time were urged to choose a "short book" for story time, and even though it was brief, the reading still seemed rushed. Later, when a few children lingered at the lunch table, they were reminded to "finish eating because the bus will be here soon." In this statement and many others like it, children at Little Lake were encouraged to develop time perspective. Through their language, the teachers at Little Lake indicated that events follow one another sequentially, and repeat in a pattern cyclically. This was accomplished via informal interactions as well as being part of classroom routines, such as the calendar routine. At group time, a child was designated as the helper for the day, and pointed with a metre-stick to the day of the week on the calendar. This was repeated by naming the month in both English and the indigenous language. At Sunbeam as well, children recited the days of the week in unison, following their teacher's lead without the aid of a printed calendar.

At Tshwane, time did not appear to govern the length of lessons, nor was it an issue of concern that teachers felt children needed to become aware. In fact, several lessons were observed to last longer than the children's interest. The lesson would peter out, marking the shift to another activity, and the choice was made by the teacher on the spot, rather than according to the schedule or the clock. Similarly, the calendar on the wall did not attract much attention.

A number of researchers have offered cultural interpretations of the development of time perspective. Jones and Brown (2005), drawing on McGrath (1988), distinguish between a temponomic society in which time has high value and what they call a temponostic society in which time is viewed indifferently. The implications for each perspective are wide-ranging and are "linked to different strategies and preferences for achieving health and well-being, socializing children, and structuring family dynamics" (Jones & Brown, 2005, p. 307). Hall (1966) distinguished two culturally-based ways of "handling time" that in turn impact the "structuring of space" (p. 162). In monochronic time, activities are compartmentalized, whereas in polychromic time activities occur simultaneously: "the monochronic person often finds it easier to function if he can separate activities in space, whereas the polychromic person tends to collect activities" (p. 162). Hall continued, explaining that "to reduce the polychromic effect" for a monochromic people—and thereby lessen anxiety—"one must reduce involvement, which means separating activities with as much screening as possible" (p. 162). The distinctions between time perspectives are useful for thinking about time at home versus school. The temponomic perspective, with its orientation on future events, is closest to the way time is treated in school, whereas in some cultures, the temponostic perspective may be a better match with children's experience of time at home. Moreover, following Hall's analysis, partitioning the preschool environment into learning centres is consistent with "monochronic peoples" need for low involvement and physical contact, whereas space at home may be open and multipurpose, with sleeping, dining, and lounging taking place in the same room. The use of partitions in preschool is described in detail later in this chapter.

Time at preschool can also be considered in relation to the overall length of the program day. Sunbeam and Little Lake follow the western nursery school and kindergarten tradition of operating for a half-day only. Half-day programs originated partly as a cost-saving measure in the late-nineteenth century, permitting overcrowded urban schools to accommodate double shifts of students. The benefit of full-day kindergarten is supported by research that indicates a greater impact with a longer program, provided that children are arranged in smaller groups (Zvoch, Reynolds, & Parker, 2008). Nevertheless, half-day programs are predominant, a feature that gives preschools a different school cycle from that of the primary school. In rural areas in Canada, where children are bussed to school, the half-days are sometimes combined and children attend every other day, on 2 days one week and 3 days the next.

Connelly and Clandinin (1990) identified 10 distinct school cycles, including the "within class cycle" (the schedule of lessons) and the "day cycle." With its differing day cycle, the children in both the band kindergarten and at Little Lake must shift locations at lunchtime: the school bus brings children from the band school to Little Lake at noon, and returns to the school with children from the morning preschool program. The children thus receive a double dose of kindergarten, though without any ongoing coordination between the teachers in the two settings. This is a typical situation, as noted by Kagan and her colleagues (2006), who found in their research that the "horizontal alignment" of the "content of the standards, curriculum, and assessments" between programs is mostly uncoordinated (p. 29).

The day-cycle at Sunbeam similarly operates on the half-day model. The half-day program is also the predominant mode of U.S. Head Start, which was the model for both for India's ICDS and Canada's AHS services (see Britto & Gilliam, 2008). Other cycles are unique to the case study preschools, for example, the holiday cycle, which at Sunbeam includes a number of festivals in September and October, during which the anganwadi centre is closed. At Tshwane the preschool operates from early morning until mid afternoon for most children, and until late afternoon for a few, to resemble an after-school day-care model.

Transitions

Transition has two common meanings in the preschool field, signifying a change from one early childhood setting to the next (cf. Prochner, Cleghorn, & Green, 2008)—home to preschool, preschool to child care, kindergarten to grade 1—as well as a teaching strategy used within classrooms to manage the shift from one activity or lesson to the next. Concerning 'within-classroom' transitions, Beaty (2004) describes how they can be managed in such a way to "prevent a mad rush for the activities and squabbles over the centre necklaces" (p. 325). In this situation, the transition is considered a means of orderly dismissal from group time. A transition can be managed using a transition activity or transition statement. The latter is described by Machado and Botnarescue (2005) as a "planned verbalization that moves young children from one activity to the next." The authors provide the following example: "people with curly hair stand up" (p. 177). Teachers may also choose to provide children with a warning in advance of a new activity, using bells, whistles, playing a chord on a piano, or turning off and on the lights.

Transition activities and statements were used in some instances in the case study preschools, such as verbal warnings prior to clean-up time at Little Lake. Common at both Little Lake and Sunbeam was the teachers' use of exercises to regulate children's bodies for gaining attention prior to a new activity. At Little Lake, these had a relaxation element similar to the Montessori's (1912) use of the silence game. Some periods of physical exercise at Sunbeam were regular activities in themselves, and not only transition activities. Whether regular or transition activities, physical exercises at Sunbeam were bolder, often moving children to heights of emotion before a sudden call for silence. This fits Alexander's (2000) description of the quick start-up of lessons in India where children were expected to, and did, rapidly shift their attention at the start-up of a lesson.

In cases where there is a delay between lessons or activities in school, children are made to wait, which, as Phillip Jackson (1966b) has pointed out, is an inevitable outcome of being part of a crowd. Jackson (1966a) further explains that by waiting, students experience the "denial of desire." We ask, how well does Jackson's analysis apply in classrooms for younger children, and in particular, the cross-cultural preschool settings within our study? Wait times between activities at Little Lake were generally filled with activities. These were different from transitional activities with the purpose of managing the children's orderly movement. Instead, these activities were clearly filler, deemed necessary due to one activity ending earlier than was planned. This type of activity is sometimes called a sponge activity, designed to soak up otherwise wasted time (Hunter, 2004). An example is the use of books after lunch and before the bus arrives to take children to the band school kindergarten. After children gathered their backpacks, shoes, and jackets, they lounged on the carpet looking at books on their own or with a teacher. The children were then called to line up at the door, and after several minutes passed without the bus arriving, the coordinator gathered the children and took them outdoors to fly a kite in a nearby field. The impression at Little Lake is of an unbroken string of activities arranged across the program day.

At Sunbeam the AWW set the pace of activities to fit the timing of the two mealtimes. After the story ended, she continued her questioning and recapitulation until signalled by the AWH that the food was ready to be served. There were, however, a number of occasions when the AWW paused in the program, creating small breaks between activities in which children's attention was permitted to drift away from the teacher. During these breaks she would stand, walk about, straighten children's clothing, and help them remove their sweaters, or move them into position. The program's rhythm moved between prolonged periods of focused attention on the teacher, and release, during which children were boisterous and even wild, running about and shouting. These occasions generally ended with an authoritarian gesture from the AWW, for example, a raised voice or a clapping of hands.

Curriculum

The formal curriculum occupies physical and temporal space differently in preschool and primary classrooms. The physical space in many primary classrooms in western countries is open and multipurpose, whereas the time allocated to each subject in the curriculum is clearly marked out. While many primary classrooms have learning centres, they are likely to be fewer in number and supplementary to the program, such as a library, writing, or technology centre (Auger & Rich, 2007, p. 158). In preschool, the physical space is partitioned and the time allocated to particular subjects is subsumed in the schedule as free play, variously known as activity time or centre time. Subject area content is described in a general way, although skills are often carefully articulated. Thus Beaty (2004) suggests that in an extended study of trees, children might learn about Native Americans one day and build a house for a guinea pig in the block centre on the next. Spodek (1988) has explained this as confusing developmental aims for knowledge. In his words, "developmental theory essentially provide information on the appropriateness of educational method, the *how* of what we teach, not on educational content, the substance of *what* we teach" (p. 10, orig. emphasis). And as we show in the present study, how and what we teach is also influenced by educational context.

It is normally the case in primary schools that more time is given to certain subjects, a situation described in policy directives and required in law. An example is in the province of Alberta in Canada, where language arts are allocated 30% of instructional time, mathematics 15%, and science, social studies, art and music (combined), and health and physical education, are each given 10%, with the remaining 15% for other subjects such as religious instruction or drama (Alberta Education, 2008, p. 31). In contrast, there are no time requirements for individual subjects in kindergarten.

In the western preschool model, the temporal space, as described in the earlier discussion of time, is dominated by a long period of uninterrupted play in a well-ordered physical space. Children are made aware of the spatial ordering of the curriculum by the naming of various areas within the classroom as specialized learning centres. Western experts believe learning centres should be distinct so children are not confused in their choices for play (Beaty, 2004). Some learning centres take their name from materials and others from the subject matter. Beaty lists materials-based centres as the block building centre, book centre, computer centre, sand and water centre, woodworking centre, cooking centre, and subject specific areas such as the manipulative and math centre, art centre, large motor centre, music centre, science and discovery centre, and writing centre. The dramatic play centre is unique as a learning centre designated by the type of play children are expected to undertake, although elsewhere dramatic play is described as a subject area, along with science and literacy (Krogh & Morehouse, 2008). Krogh and Morehouse explain further, that dramatic play is useful as a means to other ends. Through their "dramatic play experience" children acquire ideas from subject areas such as art, language, science, social studies, and mathematics.

Child development goals are used to integrate the curriculum across the learning centres. This approach is called a 'whole child' view of curriculum (Hendrick & Weissman, 2006), with its focus on activities fostering cognitive, social, emotional, aesthetic, and physical development. However, a vision of the whole child is weakened by the recommendation that the room "be divided into areas, with each providing opportunities to satisfy the developmental needs of children" (Eliason & Jenkins, 2003, p. 41). As the various areas target specific development, it becomes important for children to rotate through the entire classroom space to achieve a well-balanced, integrated development. Depaepe and Laevers (1992) explained this as the "dosing principle," in which "teachers feel that children should get a regular 'dose' of each activity which is deemed good for them" (p. 98). If it is observed that a "child avoids a particular area over a period of time, the teacher should encourage the child to use this area. Avoidance may be an indication of insecurity or unsureness with the particular area" (p. 41). Teachers are advised to use contracts with children to ensure they participate in all learning centres, adding a bureaucratic element to their free play.

Experts warn against having large, empty spaces in the classroom as a potential problem, "encourage[ing] children to run around wildly or aimlessly" (Beaty, 2004, p. 71). Most classroom layouts do include a whole-class meeting area. Dietze (2006) designates this as a space for "large-group learning dialogue" (p. 155) emphasizing that it is not to be used for direct teacher instruction. This large area is often used for other activities requiring a space free of furnishings, for example, floor blocks, as suggested by Beaty (2004). This reflects the importance of blocks in the early childhood classrooms from the time of Froebel (Hewitt, 2001). Large unit blocks require sufficient space for children to build structures they can play within, while engaging in dramatic or pretend play with their peers and developing language, problem-solving skills, etcetera. Sufficient space for blocks and room for groups of children is required—block play is deemed most beneficial when it is social. Cohen and Uhry's (2007) study concluded, "block play provides the social activity setting in which children practice social skills and learn the skills needed to be a member of the culture as a social being" (p. 313).

The space for curriculum in the case study classrooms partially reflected the dominant western view at Little Lake and Tshwane, and not at all at Sunbeam. Tables and chairs at Tshwane were grouped in the centre of the classroom, with learning centres placed along the walls of the classroom, more in keeping with primary than EC classrooms. In primary classrooms free play is often used as a reward for students finishing their work early. "They may use the centres when they finish the 'important work of the school'" (Trawick-Smith, 2006, p. 178).

The way teachers should organize learning is sometimes clearly specified in curriculum documents. An official curriculum is issued by a government agency "prescrib[ing] how and what is to be taught" (Marsh, 1997, p. 4), such as the national curriculum created by the Ministry of Education of South Africa. One role of an official curriculum is to organize content in relation to learning outcomes for assessment purposes, often within traditional subject areas, called learning areas in the South African case. Exceptions to the subject area organization in national curricula include New Zealand's program, *Te Whãriki*. There, many options exist for teachers to organize learning within actual classrooms, for example, via projects, themes, or the study of problems. In the field of early childhood education, in contrast with primary or elementary education, classroom teaching is sometimes aligned with what is called a curriculum model or program such as High/Scope or Montessori, though this was not true in the case study settings.

There was evidence of a more general theme-based approach to curriculum in use at Little Lake. Children explored topics related to the season, such as butterflies, which were depicted in teacher-led art activities. Art, as a subject, took place at designated art and craft tables. The theme was not carried over into other activity areas.

While learning through play suggests curriculum integration across subject areas, the typical organization of preschool space into learning centres often works against integration. Thus writing occurs in the 'writing centre,' music in the 'music centre,' and so on, providing early experience with the correspondence between the organization of learning and the organization of work in the society at large (Bourdieu & Passeron, 1977). The teachers at Little Lake meant for children to carry concepts with them to apply in their play at the various centres, but there was little evidence that they were able to do this without prompting from their teacher.

In terms of the range of subjects in the programs, at Little Lake, shapes and colours, etcetera, are stressed by the coordinator as important for children to learn as preparation for school. In many teaching situations, these topics are briefly touched upon while the larger focus is on motor skill development, listening to and following instructions, and perseverance.

Fantasy play is an area of the standard preschool curriculum that has little prominence at Little Lake AHS. The house area is set up as a domestic scene, and the play observed in the video-recording was not sustained.

At Sunbeam, story telling, games, and singing are afforded equal time and space. The AWW frequently shifts between activities involving controlled movement, as modelled by her, and being quiet and still.

At Tshwane the time was divided fairly evenly between whole group activity directed by the teacher and singing-dancing games, and small group work at tables (colouring, pasting, and cutting).

The Range of Subjects Across the Settings

Research has shown that the implementation of developmentally appropriate practice in a program, even within the standards required for accreditation by the National Association for the Education of Young Children, will not necessarily result in an educational program for children (Dickinson, 2002). One reason for this is that the indicators used in the accreditation "completely ignored learning in the academic content domains, and instead focus on pleasant interactions and self-regulation" (Zan, 2005, p. 89).

This was not the situation at Little Lake, where teachers created a number of opportunities for children to directly practice basic math and literacy skills. Children spent long periods during free play, sitting side by side, completing counting and shape recognition tasks with the assistance of a teacher. The direct study of shapes, colours, numbers, and letters is criticized in EC in the west, as being irrelevant to children's lives (Feeney, Christensen, & Moravcik, 2001, p. 330) and potentially harmful to later development (Gestwicki, 1999). However, it is conceived at Little Lake as an important part of a readiness curriculum, reinforcing kindergarten activities and preparing children for grade one activities.

The pattern was similar at Tshwane but perhaps less formalized. Little formal instruction was observed while children were cutting, pasting, or playing with small, differently shaped blocks.

Sunbeam offered what is termed a non-formal program in India, in contrast to the formal teaching found in many private preschools with their focus on reading and writing (Mohite, 1993). Children were taught colours, the names of animals, etcetera, through songs, games, and stories. The overall emphasis was on oral literacy and healthy physical development.

Noticeably absent in the case study preschools was adult involvement in or encouragement of children's pretend play. As noted above, dramatic play in western EC classrooms is located in a learning centre and classed as both a play and learning activity. Its importance for children's mental health and social development was established by the work of Susan Isaacs and others working in the psychoanalytic tradition in the 1920s and 1930s (Hartley, Frank, & Goldenson, 1952). More recently, with reference to Vygotsky's historical-cultural theory, dramatic play has been touted as the "leading activity" in the preschool years; that is the activity that leads child development within modern industrial societies (Duncan & Tarulli, 2003). Mature play of this sort requires guidance; it does not come to children naturally. As explained by Bodrova and Leong, (2005), dramatic play is "not a spontaneous activity inherent to early childhood." It is instead an "outgrowth of specific interactions young children have with their older peers and adults" (p. 441). There are differences, however, in the importance given to informal (home settings) and formal (school settings) pretend play by parents and teachers in relation to culture and educational philosophy. An example of the latter is the project approach described by Katz and Chard (2000), in which dramatic play mimicking real-world situations is favoured.

A similar bias is shown by fundamentalist religious groups such as Old Order Mennonites (Carlson, Taylor, & Levin, 1998), and other cultures oriented toward the collective, in which pretend play involving fantasy scenarios is believed to focus on individual needs, wishes, and desires. While children everywhere may enjoy pretend play, adults may choose to encourage it or discourage it. Findings from studies in cross-cultural psychology emphasize that the way play is supported by parents and teachers relates to values and beliefs concerning appropriate childhood socialization. In their survey of the literature on pretend play, Göncü, Patt, and Kouba (2004) note that adult involvement in children's pretend play is "closely related to their level of schooling, income level, and sources of income" (p. 428). In village communities in India and Guatemala, such adult behaviour is seen as either "inappropriate for adults or a waste of time due to their workload" (p. 429). While the children attending Little Lake and Sunbeam may have engaged in pretend play out of school, there was little direct facilitation of it within the programs. At Little Lake, the physical space for dramatic play was minimal, consisting of a small house and doll centre. At Sunbeam, dramatic musical play was led by the teacher with children following her movements as a group. At Tshwane, pretend play was expected as a natural occurrence in the house corner, however teacher involvement was not observed, indicating that pretend play was not seen as a teaching opportunity, a chance to observe children's cooperative behaviour, or to inform the teacher of children's social development.

NOTES

[1] A National Campaign for Sanitation and Hygiene Promotion with focus on Hand Washing was initiated by the Department of Drinking Water Supply, India. The campaign website cites statistics indicating that "In India, only 53% washes hands after defecation and only 38% washes before eating which is even less among those who prepare food which is 30%" (http://ddws.gov.in/handwash/contentpage.aspx).

CHAPTER 7

THE MEANING OF DIFFERENCE

In this chapter, we reflect analytically on a few particular aspects of the foregoing chapters, in terms of difference across the three country contexts. We ask, what is the meaning of observed differences, and when do overt differences simply screen out similarities? The reader will recall that one of the aims of this book was to show how apparent differences reflect common societal concerns. In each of the case study preschools, one focus has been on young children's preparation for school in a changing world. Thus on the one hand, we see global trends that reduce obvious differences in the way early childhood education is described in policy documents, for example, and on the other hand we see differentiation persisting, sometimes subtly, sometimes intentionally, in day-to-day practice. It may be that superficial differences conceal similarities and superficial similarities conceal more fundamental, deep culture differences. To begin, we will return to the earlier descriptions of how very different the physical location and indoor-outdoor space was from one preschool to the other. Next, we will take a close look at each of the preschools' daily schedules, examining the allotment of time in terms of emphasis on care or teaching activities. Then we return to a discussion of possible policy–practice gaps in each setting. Finally, we re-visit the topic of indigenous and western influences on ECCE practice.

WHAT DID THE PRESCHOOLS LOOK LIKE, INSIDE AND OUT?

In reminding the reader of what the preschool spaces looked like, indoors and out, we consider again the meaning and relationship of those spaces to the children's daily lives at home. To what extent was there familiarity between the preschool and home, in terms, for example, of freedom to come and go, designated space for children to play, the organization of equipment and furniture, and the norms governing the relationships between children and adults?

Little Lake was situated in a semi-rural First Nations reserve, some 100 kilometres from one of western Canada's major cities. The preschool shared the space with an administration building, however the two spaces were clearly separated. The large outdoor play space, created for the sole use of the preschool, was enclosed by a wire fence. The ground cover was sand with a few bushes at the side of the single story building. There was climbing equipment, slides, areas for sand play, and ample room for group games. When outdoors, the children were supervised by staff at all times. The entire area had the appearance of a North American preschool playground, identifiable as such by any passer-by. One had to be there, however, to observe that the way children and adults interacted within that playground space was quite different from what might be expected in the typical North American playground: there was little rowdiness, the children played quietly, and the teacher sat on the ground with them as they played in the sand.

Inside, the space was also organized in fairly typical, western preschool fashion with a large carpeted area for whole-group story telling and interest areas separated by low storage cabinets and shelves from which the children could choose their activities at designated times. The walls were brightly decorated with didactic materials and the children's art work, at levels the children could view with ease. Again, within this indoor space, interaction between children and adults was relatively quiet and shifts from one activity to another were carried out smoothly. What was difficult to determine was the extent to which the sheer low numbers of the preschool group and child-adult ratio determined the pace and tone in the classroom.

Little Lake preschool and the children's single-family homes were in many ways physically very different places. At home children could come and go much as they pleased; some homes, while quite distant one from the other, would contain play equipment out of doors, others would not. Inside, space would be shared by all family members with drawing, writing, or art work done on the floor or dining table, when such materials were available. However, the relationship with adults both at the preschool and at home would not be considered very pedagogical in nature. The teaching of skills and expected behaviours tended to be rather casual, with reliance on demonstration and modelling rather than on verbal instruction or admonishment. In fact, the teacher's relationship with the children was more like that of an aunt or granny, suggesting similarities between the home and preschool's norms governing child-adult relations.

In stark contrast to Little Lake, Sunbeam's outdoor space was public space, simply the courtyard between the many row-type attached houses of the compound, one of which was used as the preschool. There was thus no designated outside space for children to play while under the supervision of the anganwadi worker or her helper; rather, the space in front of the preschool and houses was the space where all children in the community could gather and play. As such, the space was shared with the community's adults as they came and went about their daily chores and activities. Supervision of children while outside the home or the preschool was therefore somewhat communal or culturally shared.

The inside space of Sunbeam was also in marked contrast to that of Little Lake. The dimly lit, stuffy room that held upwards of 30 children of mixed ages was approximately 4.5 by 6 metres. There were no interest areas or space for free play; rather, all activities were carried out with the whole group, whether that was for direct instruction or for a circle game. There were few materials except for posters and the teacher's handmade picture book, both located well above the heads of the children. The inside space of Sunbeam would have been very familiar to the children, whose nearby homes were in fact identical in layout. Similarly, the relationship of the children to adults was surely familiar in terms of language spoken and manner with which the anganwadi worker kept the children under control; however, while at the preschool children were not free to come and go as they might have been while under the eye of a parents or other adults in the compound outside. The time spent in the preschool was clearly preparation for real school. Play was not part of that; play would have been expected at home as what children naturally do.

Tshwane preschool conforms more closely to the description of Little Lake than to that of Sunbeam, however there are many differences too. The outdoor space at Tshwane was very large, a compound of about an acre in size. It contained parking space for several cars, a vegetable garden, and a large play area with some metal climbing equipment. The whole area was enclosed by a high wire fence with a gate for cars to enter. When outside during recess, the children were casually watched over by teachers, but the adults did not interact with the children unless the issue was one of safety or a squabble. Tshwane preschool was the most school-like of the three preschools, resembling, to some extent, a small North American school. The similarity was limited however, since beyond the surface features of a western preschool and its activities, there was much that reflected the persistence of traditional South African culture, norms, languages, and activities. Thus our impression was that especially in terms of adult-child relationships, this preschool was a very familiar place for many children, a place where, for the most part, they were gently cared for and treated with loving attention. Despite the physical set-up and typical preschool routines, pedagogical matters actually seemed to take something of a secondary place to a more traditional socialization centred on building relationships in the context of a culture that promotes and supports interdependence and communal responsibility (Kağitçibaşi, 1996, 2007; LeVine, 2003; LeVine et al., 1994).

SCHEDULING OF A PRESCHOOL DAY

Table 7 below shows the schedules of the three preschools in such a way that comparisons can easily be made. Close analysis suggests that the differences are in fact very minor. As the shaded areas of the table show, while Sunbeam's day starts and ends later, the scheduled time for teacher-child interaction (which may be considered teaching time) is about the same in each: nearly 2 hours at Little Lake, out of a total of 2 hours and 45 minutes, 2 hours and 45 minutes at Tshwane out of a 5 hour day, and 2 hours 15 minutes out of a total of 3 hours at Sunbeam. The proportion of time spent on care activities was most significant at Tshwane, pointing to the preschool's predominantly paediatric function. When the schedules of these three preschools are compared to two others, as in Table 8, we find the Montreal preschool to have the most pedagogical emphasis with 2 hours and 45 minutes of teacher-directed time devoted to learning or learning-related activities out of a total time of 3.5 hours, while the Calgary Head Start schedule specifies time for Art and Library centres and a total of teaching time of 2 hours in a 3 hour day.

Although it would be necessary to carry out another study in these three preschools in order to determine with precision how closely the daily schedules were actually followed, the Grade R teacher at Tshwane reported that she followed the schedule loosely, and indeed preferred her own schedule. The Little Lake

Table 7. Scheduling, Canada, South Africa, India

time	**Little Lake**	time	**Tshwane**	time	**Sunbeam**
		7:00	Staff arrival		
		8:00	Pupils arrive		
8:30	Staff arrival	8:10 - 9:00	Independent activity		
9:30	Arrival of children				
9:35	Snacks (breakfast)	9:00	Breakfast		
9:45-10:35	Morning circle; sweet grass, prayer; greetings; songs; special announcements	9:30 - 10:00	Morning 'rug-time': greetings, devotion, weather, discussion		
10:35-10:45	School readiness	10:00	Story, music, movement	10:30	Staff arrival
10:50 - 11:05	Gross motor	11:00	Developmental 'rug-time'	10:45	Arrival of children
11:10-11:20	Story time	11:30	Pre-reading skill, pre-writing skill, number concepts	11:00-11:30	Prayer, attendance, general discussions with children
11:20-11:40	Group work	12:00	lunch, rest	11:30-12:45	Classroom activity (music, chart reading, number concepts)
11:45-12:00	Lunch	1:00 p.m.	Departure	12:45-1:00	Free play
12:15	Home time			1:00-1:30	Meals
				1:30-2:00	Quiet time - stories and discussions followed by departure

schedule was sufficiently open to allow for the flexibility in timing and shifts that were observed, while overall the schedule was adhered to. At Sunbeam, adherence to the schedule was most constrained, again perhaps because of the very limited space, large numbers of children, and high child-teacher ratio.

Table 8. Scheduling at Calgary Native Head Start and a Montreal Preschool

time	**Calgary Native Head Start**	time	**A Montreal preschool**
8:30	Hot breakfast	8:15-8:30	Outdoor supervision
8:45	Circle time (using lesson plan)	8:30-8:45	Arrivals
9:15	Art centre	8:45-9:15	Gross motor activity
9:45	Sand and water centres	9:15-9:45	Learning centres
10:15	Library centre (story time)	9:45-10:00	Morning circle
10:30	Nutritional snack	10:00-10:30	Teacher directed small group activity
10:45	Gross motor centre (activity games)	10:30-11:00	Snack time/show and share
11:00	Fine motor centre (manipulative skills)	11:00-11:30	Teacher directed small group activity
11:15-11:30	Free play until picked up by parent	11:30-12:00	Closing circle and outdoor play

This analysis of the schedules (Table 7) and their comparison to two other preschools in Table 8 suggests that there is a global view of what children need to be doing in a semi-formal or formal preschool setting. There is not much variation, except that which is dictated by physical space, numbers of children, and the weather. One might expect that teacher training or qualifications would also make a difference, but this does not seem to be the case. In fact, we would take a controversial position on this and argue that teachers' care and concern for the welfare of children in this preschool age group is rooted in culturally-based child-rearing priorities. This may count as much or more than training. When training is more extensive and greater qualifications are required, it is perhaps more a function of a developed country's economy than an indicator of the quality of an ECCE centre.

POLICY – PRACTICE GAPS

The reader will recall that policy was referred to as a statement, plan, or guide for action. Policies set out the position that a group such an education ministry, school board or local authority takes on a particular matter. Education policies are usually written down in various documents that can be analysed to determine how a policy has developed, what the influences on it have been and the direction it points to in terms of desired developments, changes, or outcomes. Curriculum policy documents, for example, portray the kind of citizen and society that is envisioned in the future.

Our particular concern in this book has been with policies that relate to the care and early education of preschool children living in relative poverty, in times of social change. In that policies are not laws, but more often can be seen as evolving guides for action, it is not surprising that an analysis of policy and practice would reveal some gaps. It is well to remember that such gaps are to be found everywhere, not only in the kinds of settings that are the subject of this book.

Little Lake – The Example of AHS

Aboriginal Head Start (AHS) government-supported early childhood programs for First Nations, Métis, and Inuit children in Canada were modelled initially on Head Start compensatory programs in the United States, designed originally for inner-city, ethnic, and racial minority non-Aboriginal children. AHS programs have increased dramatically over the last 15 years, providing evidence of considerable change in attitude since the time when Aboriginal children were to be taught English in order to be ready for school and to be able to compete on an equal footing with their English-speaking peers. AHS programs for preschool children now aim to regenerate lost or nearly lost Aboriginal languages and the cultures that those languages reflect. The idea is that children who are aware of their cultural and language roots will have clearer self-identities and be better prepared to live comfortably in both worlds, the Aboriginal, whether that is on-reserve or off-, and in the larger Canadian society beyond. This change in attitude as to what is best for Aboriginal children parallels the emergence of Canada's multicultural policy and of the general acceptance in the society at large of many other cultural, ethnic, and religious groups.

The shift from the dominant society's attempt to assimilate Aboriginal children to acknowledging and encouraging the revival of their languages and cultures, reminds us of the vast social changes that First Nations peoples have experienced. While the cultural, genocidal impact of past oppression in the name of assimilation is well known, our research sought to pinpoint some of the lingering, subtle effects of that oppression in the light of the present climate of acceptance of cultural differences. Briefly, those effects may be seen in the still complicated relationship that First Nations and other Aboriginal peoples have with Federal and Provincial authorities, for instance in the financial limits that are placed on their autonomy and self-governance (Battiste & Barman, 1995; David-Cree, 2004). At the level of the preschool classroom we saw little of this, however in discussions with teachers and community leaders the situation was still clearly a concern. In particular, there was considerable difference of opinion as to the most desirable approach to be taken in preschool and schools, with awareness of the reality of the larger society's standards and norms likely to increasingly dominate Aboriginal peoples' education and life opportunities. This was evident at Little Lake in its emphasis on the development of skills and knowledge for the future: the intensive work to prepare children for kindergarten and grade 1 by tutoring them in numbers and the alphabet and teaching them social behaviour skills associated with being a pupil. It is of note that despite this admirable effort, many children were reported to be unruly by school staff, and 'not ready for school' with a considerably high grade 1 rate of failure. It may be that once Aboriginal children enter formal schooling the standards and norms governing behaviour and performance become those of the dominant society, whether or not the school is on- or off-reserve and Native run or not. Thus the continuity between home and preschool socialization that was observed at Little Lake, especially in terms of the lack of explicit expectation for verbal interaction and the implicit expectation that learning occur through observation rather than through verbal instruction, may shift abruptly with the start of primary school. There, Aboriginal children may be seen as language delayed and thus not ready for school. This analysis of the situation was hinted at by the previously mentioned government report of a high percentage of Aboriginal children with disabilities, the greatest percentage being language-related. With relevance to the INAC push for standardized testing referred to earlier, we ask how are the norms established for the testing of Aboriginal children's speech development when it is observation rather than verbal skills that are traditionally valued in the home and reinforced in the preschool? In addition, INAC funding does not support ESL for children transitioning to English language instruction, thus it is not surprising that Aboriginal children are at undue risk of being labelled as in need of special education.

Although AHS programs are government supported, they are locally controlled. As such, the goals at the local level are varied, according to each community's own perceived needs. While the emphases differ, all are developed with the six integrated components mentioned earlier, including Aboriginal culture and language, school readiness, parental involvement, and health promotion. From our observations at Little Lake, it appeared that practice supported this policy which emphasized the promotion of Aboriginal children's identities within the broader context of Canada's official policy of multiculturalism.[1]

Sunbeam

India's current national policy context, similar to that of South Africa, sees children and the investment in ECCE in terms of human resource development. The Constitution of India empowers the State to favour economically disadvantaged groups, including girls. Young children are seen as vulnerable and early experience is considered to lay the foundation for future development. Children have the right to an enabling environment; the role of the mother is seen as critical. At one time, the focus was on child welfare; however, for the last 25 or so years there has been a shift to child development and to finding ways to prepare children for school that will result in less early school dropout and better achievement. One strategy to achieve these aims is through the Integrated Child Development Services (ICDS) for mothers and children aged birth to school-age.

ICDS places importance on community involvement in resource mobilization, planning, and implementation. The approach is said to be child-centred incorporating the playway philosophy and activity-based learning, as described earlier. Playway as pedagogy emphasizes individual children's development through adult-guided games, songs and stories, and work with materials. The Indian playway method is distinctive, involving more adult direction than would be common in many western preschools (Prochner, 2002, 2009b). This follows cultural expectations regarding the adult-child interaction, as explained by Katz, Mohite, and Shastri (2009) in relation to project work in Indian preschools.

> Adults are considered authority figures and are supposed to know more than children. Therefore, rather than discussing things with each other and contradicting each other, children sought the teacher's opinions. This is very natural in the India situation. In fact, children would be satisfied with an answer only if and when it was confirmed by the teacher. (p. 51)

Within ICDS programs, any version of playway would be the exception rather than the rule. In any case, playway methods are out of step with expectations for teaching and learning in Grade 1. As seen at Sunbeam anganwadi, the educational goal was more on preparation for Grade 1, including what is to be expected in classrooms in terms of numbers of children, the role of the teacher, and expected behaviours for children.

Tshwane

South Africa's education policy context is one that looks to its education system for development, economic growth, and success on a par with the world's so-called developed nations. Education is also seen as essential to poverty reduction and to redressing the wrongs of the past that most sorely affected the black numerical majority. Children are at the centre of this integrated effort that links education with health and culture.

The ECCE policy context in South Africa is of three levels: the central state, the provinces, and the local authorities. The central state, the Ministry of Education (MoE), is engaged in overall policy development, planning and coordination. The provincial Departments of Education (DoE) are to develop delivery systems and implement policy, and the local level is responsible for providing facilities and local monitoring of programs (Report on National ECD Policies and Programmes, 2001, p. 28). Pre-primary education refers to pre-grade 1 education for learners birth to 6 years of age (UNESCO, 2006). Pre-primary programs are of two types: Grade R (reception year) which refers to the school preparation year for 5-year-olds, and pre-Grade R programs that cater for children 0 to 4 years of age. The reader will recall that Grade R was introduced in order to provide a universal pre-primary preparation for all so that previously disadvantaged children would start Grade 1 on an equal footing with their previously advantaged peers. Although slow to be implemented, the aim was to move all Grade R classes out of EC centres and into primary schools by 2010.

This change in policy for preschool education is bound to have a trickle down effect on the EC centres which, until recently, housed most of Grade Rs, creating something of a policy-practice gap in the near future. Our recent study has indicated that this top-down push will likely see 4 year olds as the group to be prepared for formal schooling with less child-centred learning and more direct instruction (Cleghorn & Prochner, 2008; Prochner & Cleghorn, 2005). The extent to which this will include earlier and earlier introduction to English, due partly to pressure from parents, remains to be seen. It also remains to be seen how the MoE will promote a bilingual or multilingual school system that gives space for the nine official African languages, in addition to English and Afrikaans.

Another change in policy is to provide more specialized services for children with disabilities and illnesses such as HIV/AIDS, which assumes that the way such children have been treated is inadequate. As Nsamenang (2007) found, the communal/community approach that we saw in action at Tshwane preschool appeared to be working well, and it was not portrayed as unusual. Thus in the months or years to come, this change from the indigenous to the western manner of treating children may create a new gap with less community involvement and less community acceptance of such children as they become increasingly categorized and labelled, and services become increasingly institutionalized.

South Africa's language policy serves to promote unity and diversity. The reader will recall that the policy favours, but does not mandate, initial instruction in the mother tongue, while placing nine African languages on an equal footing with English and Afrikaans. At the same time, increasing numbers of parents want their children taught in English, as early as possible. This is sure to be difficult to respond to since only about 20% of South Africa's population reports English as the first language. This also means that many teachers may be ill at ease teaching in English, while at the same time facing very linguistically-mixed classrooms: a recent informal survey in one school found 17 different languages represented, including French and Portuguese among refugee children from the Democratic Republic of the Congo and Mozambique (see Table 9). We will return to this topic in chapter 8 when we discuss South Africa's outcomes-based education curriculum policy in the context of globalization.

The policy context of preschool in South Africa can thus be viewed in light of recent social and political changes. As outlined in chapter 3, the end of apartheid in 1994 put a halt to official racial segregation, which saw the population divided into Black, Coloured, Asian, and White racial groups with strict laws governing the conditions under which black people could live, work, and be educated. Nine African languages, in addition to English and Afrikaans, are now designated as official, ending decades of control by speakers of English or Afrikaans. Schools are being integrated, black teachers now may teach in former all-white schools, and white teachers are being deployed to previously all-black schools. In the former homelands where black people had been required to live, those who can afford to do so now send their children to racially-mixed, better equipped schools in the city suburbs. Despite these demographic changes the legacy of apartheid can be seen, at times, in the values and attitudes that have become part of the thinking of some parents. As mentioned, there is an increasing demand for instruction in English and some white parents are resisting racially integrated schools by sending their children to elite government or private schools where white children are still more numerous. It is thus difficult to persuade parent groups, and even some educators, that children will do better in school if home languages find support within the school, while ensuring that children acquire literacy and numeracy as well in English (Benson, 2004; Bunyi, 1999; Cleghorn, 2005; DoE, 2008; Evans, 2006; 2007; Evans, Cleghorn & Sarkar, 2009; Prochner & Cleghorn, 2005; Soudien, 2007).

Table 9. South Africa's Multilingualism: One School, March 2009

L at home	Class A	Class B	Class C	Class D	totals
Afrikaans	1	1	0	1	3
Bemba	0	0	1	0	1
English	1	1	1	4	7
French	1	0	7	2	10
Lingala	0	0	2	0	2
Ndebele	0	1	0	0	1
Northern Sotho	12	9	8	16	45
Portuguese	0	0	1	0	1
Shangaan	1	1	1	0	3
Shona	1	0	0	0	1
Southern Sotho (pedi)	0	4	0	6	10
Swahili	1	0	1	1	3
Tigrinya	0	1	0	0	1
Tswana	9	11	4	0	24
Venda	6	3	0	0	9
Xhosa	0	1	5	1	7
Zulu	4	4	4	8	20
N in class	37	37	35	39	
N different languages	10	11	11	8	

It is not surprising that in Tshwane's policy context we find a direct contrast in goals to those described earlier for AHS as represented by Little Lake. As the reader saw in chapter 2, injustices of the past in both Canada and South Africa have resulted in very different meanings being attached to racial and ethnic difference. In the Canadian Aboriginal setting, the EC program is meant to enhance personal and group identity (as distinct from that of the majority), while in South Africa the aim is to reduce difference by fostering equality between the races in the name of national unity and long-awaited equity, especially for the black majority. While Canada and Canadian Aboriginal groups celebrate diversity, South Africa aims to develop a national identity, to celebrate oneness, to bring about a uniformity that softens the former harsh meaning of racial difference.

Thus, in contrast to the community of Little Lake, where cultural and linguistic difference is celebrated, the opposite is the case in South Africa where the attempt is, understandably, to erase the signs of difference in the name of a new national identity, uniformity, and equal opportunities for all. Although both Canada and South Africa have racist histories, it was only in 1994 that South Africa's system of apartheid was dismantled. Canada's racist policies regarding First Nations peoples were perhaps more subtle, in that they were cloaked in protective rhetoric, marginalising Aboriginal groups and impoverishing them on reserves while denying them their rights if they chose to live off-reserve; as well, First Nations women who married non-Aboriginal men lost the rights accorded by their Aboriginal status. Aboriginal status was removed if they went to university, joined the Armed Forces, or voluntarily enfranchised.

Earlier the term indigenous was defined two ways, as a body of knowledge associated with long-term occupancy of a certain place (Dei, Hall, & Rosenberg, 2000 p. 6) and as the dynamic way in which the residents of an area have come to understand themselves in relationship to their natural environment (Semali & Kincheloe, 1999, p. 3).

We prefer to look on the interplay between indigenous knowledge and so-called western knowledge in terms of transitions, of which there are in fact many kinds. For each setting we asked, what occurs in practice when western ways of knowing come into contact with indigenous (local) ways of socializing and working with children? How does each setting come to terms with opposing global trends: the trend towards uniformity of practice, towards western definitions of what constitutes quality in ECCE, and the trend that celebrates and promotes diversity? What happens to local conceptions of childhood, of how children learn best? What are the mechanisms through which western ways of knowing influence local ideas and practices? Do gaps between policy and practice widen? In addition to these questions, we were interested in the kinds of child development and other theories that preschool teachers had been exposed to during their training, for contained within those theories and the manner in which they tend to be taught, lies the western conception of the child and of childhood (Dahlberg, Moss, & Pence, 2006; Hatch, 1995, 2004; Nsamenang, 2007; Serpell, 1992).

Little Lake

Aboriginal Head Start Canada has far-reaching aims to change the fortunes of young First Nations, Métis, and Inuit children. This is to be done via a part-time preschool staffed by EC workers with varying types and levels of training, and in connection with community as well as provincial standards of whatever is defined as quality ECCE programming. It is further intended that preschools will attend to culture and language, education and school readiness, health promotion, nutrition, social support, and parental and family involvement. It is not at all clear that parents perceive the preschool as hub for this range of services, which would otherwise be available from health workers, social workers, certificated teachers, and so on, in specialized services. The AHS strength at Little Lake is in the degree to which preschool assists children in making an effective transition from home to school; in short, for children to see themselves as successful learners. This is more likely to occur when the skills, knowledge, and behaviour that children bring with them from home is built upon and not replaced by what is learned in school. The EC staff at Little Lake endeavoured to support children's successful transition by specifically teaching a type of pupil behaviour—for competency in the foreign culture—in the context of supportive and culturally familiar adult-child relations. Western cultural influences were pervasive in the preschool, but not dominating in relation to Aboriginal culture. The EC staff could be seen to interpret the significance of the events, materials, and activities in preschool for the children, with the aim being their future school success.

Sunbeam

According to Mohite (1993), gaps exist in targets specified by policies, programs, and targets achieved at the present time. The cause of these gaps is thought to be fragmentation and lack of coordination between different government departments and agencies. There are also gaps between professional educators' westernized views of children's early learning requirements and those of parents and local educators: parents want their children to begin reading and writing in preschool and do not consider play a valuable source of learning. In fact, play at school is considered to impede learning and maturation. Thus the links between developmental aims as stated in policy and curriculum documents and practice are not clear, perhaps because of limits in the training of anganwadi EC workers, which assumes an understanding of the link between child development theory and practice.

In fact, there are vast differences in conceptions of the teacher-child relationship: anganwadi workers prefer large groups of children and prefer to teach to the group. Thus play activities have been observed to involve the whole group in singing, games, and question-answer routines.

Tshwane

In South Africa in 1995 the Minister of Education said that the terms of the 1996 Constitution start as *intervention* with young children: to correct the wrongs of apartheid, to build a democratic and egalitarian country, and to ensure the human rights of all. The vision of the child then is one who has a name and nationality from birth (identity), parental or alternative care, basic nutrition, shelter and health care, protection from maltreatment and the right to a basic education in the language of their choice.

In the preschool where this study was carried out in South Africa, children's rights were displayed on posters in the central hallway along with posters about HIV/AIDS and posters showing Mickey Mouse. Thus serious local concerns and trends were juxtaposed with Disneyfication, an aspect of globalization. Attitudes towards children were displayed in a poster outlining children's responsibilities:

to keep the school clean, to not waste food, to show love, and to study—hinting perhaps at the more traditional holistic and communal orientation of African values. However, again in contrast, the world that the child is being prepared for is one in which they are to be given the tools to compete on the international market, to access the world stage and make the country grow and succeed. These aims are to be achieved through the newly revised national curriculum of which outcomes-based education (OBE) forms the basis. Although we will say more about OBE in chapter 8, it would appear that early childhood programs in South Africa are indeed "taking their cues from imported models that reinforce shifts from the collective to the individualistic, production-oriented culture of the West" (Myers, 1992, p. 29).

What occurs in practice? Is there evidence of a gap, between language or other policy and practice? Perhaps the most telling gap appears in the role of books in the classrooms and in the lives of preschool children. The books observed in the Grade R classroom, such as *Hattie and the Fox* by the Australian author Mem Fox, were all imported from the West[2]. We saw little evidence of a storytelling tradition in the teachers' use of books with the children. Rather, they were used for English vocabulary building, even if the English text was pasted over with the children's home language. This resulted in some code-switching during the lesson, as had occurred during the lesson on naming the body parts; the lesson was taught in Setswana but the body parts were labelled in English. While somewhat haphazard, the occasional use of the home language in the classroom may well have had the effect of according value to the children's home language. Nevertheless, since books were not accorded value in the classroom as a source of pleasure, we ask how a culture develops from its oral tradition and love of story *telling,* to add a love of story books and learning *from* books?

To conclude this chapter that asks the meaning of difference but does not pretend to answer the question fully, we offer another observation from Tshwane's Grade R classroom of western-indigenous culture contact. A game was played in the local language. The teacher and the children were fully engaged in it, happy, with laughter, loudly and rhythmically repeating the refrain, in a sing-song chant. With the shift to a circle game using English, the children's and teacher's body language became stiff and the children's attention soon wandered. Here we would say that the meaning of difference lay in the affective domain. More will be said in chapter 8 about the centrality and importance of language issues in these early childhood classrooms.

NOTES

[1] "There cannot be one cultural policy for Canadians of British and French origin, another for the original peoples, and yet a third for all the others, for although there are two official languages there is no official culture" (Trudeau, 1971, pp. 8545-8548).

[2] It may be relevant that the author was raised in Zimbabwe by missionary parents. She left Zimbabwe at age 19.

CHAPTER 8

GLOBALIZATION REVISITED

In this final chapter, the aim is to highlight the ways in which the socio-cultural lens that we used to understand and describe Sunbeam, Tshwane and Little Lake preschools, brought to the fore the influence of globalization in each. We defined globalization primarily in terms of the varied ways in which events, policies, activities, attitudes, and beliefs in one part of the world become part of the thinking, beliefs, policies, and behaviours of people in another part of the world. We suggested that globalization could be expected to manifest itself in varied ways: on the one hand, creating shared meanings about what is best for children to thrive and be ready for school; and on the other hand, causing clashes between western prescriptions and locally-rooted approaches to working with young children. We then located each setting with regard to its respective historical experience with colonization and its context of social change: in India, mainly technological developments with associated social changes, in South Africa, changes in the racial social structure, and cultural regeneration in the Aboriginal community in Canada. We have thus given ourselves a tall order by posing the following question: with particular reference to the influence of globalization and to the interaction between the local and the global, what sense can be made from the discussions about curriculum policy (chapter 3), social relations (chapter 4), materials and space (chapter 5), and the interplay between paediatric and pedagogical approaches (chapter 6) at Sunbeam, Little Lake, and Tshwane preschools?

In the pages that follow, the discussion will draw from the foregoing chapters to take up three topics. Firstly, what do the three settings tell us about the current global academic discourse about quality in ECCE settings? Secondly, what has been learned about global prescriptions regarding early childhood curricula? Thirdly, what have these settings contributed to our thinking about transitions: from preschool to regular school, from the local to the global? The chapter ends with a few tentative recommendations.

Quality Issues

Prior to embarking on a discussion about issues of quality in ECCE settings, it is important to reiterate the fact that in no way whatsoever was the study that this book stems from concerned with assessing the quality of the three settings. Indeed, the socio-cultural approach that we used in the research sought to understand differences in conceptions of the child and childhood; we sought multiple perspectives on how to work with children in a range of contexts. We did so from a position of concern, shared by several others, that the ECCE field is "dominated

123

by meta-narratives underpinned by psychologically-based discourses such as developmentally appropriate practice (DAP) ... spoken in the English language, ... that western psychological approaches do not necessarily transcend borders" (Lewis, Macfarlane, Nobel & Stephenson, 2006, p. 25; see also Ball & Pence, 1999; Dahlberg, Moss & Pence, 2006; Hatch, 1995; Moss, 1994; Nsamenang, 2007; Serpell, 1992). As we proceeded through the fieldwork, and despite our considerable prior research experience in diverse settings, we still had to reflect on our own taken-for-granted notions about such matters as the way ECCE spaces are to be organized, and the aesthetics of material resources. As we did so, we came to a fuller appreciation of what quality might mean in diverse settings. In fact, although we are tempted to ask if it is a useful notion at all, it remains an important issue to consider. In the words of Moss (1994):

'Quality' is an international buzzword, not only in early childhood services but in connection with every kind of product and service. Yet in its mantra-like repetition, the word is in danger of being rendered meaningless. It attracts widespread support—for who could not want 'good quality'—unless and until we have to say what we actually mean, at which point it becomes far more elusive. (p. 1).

This being said, we agree that while teachers, parents, and researchers may lean towards contextualized definitions of quality in ECCE settings, the reality is that politicians and governments rely on information from the field to create guidelines for establishing national norms and standards for all levels of schooling (Myers, 2005). Thus it may be another aspect of the influence of globalization that countries such as India and South Africa increasingly look to their national governments for local support of ECCE programs, while national governments look to the West for policy and curriculum guidelines.

Earlier it was noted that early childhood discourse exhibits considerable difference of opinion about what the view of the child should be, and what the pedagogical/paediatric priorities of early childhood settings ought to be: protection of child rights and safety, school readiness, or healthy development? Matters of quality appear to get caught in the middle of the two opposing trends mentioned earlier: a world-wide increase in recognition of the validity of local, indigenous ways of knowing about, and working with children on the one hand, and a persistence of western dominant discourse that militates against the inclusion of indigenous knowledge and activity in ECCE settings on the other hand. The forces of globalization, via the western dominant voice, would, however, appear to be winning out by virtue of education policy-borrowing, in the content of teacher education courses, in workshops for practicing teachers offered by international NGOs, and through the content of textbooks written by or primarily for educators in the West, in English, usually with the western-centric assumption that the reader is a first language speaker of American English (Peacock & Cleghorn, 2004).

The forces of globalization regarding quality issues in ECCE can also be seen in the preoccupation of international organizations such as UNICEF and the World Bank, which establish indicators of what it is that the world's children require in order to be healthy, to be protected from harm, to develop, and to achieve their learning potential. This is supported by the 1989 Convention on the Rights of the Child which commits countries to translate international standards into domestic law and national practice. The problem arises in the efforts to define international standards and to arrive at locally appropriate indicators. For example, Evans (1996) in the *Coordinators' Notebook*, published by the Consultative Group on Early Childhood Care and Development, provides six different examples of systems for assessing quality in early childhood environments. One of these, based on the High/Scope Perry Preschool study, mentions five elements of effective programmes, which include the use of developmentally-appropriate curricula that support children's self-initiated learning activities, and classes with a ratio of less than 20 3 to 5 year olds for every pair of adults (Schweinhart, Barnes & Weikart, 1993). Another model, summarized by Woodhead (1996), mentions an environment full of specially-constructed physical materials, objects, tools, and activities, to which children are given relatively free access. And, perhaps the most widely known quality scale, the Early Childhood Environment Rating Scale (Harms, Clifford, & Cryer, 2005), though recently adapted to different cultural settings (Aboud, Hossain, & O'Gara, 2008; Sheridan, Giota, Han, & Kwon, 2009), provides what is in effect an observation grid for assessing the presence or degree of compliance, on a five point scale, of a number of criteria such as personal care routines, language-reasoning experiences, and creative activities. If we were to extract key words from this paragraph and apply them to our three preschools the result would be something like what appears in Table 10 (P= present; A= absent; PA= partial, teacher controlled).

Table 10. Quality Considerations in the Three Preschools

Item	Little Lake	Sunbeam	Tshwane
Self-initiated activities	P	A	PA
2/-20 ratio	P	A	A
Free access materials	P	A	PA
Personal care routines	P	P	P
Language reasoning activities	P	A	A
Creative activities	P	A	P

Evidently, criteria such as these could be applied to Sunbeam and Tshwane preschools with only the most negative of assessments, yet from our perspective all three preschools fit well with community expectations and dovetailed the activities and interaction with children in locally acceptable ways. In fact, the criteria outlined in the 1996 *Coordinators' Notebook* exclude the sense of community that clearly characterized several of the ECCE centres we visited both in India and in South Africa, the pride with which accomplishments were reported to have been made with such few resources, the inclusive attitude of teachers and preschool directors towards the children and their parents, and so on. It is of note that these functional characteristics are difficult to observe directly and to quantify, but that does not negate them. Similarly, at Tshwane, we noted the ease with which children who were known to be HIV positive or have disabilities, were included and not labelled as a problem. A community spirit and shared sense of *care* was pervasive not only at Tshwane but at the other centres we visited too. We doubt that this possible evidence of the African philosophy or value *ubuntu*[1] can be easily extinguished through globalization or otherwise.

Admittedly, our familiarity with the literature on quality assessment indicators remains limited; however, the debates are important: should the focus be on child development or on the conditions of early childhood care and education? Who should decide a preschool's program: representatives of international organizations or local communities? How should indicators of quality be used: to advocate for children's services, to evaluate existing programs, to generate local discussion about what children need? Rarely is the fundamental question asked: Why are international indicators sought? What larger purpose do they serve, and for whom?[2] Perhaps international and local indicators of quality are not only different but unrelated phenomena. For example, what seems to stand out within the concept of international standards is a glaring deficit view of non-western ECCE programs. In addition to the deficit view underlying the idea of intervention, if not many interventions themselves, a deficit view of ECCE programs, activities, and aims that deviate from the western standard, however that is defined, pervades EC discourse. It is still rare that policy makers or educators speak of school readiness in terms of readying the school for the child, rather than the child for the school. For example, with regard to school readiness, Dickinson (2002) states:

> Children who come to school from literacy rich pre-school and home environments have a 1000 hour advantage … Catch-up is possible given two years of extra support in phonemic and literacy awareness … immerse children in books that deal playfully with speech sounds. (pp. 27-28)

What is missing here too is the fact that the literacy rich (middle class) home environment links the child affectively to books. This is what reading bedtime stories is about (Bettleheim, 1977); this is what many western middle class educated parents do with their children at bedtime. If indeed the world's children are expected to be ready to read (usually in English) by grade 1 (a questionable expectation in itself), one must then ask how the affective link to the meaning of print may be replicated when reading to children at home is not part of the culture, but oral story telling is. Surely there are other than interventionist, compensatory strategies to insure that those (majority world children) who start school 1000 hours behind (behind what, whom?) are not doomed? Surely there is value to be found for school readiness within the oral tradition?

Although the notion of international standards may be appealing, ideas such as developmentally appropriate practice and play-based learning and teaching are not universally appreciated. In fact, even national standards may be an unrealistic aim when rural and urban differences in the majority world are considered, along with the cultural and linguistic differences that tend to coincide with such regional differences. There is little to suggest that national or international standards can be realized, based as they are on ill-defined purposes and on inadequate cross-cultural research evidence; rather, they are based on research that is fundamentally biased in favour of western-centric beliefs and *regimes of truth* (Foucault, 1980) about what is good for the world's children, and inadequately examined assumptions about what constitutes good practice.

In a similar vein, taken-for-granted beliefs about school readiness permeate mainstream discourse, based as they are on assumptions of universal stages of child development and children's needs (Graue, 1992; Shallwani, 2009). Increasingly, one not only finds reference to a seemingly universal set of skills and knowledge that children need to possess prior to starting school, but there is more and more reference to formal testing for school readiness. In this regard then, globalization seriously risks increasing the majority-minority inequities by marginalizing majority world children as 'not ready' in relation to standards set for minority world children.

As Tobin (2005) argues, there are many different ways of working effectively with young children, there are many different ways of protecting them from harm, and there are many different ways of preparing them for the schools that exist in their own environments. As evidence for this position, Tobin draws on his research in Japanese preschools and his more recent studies of immigrant children in Europe. Citing the Japanese preschool setting, Tobin notes that if our theories of quality early childhood education are correct, the ratios, class size, non-intervention by Japan's teachers in children's fights and other practices should produce children who are socially, linguistically, and cognitively impaired (Tobin, 2005, p. 422). There is, however, nothing to suggest this in the results of international cross-cultural studies of achievement (Mullis, Martin, & Foy, 2008). The point is, children are generally well prepared in preschool settings for the experiences they will encounter when they attend school in their own communities, providing that the school represents the community rather than the trappings of the colonial era. This does not, however, suggest that when communities and their schools are severely impoverished, when teachers are inappropriately trained for effective work in their own settings, and when children are treated harshly, that nothing should be done. Then the discourse of children's rights and international standards would have at the core diversity of beliefs, attitudes and preferred ways of working with children.

Our findings suggests that globalization may have had the effect of undermining confidence in the local, quite functional, practices of teachers in countries such as India and South Africa; the reader will recall the teacher at Tshwane preschool who was embarrassed to admit (to the researchers who were surely perceived as outside 'experts') that she did not follow the daily schedule provided by a western NGO but preferred her own, which was literally hidden underneath.[3]

Global Prescriptions about Curriculum

The highly varied influence of globalization in each preschool setting was evident from the comparative analysis of curriculum elements, the daily schedules of activities, and the presence and use of materials. For the moment, let us take the tension between play-based versus teacher-directed instruction, where the former is associated with western ECCE theory and practice and the latter linked with traditional cultures and majority world values and beliefs. The notion of play-based learning at Sunbeam was embedded in the non-formal playway approach as learned in ICDS training workshops, and adapted to Sunbeam's situation. As practiced at Sunbeam, activity was entirely teacher directed, with the children responding in unison in a playful manner. There was no physical space for small group work, child-initiated activities or free play, though free play was an item in the daily schedule. The physical space was sparsely decorated with a couple of posters, placed high above the children's line of vision. Preschool was about learning the teacher-led routines in a crowded space, with young children being readied for a type of schooling where the crowding and the routines would be familiar, as would the authority of the teacher. There was no hint of doubt on the anganwadi's part that her approach was the correct one, surely to be approved by parents whose homes and outdoor courtyards were within reach of her work with their children.

At Little Lake, the approach was in direct contrast to that of Sunbeam, with less than 12 children in a large space designed for small group as well as whole group work, and with much individual attention given by the teacher and her helper. In addition to the teacher's helper, the cook and the bus driver helped out informally. The content of story telling and of materials posted on the walls were clearly intended to foster awareness of Aboriginal cultural heritage and language. Classroom materials also portrayed quite typical North American preschool culture with, for example, weather and number charts which children could view easily. Outdoor play, while supervised, gave vent to the natural inclinations of children to learn informally and through manipulation of natural materials such as sand. Thus at Little Lake a western view of ECCE combined with the ideology of cultural regeneration, which signals a relatively recent change from Canada's earlier history of attempted eradication of First Nations difference through forced assimilation (Schissel & Wotherspoon, 2003).

Again in contrast, Tshwane preschool curriculum may have been influenced most by globalization due to the preponderance of imported or donated western materials, as well as the training and recommendations of foreign NGOs regarding practice. In addition, and not unlike the situation just described at Little Lake, the preschool in South Africa was feeling the effects of recent social change, which included the frequent MoE mandated changes to the national curriculum. The reader will recall that one aim of curriculum reform was to foster equality between the racial groups, the lines being erased of the apartheid-induced meaning attached to racial difference. The result in the Grade R classroom was a somewhat random cultural and linguistic mix of the local and the global that perhaps could have benefited from being made explicit by teacher educators. As the Interim Policy for Early Childhood Development (DoE, 1997, p. 2) noted, "the long history of discriminatory provision in this [ECE] sector delivers a set of conditions that make it difficult to provide a quick-fix solution". This is because poverty and racial segregation persist in the still all-black former townships even while various measures have been introduced to allow for affirmative action. Indeed, the notion of the quick-fix sounds very western, and rarely occurs in the West in any case.

Another issue relates to the predominance of western prescriptions in South Africa's national curriculum. Although the current language of instruction policy endorses the idea of additive bilingualism, little is said about how the policy might be implemented. Rather, the many different languages and cultures of South Africa are simply to be respected. The apparent ambivalence about maintaining home languages may be due to South Africa's concern to unify the nation since the legacy of the apartheid era lingers with its emphasis on strict social, economic, and legal boundaries between the racial groups. Nevertheless, the situation is alarming: in the name of unity there is the potential destruction of local cultures, languages and values as these relate to family, community, and the raising of children. When local languages are lost the need for regeneration later on can become acute, as is the case in many of Canada's Aboriginal communities. Indeed, recent initiatives, some developed through community-university partnerships, emphasize the importance of strengthening culture and language while simultaneously ensuring access to a globalized world (Ball, Definney, & Pence, 1999).

Until recently, all Grade Rs were included in ECE/D programs, about 85% of which were community- or home-based, many operated by church groups and non-governmental organizations. As described earlier, the MoE (central government) and DoEs (provincial governments) are in the process of removing Grade R from these settings and phasing them into the public primary school system, in order to provide access for all to a year of preparation for primary school, in line with efforts to democratize the country and educational opportunities. Grade R teachers are to be provided with specialized training and the DoE is further developing, in conjunction with the Department of Health and Social Development, an integrated service for children age 0 to 4. While slow to be implemented, the national goal is for all children entering grade 1 to have participated in an accredited Reception Year Programme by 2010. At the local level there may be consequences, however, for children in the preschools. In fact, we observed in one ECCE centre the 4 to 5 year olds being offered the Grade R curriculum. In turn, it can be expected that as previously mentioned, 3 year-olds may increasingly be involved in school readiness activities. It is debatable that the presumed benefits of such change can be justified in terms of the principles underlying the compensatory interventions of programs such as Head Start.

Several South African education researchers have raised an alarm, based on their study of problems with OBE in other countries (Jansen, 2002; Ogunniyi, 2005; Sanders, 1999). As was noted earlier, OBE in South Africa has not been easily adopted or understood. Not only is its philosophy not clear to some, but the implementation process is difficult. As with all reforms in education, some teachers are comfortable with the results of how they have always taught and see no need to change. Others have difficulty with the OBE guidelines. With no prescribed content, some teachers do not see how the objectives can be met. A major risk with OBE is that it will lead to more testing, to determine if objectives have been met, rather than less, and to an inclination to put a cap on what is taught if the learners appear to have achieved specific objectives. As one teacher is reported to have said: "How can I stop my students from going ahead to the next level?" (Sanders, 1999, p. 388).[4]

The Impact of Policy Borrowing From the West

South Africa's policy of outcomes-based education provides an example of the way in which globalization enters the minds, attitudes and behaviours of educators. OBE is a controversial approach, being tried in many parts of the world where the verdict is still to come in. On the surface, it comes across as a one-size-fits-all approach. The developmental stages and expected outcomes are clearly defined for each age group from birth onwards. The model of OBE adopted by South Africa is based primarily on that of New Zealand with elements from the USA (Botha, 2002; Jansen, 1999; Spreen, 2001). School subjects were to make way for learning areas, and constructivist methods based on work that was relevant to students' lives were to be used. Learning was to be lifelong with all qualifications, including vocational skills, to be officially recognized.

As mentioned earlier, the 1995 Constitution and then the new National Curriculum provided the policy framework for the education of all South Africans from birth, for lifelong learning. The government sought to develop an education system that would be equitable and able to compete internationally. Children were seen as the key to development and economic growth. South Africa thus borrowed, adapted, and adopted OBE as its national standard for all levels of formal schooling, including the Grade R, the focal group at Tshwane. The reader will recall that the Grade R curriculum seeks to create a lifelong learner who is confident, literate, and multi-skilled, with the ability to participate in society as an active citizen. As mentioned above, the principles of OBE were observed to be filtering down to the preschools because of their history of housing Grade R classes and the fact that preschool classes for 4 year olds will inevitably become the new school preparation year once the plan to move Grade R classes into primary schools is fully implemented. Thus additional details about the Grade R curriculum as described earlier are relevant here, especially since OBE collides head-on with South Africa's language policy in the classroom.

Language Policy Meets Outcomes-Based Education

South Africa is a multilingual, multicultural country with 11 official languages (Afrikaans, English and nine African languages). The national curriculum policy calls for the mother tongue to predominate in the early years of schooling with slow and well-planned introduction of what is referred to as the first additional language[5] from the start. A high level of proficiency in at least two languages is the goal (Webb, 2002). The first additional language is increasingly English, although in some regions Afrikaans predominates. Much as we observed in English lessons at Tshwane preschool, the emphasis at first is on listening skills, using formulaic language (greetings), repeating frequently used words and phrases, responding to simple questions with one or two word answers, singing simple songs, and performing action rhymes.

The language policy for the foundation phase (Grades R to 3) and our analysis of policy documents suggest the presence of potential confusion between policy and practice. Despite the policy that the mother tongue is to predominate in the first few years, the national curriculum states that by Grade 4 a reading vocabulary of several thousand words in the additional language is expected. If this level of vocabulary is to be achieved by Grade 4, it is likely that the instructional language will be stressed over the mother tongue from the start. However, and further to the foregoing, the curriculum also spells out the OBE learning outcomes for listening, speaking, writing, reading and viewing, thinking and reasoning, language structure and use, little of which was observed during our fieldwork. At the same time, the curriculum implies that learners should achieve similar levels of competence in their home and additional languages by the end of Grade 9, but does not specify the kind of bilingual program that could bring about such results. The means by which each of the OBE learning outcomes is to be achieved are not spelled out. There is passing mention of an oral tradition and indigenous African values. As a national curriculum it cannot easily be adapted to the rural, semi-rural or urban life-styles and experiences that children bring to school. Despite plans to provide training for Grade R teachers, Grade R teachers tend to be hired from the pool of Grade 1 teachers who have been trained for primary school teaching, not for ECE.

A national curriculum is a way of constructing a national identity where certain cultural values are promoted and others are not (Bernstein, 1971, as cited in Stephens, 2007, p. 122). However, a contradiction lies in the fact that the curriculum policy documents refer to the importance of home languages, cultures, and literacies while OBE stresses individualism, rationality, and progress, as well as the compartmentalization of knowledge in direct contradiction to African values, where the focus is the ethnic group, spirituality, and a holistic worldview. As a final note on this topic, according to Stephens (2007), there is

> no articulation of an alternative view that traditional life might equally be of value in the so-called modern world....the relationship between education and economy looms large on a rationale for a transformative educational policy to accommodate the neo-liberal capitalist economy; traditional cultures and values are relegated to a secondary role (p. 250).

From Home to School: Border Crossing and Complex Encounters

In this section we are attempting to add theoretically to the topic of children's transitions to the world of schooling, drawing as we do so from the three preschool settings. Transitions are here discussed as *complex encounters*, defined as encompassing the linguistic, cultural, and conceptual shifts that accompany the process of acculturation through formal schooling to western ways of knowing and behaving. Clearly, this process was more evident at Tshwane and Little Lake than at Sunbeam.

There are important lessons to be learned about home-school transitions, especially from South Africa where, despite 11 official languages, the transition to formal schooling usually includes a shift from the home or community language to instruction in English. While South Africa's language-in-education policy advocates initial instruction in the mother tongue, many parents want their children exposed to English as early as possible. In addition, the language that preschool teachers use when introducing children to the written word tends to be the language that children will most likely be taught in at school. Thus the push towards the use of English, the de-facto language of instruction (LoI) comes from several directions. In South Africa it is evident that early learning and the establishment of emergent literacy[6] is linked to and complicated by the spread and increasingly global power of English (Cummins, 2000a; Heugh, Siegrühn & Plüddemann, 1995; Phillipson, 1992; Tollefson, 1991).[7]

As mentioned earlier, only 20% of South Africans report English as their first language. This means that many of South Africa's teachers are not only second language speakers of English, but often do not know the children's home languages. How can teachers attend effectively to children's learning needs under such circumstances? How can they teach effectively if they lack security in the LoI but feel bound to use it? A similar question might be asked in reference to preschool teachers in India. Although at Sunbeam the anganwadi and the anganwadi helper used the children's home language, a dialectical variation of Gujarati, there was a rapidly changing world not far beyond the preschool community that children would soon encounter, one that at a minimum they had been exposed to via television. Though not yet actively transitioning in their daily lives to that world, we saw no hint at Sunbeam that children were being prepared for it. In contrast, at Little Lake, the two worlds met within the classroom, via the activities and indigenous rituals, through the typical North American preschool organization of space, in the indigenous and western learning materials and decorations on the walls, and in the routines and overall ethos of the setting.

Children's transitions from home to school may be seen in terms of border crossings. This concept allows for a closer examination of the home-school transition in terms of complex encounters. The walk or ride from home to school may in itself involve a literal kind of border crossing from the residential to the institutional; however, border crossing here refers more accurately to the ability to shift conceptually, culturally, and when possible, linguistically, between worldviews (Aikenhead & Jegede, 1999; Cobern, 1998; Giroux, 1992; Nsamenang, 2004; Serpell, 1993). When the environment of the preschool has been influenced through globalization by western ways of knowing, different worldviews meet in the classroom. The lines between the worldviews need to be distinguished, as was occurring at Little Lake, for meaningful learning to take place. There it appeared that the children were being prepared to go back and forth between the two with relative ease (Anderson-Levitt, 2003; Dachyshyn & Kirova, 2008). At Tshwane, despite the use of both English and Setswana in the classroom, it appeared that this aspect of the children's experience was not at the forefront of the teacher's consciousness, and thus the crossings were not being made explicit for the children. This is an area, therefore, that we identified that could be included in teacher preparation courses or in in-service workshops, since teachers too need to border cross in order to be alert to the shifts that their learners are experiencing.

Border crossing may be facilitated in several ways; for example, by careful selection of posters and didactic materials for the classroom. The materials should illustrate the different home-school worlds and provide stimuli for discussions about home-school language or cultural differences. Tshwane preschool was replete with materials that might have been used for this purpose, but they were not. For example, several posters in the preschool hallways contained images of Mickey Mouse along side information about HIV/AIDS. The only doll in the play-house corner was white, yet the children were all black. The poster for teaching body parts was labelled in English, however the lesson was taught in Setswana. These were clearly complex encounters for the learners.

Teachers' abilities to engage in border crossing may be facilitated when they are able to use both the LoI and the learners' home languages to code-switch in systematic, purposeful ways. When children do not understand what has been said in English, a word or two in the home language will establish meaning quickly. Code-switching allows for meaning to be negotiated, for untranslatable ideas to be clarified, and for children's home languages and cultural identities to be validated within the classroom (Arthur, 1994; 1996; Brock-Utne, 2003; Cleghorn, 1992; Dube & Cleghorn, 1999; Eastman, 1992; Evans et al., 2007; Merritt, Cleghorn, Abagi, & Bunyi, 1992; Myers-Scotton, 1993).

Another recommendation coming out of our work is thus related to teachers' needs for tools to understand what children are experiencing as they begin the process of *acculturation* towards western ways of knowing and individualistic ways of behaving (Waldrip & Taylor, 1999). They need strategies for bridging the gulf between their own, the school's, and the learners' worldviews. They need tools to prepare children for the world far beyond the preschool.

Early Literacy Preparation: A Complex Encounter with Power Dimensions

Preparing children to read starts with conveying the meaning of print. Some see this as a relatively simple, universally established matter of teaching ABCs while others view the process as contextual and complex, combining the oral, visual, and the written, always taking place within a context of power relations. The New Literacy Studies (NLS) group in England, the United States, and South Africa note how the meaning of print in one part of the world may be very different from another: the printed word may be considered sacred, or the paper it appears on may be considered as valuable fuel for the cooking fire. The NLS plural conception of literacy underlines the persistence and importance of oral literacy in parts of the majority world where an institutional, textbook-based western form of schooling was introduced in the context of the power structure of colonization (Somjee, 2000). Thus, in addition to the implicit power dimension associated with the notion of international standards in ECE, educators need to be aware of the power dimension of literacy learning. They must ask whose literacy is being taught, in what language, and why (Barton, 1995; Barton, Hamilton, & Ivanic, 2000; Brandt & Clinton, 2002; Collins & Blot, 2002; Gee, 1986; 2000; 2008; Kim, 2003; Ong, 1991; Prinsloo & Breier, 1996; Street, 2001a & b; 2003; 2004). Due to the high value placed on oral language skills in many parts of the majority world, emphasis on L1 oral skills in the early years may be the best resource to tap, for story telling, and for connecting children in due course to the meaning of print.

SOME CONCLUDING THOUGHTS

In this final section we will venture further, but timidly, into the territory of recommendations. In this we will first address a matter of policy at the national level. Then the discussion will turn to the implications for educators, teacher educators, and community leaders.

It is understandable that a government should aim to develop its economy and to be competitive in today's world; however, relying on the education system as the main vehicle for achieving these aims may be short-sighted. Much that is of value that is rooted within a country may be lost. What comes immediately to mind here is that South Africa's OBE, borrowed from the West and implemented in a top down manner as a panacea for the country's ills, would appear to conflict with a language policy that recognizes 11 official languages and a stated belief in preserving home languages. Nowhere is it spelled out exactly how the aims of these two policies can be achieved. In such a multilingual country, language issues are extremely important and must be addressed explicitly if school completion rates are to be increased drastically. It is well-shown in the research literature on bilingual education that starting with very young children, in-school maintenance of home languages in a well thought-out bilingual program of instruction produces additive results (Genesee, 2008). When home languages receive little more than passing attention in school, the risk is that in the long term community linkages will be severed along with personal identities, rooted as they are in the local. National development does not occur among people who have lost their culture, language, and identity.

What do preschool teachers need to know in order to work effectively with young children? Here we sense that there is a disjunction between the content of training, when it takes place at all, and practice. A survey of courses offered in the West to future early childhood teachers shows that the curriculum content is heavily laden with child development theory and prescriptions for practice: classrooms are to be child-centred, practice is to be developmentally appropriate, and constructivist teaching methods are to be used in conjunction with play-based teaching and learning. What we saw in each preschool setting was that teachers' good teaching instincts prevailed in ways that were culturally appropriate and locally expected. Except for Little Lake, there was little to suggest that teachers were behaving according to how they had been trained, rather they behaved according to what they felt was best for the children in their charge. At Little Lake, what was best for the children included a conscious awareness on the part of the teacher regarding the importance of cultural regeneration. Such conscious awareness of the children's needs was not so apparent at Sunbeam and minimally so at Tshwane, due no doubt to their conceptions of children's needs lying within the realm of what was referred to earlier as deep culture.

What do community leaders need to know in order to influence local schooling policies? Perhaps the best advice is not to underrate what is done locally simply because it may not look modern. Question taken-for-granted beliefs that what is done in the West is best and the only way forward to development. Listen to the country's experts who have been abroad for long enough to see that not all is well there either. Stay local, while also going global.

NOTES

[1]   Ubuntu refers to the African humanist philosophy of the connectedness between people, perhaps best characterized by the phrase 'I am because we are'.

[2]   A similar lack of fundamental questioning underlies some of the work on 'going to scale' (Vargas-Baron, 2009). The value or importance of going to scale is not sufficiently interrogated. What gets lost when successful, locally generated programs such as Escuela Nueva are transported elsewhere (Hoyos-Vivas, 2008)?

[3]   This small episode points to the tendency for data to be altered in the presence of researchers. In line with the conventions of ethnographic, qualitative methods, had we not spent many hours with this teacher gaining her trust, her actual preference might not have come out.

[4]   Sanders' research on OBE was carried out in the context of science education at the primary and secondary levels, however the comments of the teachers she interviewed corresponded to our concern that OBE might not be entirely appropriate for preschool and early school years children, nor for their teachers.

[5]   Use of the term 'second language' or L2 would imply that South African children shift only from the home language to the language of schooling, rather than acquire several languages in addition to the home language. The First Additional Language connotes the language of schooling which is increasingly English.

[6]   The term emergent literacy is used broadly here to include oral, visual, and 'written' teaching events and practices that foster children's understanding of the meaning of print: vocabulary building exercises and drills, exposure to visual symbols and pictures, and children's drawings that tell a story.

[7]   It is estimated that over 700 million of the world's children learn via English, a language not spoken at home (Cummins & Corson, 1997; Ramanathan, 2005).

AFTERWORD

GLOBALIZATION AND INDIGENIZATION: DRIVING
PRESCHOOL PEDAGOGIES HOME

'From the ground up' characterizes the compelling use of ethnography by Cleghorn and Prochner to observe the everyday routines, critical incidents, decision making processes and community interactions that make up the preschool experiences of children, parents and teachers in three case study settings. Their goal in part was to uncover tacit authority and hidden curricula, elusive and fluid, and therefore not necessarily available through participants' own accounts of their practice. Through analyses of policy, national curricula, and preschool schedules, activities, and materials, the investigators were able to discern the often subtle, dialectical and sometimes jarring patterns of local and more distal influences on care-giving, pedagogical practices, and teacher-parent communications in the daily life of the preschools. 'From the ground up' also speaks to the authors' confidence, disclosed in the final chapter, that those who are most responsible for caring for young children in their specific geo-cultural locations and familial environments are most likely to have the best idea about how to support their well-being. Through dialogue among parents and other community members, practices that are feasible and fitting for local needs and goals are most likely to be constructed.

This book is particularly concerned with policies that relate to the care and early education of preschool children living in relative poverty in times of social change. The authors use both an historical perspective and a socio-cultural lens to explore the connections among people, places, and policy that shape practices in the three preschool examples. All three are described as settings in transition—from the racialised social structure to social unity in South Africa, from cultural genocide to cultural regeneration in Aboriginal communities in Canada, and from a colonial to a post-colonial and more technological environment in India. The authors begin with interrogating the seemingly inescapable tendency of national governments in the majority world to look to the west for theories, policies, and practice standards, and often for program models that are marketed for wholesale adoption—at least on the surface—or adaption in communities far from their conceptual and cultural origins. In each study site, the authors ask what occurs in practice when western ways of knowing come into contact with indigenous or local ways of socializing and working with children. They illustrate in numerous ways the tension between a broadening recognition of the value of local or indigenous knowledge and goals for young children's development, on one hand, and the accumulation of research-based evidence as well as taken-for-granted assumptions or 'regimes of truth' (Foucault, 1980) in the West about what it means to be educated and how to achieve targeted outcomes (Stroud, 2007).

In the authors' assessment, the activities and interactions with children in all three preschools fit well with community expectations. They all advanced a sense of community and teachers took pride in what they were able to achieve in their preschools with little training and relatively few resources. Community belonging, cultural pride, and an increase in positive predispositions among parents and other community members towards meeting children's needs in culturally congruent ways are hard to measure, but this does not mean they are unimportant. Indeed, these may be the most important factors determining positive developmental outcomes. But what are positive outcomes? Cultural literacy, positive self-concept, developing home language proficiency, genuinely caring intergenerational relationships—these are also hard to measure directly, and are often excluded in prescribed standards for early childhood programs, in school readiness inventories, and outcomes-based education.

Cleghorn and Prochner suggest that the meaning of difference in preschool pedagogies lies in the affective domain, such as the pleasure that children and caregivers take in the activities of their preschool day: for example, the pleasure of a story book read at leisure and not chosen because it is short and the teacher must rush to finish it in order to keep to a prescribed and hurried schedule; the pleasure of hearing and telling stories, rather than the task of listening to stories read in an unfamiliar language; or the awkwardness of a parent talking with a teacher who is trying to follow a prescribed policy handed down from the government rather than listening to what the parent wants for their child. Affective and social qualities of caring, community, cultural safety and confidence are endangered when there is a top-down push to extend the reach of academic learning steadily downward from primary year one to kindergarten and from kindergarten into pre-kindergarten, as we are seeing in many parts of Canada, for example. Attending the trend towards downward expansion of academic programming is a tendency for both parents and policy makers to pressure teachers and children to begin to use the language of formal schooling—often English—in place of the children's home language or a common local dialect. Another consequence is often the screening, labeling, and specialized treatment of children designated as unready to handle academic learning tasks due to a sensory or physical handicap or chronic disease, and the potential for the gradual exclusion of these children from the 'mainstream.'

One of the key dilemmas that faces early childhood programs throughout the majority world—and one that is illustrated in the case study preschools—can be construed as a kind of "double bind" (Bateson, 1972). On one hand, many—if not most—parents, early childhood educators and policy makers want to prepare children for successful participation in economic and political spheres. In most settings this means learning a dominant language and achieving in formal schooling. On the other hand, these same stakeholders often assert the value and desire to preserve or strengthen local cultural knowledges, languages, and literacies. The apparent double bind is in the effort to have both at the same time: to orient preschool towards early learning and school readiness, including introducing the language of schooling and moving away from the pedagogy of learning through play that has been the hallmark of early childhood education. All three of the preschools studied by Cleghorn and

Prochner had preparation for the transition to school as a primary goal. The double bind was most starkly evident in the self-contradictory national policy framework governing preschool in South Africa.

A central flaw in resolving the dilemma by favoring the downward extension of formal schooling into preschool is that it is based on the over simplistic belief that if the task demands presented to children in preschool are a simplified but closely matched version of the task demands that children will face upon formal school entry, children will be more likely to succeed. Yet, Piagetian research has shown that the cognitive structures and logic supporting children's learning is fundamentally different during the preschool years compared to the period of primary schooling (Langer & Killen, 1998). Also, linguistic research supports providing opportunities for children to learn in preschool and throughout the primary school years in their mother tongue. This ensures that children develop reading proficiency in their first language, along with the cultural worldview and identity embodied in their mother tongue, and also lays the foundation for learning to read before the child is asked to transition to an additional language of instruction (Cummins, 2000). Further, as Cleghorn and Prochner suggest, what is at stake is the affective component of teaching and learning when children and their teachers are required to accommodate to cultural forms of learning and literacy and a language of interaction that is not the culture or language with which they are most familiar and comfortable. The authors return repeatedly to the theme of pleasure in preschool, and the affective foundation of learning to love social interaction, hearing and telling stories for enjoyment, and the thrill of discovery when children are encouraged to explore and engage in spontaneous and peer-mediated learning. What is not understood by many policy makers as well as by many parents is that when children have a strong positive identity as learners and see their own culture and language as worthy and effective for learning, they are more likely to form positive attachments to the formal education process and more likely to have the cognitive and linguistic foundational skills for success in school.

A haunting question that this volume evokes is whether preschools and advocates of quality early childhood programs are really in a position to stem the tide of westernized values and ideas about the nature of childhood and how children should learn and develop in the face of growing pressure from both parents and policy makers who foreground these values. How do we demonstrate and convince policy makers and donors that locally constructed, perhaps more subtle yet functional indigenous approaches to socialization that ground children in their cultural identity, home language and local literacies may actually provide children with the strongest foundation for subsequent learning and participation in the mainstream? To many parents and policy makers, a lack of transparent correspondence between the content and activities of preschool versus primary school may seem counter-intuitive and counter-productive to the goal of promoting the social inclusion of minoritized and disadvantaged children. Cleghorn and Prochner do not answer this for us, but their book is a strong stimulus for dialogue about how to sustain local knowledge and language while also attending to diverse parents' goals and national human resource development targets for the children's eventual participation in local labour markets and the global economy.

The hope offered in this volume lies in what the authors have characterized as subtle forms of resistance. Their examples demonstrate that practices in particular geocultural locations are not always tightly bound by formal policy prescriptions. And in some settings, such as the case of Aboriginal Head Start at Little Lake, the national policy context and local goals for children share a strong positive emphasis on indigenous language and cultural practices.

Another hopeful view is that while globalization has tended to be associated with westernization and a hegemonic neoliberalism, it can also imply interconnectedness, increased choice as a result of increased communicative possibilities, and hybridity. How can the increased communicative possibilities and economic interdependency associated with globalization be turned into opportunities for children and those who care for them, without unintended losses to community strengths? Part of the answer lies in iterative planning efforts that seriously engage parents and other stakeholders in understanding the possibilities for early childhood education, the probable consequences of various choices, and the goodness of fit between their goals and various approaches.

As Tobin and his colleagues (1989; 2009) concluded from their seminal studies of preschools in Japan, China and the United States, there are many ways to support the holistic development of young children. The point is not to eschew an imported approach just because it is foreign or to favour a local approach just because it is indigenous, swapping a colonial ideological tyranny for a homegrown variety. Rather, there is a need for a constant critical reflection among policy makers, practitioners and parents on where various preschool goals and practices have come from, what and whose purposes they are intended to serve, whether they are functional in the local context, and whether parents—who after all should be the ultimate arbiters of programs that are intended to benefit their children—agree with what their children are receiving in preschool.

Education programs to prepare early childhood practitioners and policy leaders can play important roles in strengthening the capacity and confidence of local actors and national leaders to critically examine the historical, cultural and social derivation of approaches to preschool, school readiness, and primary school, to involve local stakeholders in making choices and reshaping and reinventing both western and local practices to fit their own internally defined goals for children's development, as well as the ability and political will of state (government), substate (teachers, principals), and nonstate (NGO), actors to work together to support locally fitting early childhood programs. In settings such as Little Lake, a hybrid approach will evolve that combines traditional and modern, indigenous and transcultural approaches to create new preschool practices that are fitting to the particular children, parents and schools in a particular community. Educators and policy leaders can work as allies to help families successfully support their children's journeys to develop cultural literacy, home language proficiency, educational engagement, vocational success and social inclusion.

Jessica Ball, University of Victoria, Canada

REFERENCES

A most hopeful experiment. (1965, November 23). *Globe & Mail* (Toronto), p. 6.

Abagi, O. (2005). The role of the school in the 21st century: Coping with forces of change. In A. Abdi & A. Cleghorn (Eds.), *Issues in African education: Sociological perspectives* (pp. 297–317). New York: Palgrave-Macmillan.

Abdi, A. A., & Cleghorn, A. (Eds.). (2005). *Issues in African education: Sociological perspectives.* New York: Palgrave-Macmillan.

Aboriginal Health Research Networks Secretariat. (2008). *Newsletter.* Retrieved from http://www.ahrnets.ca/

Aboriginal Research Institute of Six Nations Reserve. (2005). *National dialogue on federal aboriginal early childhood development strategy. Draft report.* Ottawa: Distributed by Health Canada. Retrieved from http://www.accel-capea.ca/pdf/Edited%20ARI%20National%20Dialogue%20Eng%20May %2006-05.pdf

Aboud, F. E., Hossain, K., & O'Gara, C. (2008). The succeed project: Challenging early school failure in Bangladesh. *Research in Comparative and International Education, 3*(3), 295–307.

Aikenhead, G. S., & Jegede, O. J. (1999). The federal government, child care, and the child development associate: A dissenting view. *Child Care Quarterly, 2*(2), 136–141.

Alberta Education. (2008). *Guide to education: ECS to grade 12.* Edmonton: Author.

Alexander, R. (2000). *Culture and pedagogy: International comparisons in primary education.* Oxford: Blackwell.

Anderson-Levitt, K. (Ed.). (2003). *Local meanings, global schooling: Anthropology and world culture theory.* New York: Palgrave-Macmillan.

Anganwadi Workers threaten dharna. (2009, January 1). *The Hindu* (India). Retrieved from http://www.thehindu.com/2009/01/09/stories/2009010953690300.htm

Apple, M. (2003). Is the new technology part of the solution or part of the problem in education? In A. Darder, M. Baltodano, & R. Torres (Eds.), *The critical pedagogy reader* (pp. 440–457). New York: Routledge.

Apple, M. (1979). *Ideology and curriculum.* London: Routledge & K. Paul.

Armitage, A. (1995). *Comparing the policy of aboriginal assimilation: Australia, Canada, and New Zealand.* Vancouver: UBC Press.

Arthur, J. (1994). Talking like teachers: Teacher and pupil discourse in Botswana primary classrooms. *Language Culture and Curriculum, 7*(1), 29–40.

Arthur, J. (1996). Code-switching and collusion: Classroom interaction in Botswana primary schools. *Linguistics and Education, 8*, 17–33.

Ashcroft, B. (2001). *On post-colonial futures: Transformations of colonial culture.* London: Continuum.

Aubrey, C., David, T., Godfrey, R., & Thompson, L. (2000). *Early childhood education research: Issues in methodology and ethics.* London: RoutledgeFalmer.

Auger, W., & Rich, S. J. (2007). *Curriculum theory and methods.* Mississauga: John Wiley & Sons.

Babbie, E. (2002). *The basics of social research.* Toronto: Nelson Thomson.

Bainer, C., & Hale, L. (2007). *Second home: A day in the life of a model early childhood program.* St. Paul, MN: Redleaf.

Ball, J., Definney, S., & Pence, A. (1999). Evaluation of community involving ECCD training in seven First Nations communities. In E. Lowe (Ed.), *Linking research to practice: Second Canadian forum* (pp. 188–193). Ottawa: Canadian Child Care Federation and Canadian School Boards Association.

Ball, J., & Pence, A. R. (1999). Beyond developmentally appropriate practice: Developing community and culturally appropriate practice. *Young Children, 54*(2), 46–50.

Barakett, J., & Cleghorn, A. (2007). *Sociology of education: An introductory view from Canada.* Toronto: Pearson.

REFERENCES

Barton, D. (1995). *Family literacy programmes and home literacy practices*. Paper prepared for the Literacies for the Future Symposium, University of Brighton, Lewes, UK.

Barton, D., & Hamilton, M. (1998). *Local literacies: Reading and writing in one community*. London: Routledge.

Barton, D., Hamilton, M., & Ivanic, R. (2000). *Situated literacies: Reading and writing in context*. London: Routledge.

Bateson, G. (1972). *Steps to ecology of mind*. New York: Ballantine.

Battiste, M., & Barman. (Eds.). (1995). *First Nations education in Canada: The circle unfolds*. Vancouver: UBC Press.

Battiste, M. (2000). *Protecting indigenous knowledge and heritage: A global challenge*. Saskatoon: Purich.

Beach, J., & Friendly, M. (2005). *Child care centre physical environments*. Toronto: Child Care Resource and Research Unit.

Beaty, J. (2004). *Skills for preschool teachers* (7th ed.). Upper Saddle River, NJ: Pearson.

Beck, R. B. (2000). *The history of South Africa*. Westport, CT: Greenwood.

Bennett, N., Wood, E., & Rogers, S. (1997). *Teaching through play: Teachers' thinking and classroom practice*. Philadelphia: Open University Press.

Beatch, M. (2004). *Taking ownership: The implementation of a non-aboriginal program for on-reserve children*. MA thesis, Simon Fraser University.

Benson, C. (2004). Do we expect too much of bilingual teachers? Bilingual teaching in developing countries. *International Journal of Bilingual Education & Bilingualism, 7*(2–3), 204–221.

Bettleheim, B. (1977). *Uses of enchantment*. New York: Basic Books.

Bhabha, H. K. (1994). *The location of culture*. New York: Routledge.

Bhattacharjee, N. (1999). Through the looking glass: Gender socialization in a primary school. In T. S. Saraswathi (Ed.), *Culture, socialization, and human development: Theory, research and applications in India* (pp. 336–356). New Delhi: Sage.

Blauner, B. (1972). *Racial oppression in America*. New York: Harper & Row.

Bodrova, E., & Leong, D. J. (2005). High quality preschool programs: What would Vygotsky say? *Early Education and Development, 16*(4), 435–444.

Botha, M., Maree, J. G., & de Witt, M. W. (2005). Developing and piloting the planning for facilitating mathematical processes and strategies for preschool learners. *Early Child Development and Care, 175*(7/8), 697–717.

Bourdieu, P., & Passeron, J. C. (1977). *Reproduction in education: Society and culture*. Thousand Oaks, CA: Sage.

Botha, R. J. (2002). Outcomes-based-education and educational reform in South Africa. *International Journal of Leadership in Education, 5*(2), 361–371.

Brandt, D., & Clinton, K. (2002). Limits of the local: Explaining perspectives on literacy as a social practice. *Journal of Literacy Research, 34*(3), 337–356.

Brewer, J. (2004). *Introduction to early childhood education: Preschool through primary grades* (5th ed.). Boston: Pearson.

Brey, P. (1998). Space-shaping technologies and the geographical disembedding of place. In A. S. Light & J. M. Smith (Eds.), *Philosophy and geography* (pp. 239–263). New York: Rowman & Littlefield.

Britto, P. R., & Gilliam, W. (2008). Crossing borders with Head Start: An analysis of international early childhood programs. *Infants and Young Children, 21*, 82–91.

Brock-Utne, B. (2003, March 12–16). *The merits and problems of code-mixing and code-switching in the African classroom*. Paper presented at the annual meeting of the Comparative and International Education Society, New Orleans.

Budgell, R. (1998). *Aboriginal Head Start and Native American Head Start: Hands across the border?* Paper presented at the annual conference of the National Association for the Education of Young Children, Toronto.

Bunnett, R., & Kroll, D. (2000). Transforming spaces: Rethinking the possibilities—Turning design challenges into opportunities. *Child Care Information Exchange, 131*, 26–29.

Bunyi, G. (1999). Rethinking the place of African indigenous languages in African education. *International Journal of Educational Development, 19*(4–5), 337–350.

Carlson, S. M., Taylor, M., & Levin, G. R. (1998). The influence of culture on pretend play: The case of Mennonite children. *Merrill-Palmer Quarterly, 44*(4), 538–585.

Cartwrigtht, S. (2004). Young citizens in the making. *Young Children, 59*(5), 108–109.

Cassidy, D. J., Hestenes, L. L., Hansen, J. K., Hegde, A., Shim, J., & Hestenes, S. (2005). Revisiting the two faces of child care quality: Structure and process. *Early Education and Development, 16*(4), 505–520.

Ceppi, G., & Zini, M. (1998). *Children, spaces, relations: Metaproject for an environment for young children.* Reggio Emilia: Reggio Children.

Chaudhary, L. (2009). Determinants of primary schooling in British India. *Journal of Economic History, 69*(1), 269–302.

Child Development Laboratory School. (2009). *Class schedules, Lab4.* Iowa State University, College of Human Sciences. Retrieved from http://www.hs.iastate.edu/cdlab/class_schedules.php

Cleghorn, A. (1992). Primary level science in Kenya: Constructing meaning through English and indigenous languages. *International Journal of Qualitative Studies in Education, 5*(4), 311–323.

Cleghorn, A. (2005). Language issues in African school settings: Problems and prospects in attaining education for all. In A. A. Abdi & A. Cleghorn (Eds.), *Issues in African education: Sociological perspectives* (pp. 101–122). New York: Palgrave-Macmillan.

Cleghorn, A., & Evans, R. (2009, June). *Complex language encounters.* Paper presented at the Comparative and International Education Society of Canada, Ottawa.

Cleghorn, A., Merritt, M., & Abagi, O. (1989). Language policy and science instruction in Kenyan primary schools. *Comparative Education Review, 33*(1), 21–39.

Cleghorn, A., & Prochner, L. (1997). Early childhood education in Zimbabwe: Recent trends and prospects. Special issue: Children, families, and change: International perspectives. *Early Education and Development, 8*(3), 339–352.

Cleghorn, A., & Prochner, L. (2003). Contrasting visions of early childhood education: Examples from rural and urban settings in Zimbabwe and India. *Journal of Early Childhood Research, 1*(2), 131–153.

Cobern, W. W. (Ed.). (1998). *Socio-cultural perspectives on science education: An international dialogue.* London: Kluwer.

Cohen, L., & Uhry, J. (2007). Young children's discourse strategies during block play: A Bakhtinian approach. *Journal of Research in Childhood Education, 21*(3), 302–315.

Collins, J., & Blot, R. (2002). *Literacy and literacies: Texts, power and identity.* New York: Cambridge.

Connelly, F. M., & Clandinin, J. (1990). The cyclic temporal structure of schooling. In M. Ben-Peretz & R. Broome (Eds.), *The nature of time in schools* (pp. 36–63). New York: Teachers College Press.

Cummins, J. (2000). *Language, power and pedagogy.* Clevedon, UK: Multilingual Matters.

Cummins, J. (2000a). *Language, power, and pedagogy: Bilingual children in the crossfire.* Clevedon, England: Multilingual Matters.

Cummins, J., & Corson, D. (Eds.). (1997). *Bilingual education. Encyclopedia of language and education* (Vol. 5). Dordecht, The Netherlands: Kluwer.

Dachyshyn, D., & Kirova, A. (2008). Understanding childhoods in-between: Sudanese refugee children's transition from home to preschool. *Research in Comparative and International Education, 3*(3), 281–294.

Dahlberg, G., & Moss, P. (2005). *Ethics and politics in early childhood education.* New York: Routledge.

Dahlberg, G., Moss, P., & Pence, A. (2006). *Beyond quality in early childhood education and care: Languages of evaluation* (2nd ed.). Abingdon: Routledge.

Das, D. (2003). *Case study of the status of India's early childhood care and education services.* New Delhi: UNESCO. Retrieved http://portal.unesco.org/education/en/file.download.php

David-Cree, L. (2004). *Would you like to hear a story? Mohawk youth narratives on the role of the history of Quebec and Canada on indigenous identity and marginality.* Master's thesis, Concordia University, Montreal.

REFERENCES

Dei, G. J., Hall, D. L., & Rosenberg, D. G. (Eds.). (2000). *Indigenous knowledges in global contexts: Multiple readings of our world*. Toronto: University of Toronto Press.

Depaepe, M., & Laevers, F. (1992). Preschool education in Belgium. In G. Woodill, J. Bernhard, & L. Prochner (Eds.), *International handbook of early childhood education* (pp. 93–103). New York: Garland.

Department of Education, South Africa. (1995). *Education white paper no. 1 on education and training*. Pretoria: Author.

Department of Education, South Africa. (1997). *Interim policy for early childhood development*. Pretoria: Author.

Department of Education, South Africa. (2001a). *Education white paper 5 on early childhood education: Meeting the challenge of early childhood development in South Africa*. Pretoria: Author.

Department of Education, South Africa. (2001b). *Report on national early childhood development policies and programmes*. Pretoria: Author.

Department of Education, South Africa. (2001c). *The nationwide audit of early childhood development provisioning in South Africa*. Pretoria: Author.

Department of Education, South Africa. (2008). *Rev. national curriculum statement, Grades R – 9 (Schools)*. Pretoria: Author.

Department of Justice Canada. (1985). *Indian Act*. Ottawa: Author.

Dickinson, D. (2002). Shifting images of developmentally appropriate practice as seen through different lenses. *Educational Researcher, 31*(1), 26–32.

Dietze, B. (2006). *Foundations of early childhood education: Learning environments and child care in Canada*. Toronto: Pearson Prentice Hall.

Dube, R., & Cleghorn, A. (1999). Code switching in mathematics lessons in Zimbabwe. *Zimbabwe Journal of Educational Research, 11*(1), 1–12.

Dudek, M. (2000). *Architecture of schools: The new learning environments*. Boston: Architectural Press.

Duncan, R. M., & Tarulli, D. (2003). Play as the leading activity of the preschool period: Insights from Vygotsky, Leont'ev, and Bakhtin. *Early Education and Development, 14*(3), 271–292.

Eastman, C. (Ed.). (1992). Special issue on code switching. *Journal of Multilingual and Multicultural Development, 13*(1–2), 1–17.

Eliason, C., & Jenkins, L. (2003). *A practical guide to early childhood curriculum* (7th ed.). Upper Saddle River, NJ: Merrill.

Essa, E., & Burnham, M. M. (2001). Child care quality: A model for examining relevant variables. In S. Riefel & M. H. Brown (Eds.), *Early education and care, and reconceptualising play* (Vol. 11, pp. 59–113). New York: JAI.

Evans, R. (2006). The impact of presenter speech personality on learner participation during televised instruction. *Journal of Language Teaching, 40*(2), 21–34.

Evans, G. W., & Lepore, S. J. (1993). Household crowding and social support: A quasi experimental analysis. *Journal of Personality and Social Psychology, 65*(2), 308–316.

Evans, G. W., Lepore, S. J., & Allen, K. (2000). Cross-cultural differences in tolerance for crowding: Fact or fiction? *Journal of Personality and Social Psychology, 79*(2), 204–210.

Evans, J. (1996). Quality in programming: Everyone's concern. In *Coordinators' notebook* (Vol. 18, pp. 1–37). Toronto: The Consultative Group on Early Childhood Care and Development. Retrieved from http://www.ecdgroup.com/download/cc118aqi.pdf

Evans, R., Cleghorn, A., & Sarkar, M. (2009, May 22). *Complex language encounters: Observations from linguistically diverse South Africa classrooms*. Paper prepared for the Language and Literacy Researchers of Canada, Canadian Society for Studies in Education conference, Ottawa.

Evans, R., Gauton, R., Kaschula, R. P. D., Ramagoshi, R., & Taljard, E. (2007). *Classroom literacies: Understanding your multilingual classroom*. Thorton, S. Africa: Bateleur.

Feeney, S., Christensen, D., & Moravcik, E. (2001). *Who am I in the lives of children? An introduction to teaching young children* (6th ed.). Upper Saddle River, NJ: Merrill/Prentice Hall.

Fein, H. (1993). *Genocide: A sociological perspective*. London: Sage.

First Nations Child and Family Caring Society of Canada. (2005). Wen:de Report. *Are we coming to the light of the day?* Ottawa: Author.

Fleer, M. (2003). Early childhood education in an evolving 'community of practice' or as lived 'social reproduction': Researching the 'taken for granted.' *Contemporary Issues in Early Childhood, 4*(1), 64–79.

Foucault, M. (1980). *Power/knowledge: Selected interviews and other writings 1972–1977.* New York: Pantheon Books.

Freeman, E. B., & Hatch, A. (1989). What schools expect young children to know and do: An analysis of kindergarten report cards. *The Elementary School Journal, 89*(5), 594–605.

Gaskins, S. (1996). How Mayan parental theories come into play. In S. Harkness & C. Super (Eds.), *Parents' cultural belief systems: Their origins, expressions, and consequences* (pp. 364–384). New York: The Guilford Press.

Gee, J. (1986). Orality and literacy: From the savage mind to ways with words. *TESOL Quarterly, 20*(4), 719–746.

Gee, J. (2000). The new literacy studies: From "socially situated" to the work of the social. In D. Barton, M. Hamilton, & R. Ivanic (Eds.), *Situated literacies: Reading and writing in context* (pp. 180–196). London: Routledge.

Gee, J. (2008). *Social linguistics and literacies: Ideology in discourses.* New York: Routledge.

Genesee, F. (2008). Dual language learning in the global village. In D. Tedick (Ed.), *Pathways to multilingualism: Evolving perspectives on immersion education* (pp. 253–266). Clevedon: Multilingual Matters.

Gerlach, A. (2008). "Circle of caring:" A First Nations worldview of child rearing. *Canadian Journal of Occupational Therapy, 75*(1), 18–25.

Guerrero, S., & Enesco, L. (2008). *The development of racial awareness.* Germany: VDM, Verlag.

Gestwicki, C. (1999). *Developmentally appropriate practice: Curriculum and development in early education* (2nd ed.). Albany, NY: Delmar.

Giddens, A. (1990). *The consequences of modernity.* Stanford, CA: Stanford University Press.

Giddens, A. (1991). *Modernity and self-identity: Self and identity in the late modern age.* Cambridge, UK: Polity Press.

Gilliam, W. S., & Shahar, G. (2006). Preschool and child care expulsion and suspension: Rates and predictors in one state. *Infants and Young Children, 19*(3), 228–245.

Giroux, H. (1992). *Border crossings.* New York: Routledge.

Glover, G. (2001). Parenting in Native American families. In N. Boyd (Ed.), *Culturally diverse parent-child and family relationships: A guide for social workers and other practitioners* (pp. 205–231). New York: Columbia University Press.

Government of India. (2004). Department of Women, Development & Child Welfare. Retrieved from http://anganwadi.ap.nic.in/icds_programs.html

Göncü, A., Patt, M. B., & Kouba, E. (2004). Understanding young children's pretend play in context. In P. K. Smith & C. H. Hart (Eds.), *Blackwell handbook of childhood social development.* Blackwell Publishing.

Graue, E. (1992). Readiness, instruction, and learning to be a kindergartner. *Early Education and Development, 3*(2), 92–114.

Graue, E., Hatch, K., Rao, K., & Oen, D. (2007). The wisdom of class size reduction. *American Educational Research Journal, 44*(3), 670–700.

Greenwood, M., de Leeuw, S., & Ngaroimata Fraser, T. (2007). Aboriginal children and early childhood development in Canada: Linking the past and the present to the future. *Canadian Journal of Native Education, 30*(1), 5–31.

Guerrero, S., & Enesco, I. (2008). *The development of racial awareness.* Saarbrücken: VDM Verlag.

Gullöv, E. (2003). Creating a natural place for children: An ethnographic study of Danish kindergartens. In K. Fog Olwig & E. Gullöv (Eds.), *Children's places: Cross-cultural perspectives* (pp. 23–38). London: Routledge.

REFERENCES

Gupta, A. (2004). Working with large class size: Dispositions of early childhood teachers in India. *Contemporary Issues in Early Childhood, 5*(3), 361–377.

Gupta, A. (2008). Tracing local-global transitions within early childhood curriculum and practice in India. *Research in Comparative International Education, 3*(3), 266–280.

Hall, E. T. (1966). *The hidden dimension.* Garden City, NY: Doubleday.

Harkness, S., & Super, C. M. (1996). *Parents' cultural belief systems: Their origins, expressions, and consequences.* New York: Guilford.

Harms, T., Clifford, R. M., & Cryer, D. (2005). *Early childhood environment rating scale.* New York: Teachers College Press.

Hartley, R., Frank, L., & Goldenson, R. (1952). *Understanding children's play.* New York: Columbia University Press.

Hatch, A. (1995). *Qualitative research in early childhood settings.* Westport, CT: Praeger.

Hatch, A. (2004). *Teaching in the new kindergarten.* Clifton Park, NJ: Thomson Delmar Learning.

Health Canada. (1995). *Aboriginal Head Start initiative: Guide for applicants.* Ottawa: Author.

Health Canada. (2000, Spring). *Aboriginal Head Start newsletter.* Ottawa: Author.

Health Canada. (2001, Fall/Winter). *Aboriginal Head Start newsletter.* Ottawa: Author.

Health Canada. (2001). *Aboriginal Head Start in urban and northern communities: Program and participants 2000.* Ottawa: Author.

Health Canada. (2002). *Creation stories: Personal reflections about Aboriginal Head Start in urban and northern communities.* Ottawa: Author.

Health Canada. (2003a). *Aboriginal Head Start On Reserve, 2001–2003 progress report.* Ottawa: Author.

Health Canada. (2004). *Aboriginal Head Start On Reserve program: Summary of the evaluation.* Ottawa: Author.

Health Canada. (2005). *First Nations Head Start standards guide.* Retrieved from http://www.hc-sc.gc.ca/fniah-spnia/pubs/famil/_develop/2003_ahs-papa-ref-guide/index-eng.php

Heath, S. B. (1983). *Ways with words: Language, life and work in communities and classrooms.* New York: Cambridge University Press.

Helfenbein, R. J. (2006). Space, place, and identity in the teaching of history: Using critical geography to teach teachers in the American South. In A. Segall & E. Heilman (Eds.), *Social studies—the next generation: Re-searching in the postmodern* (pp. 111–124). New York: Peter Lang.

Hendrick, J., & Weissman, P. (2006). *The whole child: Developmental education for the early years.* Upper Saddle River, NJ: Pearson/Merrill Prentice Hall.

Heugh, K., Siegrühn, A., & Plüddemann, P. (1995). *Multilingual education for South Africa.* Johannesburg: Heinemann.

Hewitt, K. (2001). Blocks as a tool for learning: Historical and contemporary perspectives. *Young Children, 56*(1), 6–10.

Hirschfeld, L. A. (1993). Discovering social difference: The role of appearance in the development of racial awareness. *Cognitive Psychology, 25*(3), 317–350.

Holloway, S. L., & Valentine, G. (2000). Spatiality and the new social studies of childhood. *Sociology, 34,* 763–783.

Hornberger, N. H., & Chick, K. (2001). Co-constructing school safetime: Safetalk practices in Peruvian and South African classrooms. In M. Martin-Jones & M. Heller (Eds.), *Voices of authority: Education and linguistic difference* (pp. 31–55). Westport, CT: Ablex.

Hoyos-Vivas, L.-M. (2008). *The current Colombian education policy and its impact in the rural areas.* Unpublished Masters Thesis, Concordia University.

Human Resources Development Canada, Health Canada, & Indian and Northern Affairs Canada. (2003). *Early childhood development activities and expenditures. New addition: Early learning and child care activities and expenditures: Baseline report 2002–2003.* Ottawa: Author.

Hunter, R. (2004). *Madelaine Hunter's mastery teaching: Increasing instructional effectiveness in elementary and secondary schools.* Thousand Oaks, CA: Corwin Press.

Indian and Northern Affairs Canada. (2003). *National assessment of water and wastewater in First Nations communities. Summary report.* Ottawa: Indian and Northern Affairs Canada.

Iwata, O. (1992). Crowding and behaviour in Japanese public spaces: Some observations and speculations. *Social Behaviour and Personality, 20*(1), 57–66.

Jackson, P. W. (1966a). *Life in classrooms.* New York: Holt, Rinehart & Winston.

Jackson, P. W. (1966b). The student's world. *The Elementary School Journal, 66*(7), 345–357.

Jambunathan, S. (2006). Relationship between perception of self-competence and parenting attitudes of Asian Indian preschoolers. *Early Childhood Development and Care, 176*(7), 745–752.

Jansen, J. D. (1999). Setting the scene: Historiographies of curriculum policy in South Africa. In J. Jansen & P. Christie (Eds.), *Changing curriculum: Studies on outcomes-based education in South Africa* (pp. 3–20). Cape Town: Juta & Co.

Jansen, J. D. (2002). Political symbolism as policy craft: Explaining non-reform in South African education after apartheid. *Journal of Education Policy, 17*(2), 199–215.

Jessen, M. (1974). Early childhood education program for American Indians. *Contemporary Education, 45*(4), 278–281.

Jipson, J. (1991). Developmentally appropriate practice: Culture, curriculum, connections. *Early Education and Development, 2*(2), 120–136.

Johnson, R. (2000). *Hands off! The disappearance of touch in the care of children.* New York: Peter Lang.

Johnson, R. T., & Gaiyabu, M. (2001). Resisting normative representation in the Pacific Islands: Domestic enemies meet over coffee. In J. A. Jipson & R. T. Johnson (Eds.), *Resistance and representation: Rethinking childhood education* (pp. 279–290). New York: Peter Lang.

Jones, J., & Brown, W. T. (2005). Any time is Trinidad time! Cultural variations in the value and function of time. In A. Strathman & J. Joireman (Eds.), *Understanding behavior in the context of time: Theory, research, and application* (pp. 305–323). Mahwah, NY: Lawrence Erlbaum.

Joshi, A. (2009). What do teacher-child interactions in early childhood classrooms in India look like? Teachers' and parents' perspectives. *Early Childhood Development and Care, 179*(3), 285–301.

Kagan, S. L., Carroll, J., Comer, J. P., & Scott-Little, C. (2006). Alignment: A missing link in early childhood transitions? *Young Children, 61*(5), 26–32.

Kağitçibaşi, Ç. (1996). *Family and human development across cultures: A view from the other side.* Mahwah, NJ: Erlbaum.

Kağitçibaşi, Ç. (2007). *Family, self, and human development across cultures: Theory and applications* (2nd ed.). New Jersey, NJ: Psychology Press.

Kakar, S. (1978a). *Indian childhood: Cultural ideals and social reality.* New Delhi: Oxford University Press.

Kakar, S. (1978b). *The inner-worlds: A psycho-analytic study of childhood and society in India.* New Delhi: Oxford University Press.

Kantrowitz, E. J., & Evans, G. W. (2004). The relation between the ratio of children per activity area and off-task behaviour and type of play in day care centres. *Environment and Behaviour, 36,* 541–447.

Katz, L., & Chard, S. (2000). *Engaging children's minds: The project approach* (2nd ed.). Stamford, CT: Ablex.

Katz, L., Mohite, P., & Shastri, J. (2009). The project approach in an Indian context. In P. Mohite & L. Prochner (Eds.), *Early childhood care and education: Theory and practice* (pp. 40–51). New Delhi: Concept Pub. Co.

Kaulback, B. (1984). Styles of learning among native children. A review of the research. *Canadian Journal of Native Education, 11*(3), 27–37.

Kaur, B. (2009). Early childhood education in India from 1830s to 1940s: Leapfrogging through a century. In P. Mohite & L. Prochner (Eds.), *Early childhood care and education: Theory and Practice* (pp. 144–165). New Delhi: Concept Pub.

Kendrick, M., & Jones, S. (2008). Girls' visual representations of literacy and identity in a rural Ugandan community. *Canadian Journal of Education, 31*(2), 371–403.

Kim, J. (2003). Challenges to NLS: Response to "What's 'new' in New Literacy Studies". *Current Issues in Comparative Education, 5*(2), 118–121.

Klein, N. (2003). *No logo: Taking aim at brand bullies.* Toronto: Vintage Canada.

REFERENCES

Knudsen, D. (2000). *Alberta Aboriginal Head Start conference 2000 report.* Edmonton: Publisher unknown.

Krogh, S. L., & Morehouse, P. J. (2008). *The early childhood curriculum: Inquiry learning through integration.* Boston: McGraw-Hill.

Kuper, A. (1999). *Culture: The anthropologists' account.* Cambridge, MA: Harvard University Press.

Kurian, G. (1986). *Parent-child interaction in transition.* New York: Greenwood.

Kushner, D. (2001). The dangerously radical concept of free play. In S. Riefel & M. H. Brown (Eds.), *Early education and care, and reconceptualising play* (Vol. 11, pp. 275–293). New York: JAI.

Langer, J., & Killen, M. (1998). *Piaget, evolution, and development.* Mahwah, NJ: Lawrence Erlbaum.

Lawn, M. (1999). Designing teaching: The classroom as technology. In I. Grosvenor, M. Lawn, & K. Rousmaniere (Eds.), *Silences and images: The social history of the classroom* (pp. 63–82). New York: Peter Lang.

Leahy, W., Cooper, G., & Sweller, J. (2005). Interactivity and the constraints of cognitive load theory. In A. Peacock & A. Cleghorn (Eds.), *Missing the meaning: The development and use of print and non-print text materials in diverse school settings.* New York: Palgrave.

Leavitt, R. L. (1994). *Power and emotion in infant-toddler day care.* Albany, NY: State University of New York Press.

LeVine, R. A. (2003). *Childhood socialization: Comparative studies of parenting, learning, and educational change.* Hong Kong: Comparative Education Research Centre, University of Hong Kong.

LeVine, R. A., Dixon, S., LeVine, S., Richman, A., Leiderman, P. H., Keefer, C. H., et al. (1994). *Child care and culture: Lessons from Africa.* Cambridge: University Press.

LeVine, S. (2008). *School lunch politics: The surprising history of America's favourite welfare program.* Princeton, NJ: Princeton University Press.

Levy, R. (2008). 'Third spaces' are interesting places: Applying 'third space theory' to nursery-aged children's constructions of themselves as readers. *Journal of Early Childhood Literacy, 8*(1), 43–66.

Lewis, T., Macfarlane, K., Nobel, K., & Stephenson, A. (2006). Crossing borders and blurring boundaries: Early childhood practice in non-western settings. *International Journal of Early Childhood, 38*(2), 23–35.

Liddell, C. (1995). Mixed blessings: Effects of educational resource materials on South African children in day care. *International Journal of Early Years Education, 3*(1), 56–69.

Liddell, C., & Kruger, P. (1987). Activity and social behaviour in a crowded South African nursery: Some effects of crowding. *Merrill Palmer Quarterly, 33*(2), 195–216.

Liddell, C., & Kruger, P. (1989). Activity and social behaviour in a crowded South African Township nursery: A follow-up on the effects of crowding at home. *Merrill Palmer Quarterly, 35*(2), 209–226.

Light, H. K. (1985). Guidance of American Indian children: Their heritage and some contemporary views. *Journal of American Indian Education, 25*(1), 42–46.

Lipka, J. (2002). Schooling for self-determination: Research on the effects of including native language and culture in the schools. (ERIC Document Reproduction Services No. ED459989)

Lloyd, B., & Howe, N. (2003). Solitary play and convergent and divergent thinking skills in preschool children. *Early Childhood Research Quarterly, 18*(1), 22–41.

Lockhart, S. D., Xiang, Z., & Montie, J. (2003). Findings from concurrent observation systems. In D. P. Weikart, P. P. Olmstead, & J. Montie (Eds.), *A world of preschool experience: Observations in 15 countries* (pp. 162–196). Ypsilanti, MI: High/Scope Press.

Loo, C. (1972). The effects of spatial density on the social behaviour of children. *Journal of Applied Social Psychology, 2*(4), 372–381.

Lubeck, S. (1985). *Sandbox society: Early education in black and white America.* Philadelphia: Falmer.

Machado, J. M., & Botnarescue, H. M. (2005). *Student teaching: Early childhood practicum guide* (5th ed.). Albany, NY: Thomson Delmar.

Mac Naughton, G., & Williams, G. (2005). *Teaching young children: Choices in theory and practice.* Maidenhead: Open University Press.

Malaguzzi, L. (1993). For an education based on relationships. *Young Children, 49*(3), 9–12.

Marks, E., & Graham, E. (2004). *Establishing a research agenda for American Indian and Alaska Native Head Start programs*. Prepared for the U.S. Department of Health & Human Services. Calverton, MD: OEC Macro.

Marsh, C. (1997). *Key concepts for understanding curriculum* (Rev. ed.). London: Taylor & Francis Routledge.

Marsh, C. (2004). *Key concepts for understanding curriculum* (3rd ed.). London: Taylor & Francis Routledge.

McElhinny, B. (2007). Introduction: Language, gender and economies in global transitions: Provocative and provoking questions about how gender is articulated. In B. S. McElhinny (Ed.), *Words, worlds, and material girls: Language, gender, globalization* (pp. 1–38). New York: Mouton de Gruyter.

McGrath, J. E. (1988). *The social psychology of time: New perspectives*. New York: Sage.

McGrew, A. G., & Lewis, P. G. (1992). *Global politics: Globalization and the nation-state*. Cambridge: Polity Press.

McGregor, J. (2004). Space, power and the classroom. *Forum, 46*(1), 13–18.

Meriwether, L. (1997). Math at the snack table. *Young Children, 52*(5), 69–73.

Merritt, M., Cleghorn, A., Abagi, O., & Bunyi, G. (1992). Socialising multilingualism: Determinants of code-switching in Kenyan primary classrooms. *Journal of Multilingual and Multicultural Development, 13*(1–2), 103–121.

Merritt, M., Cleghorn, A., & Abagi, J. O. (1988). Dual translation and cultural congruence: Some exemplary practices of Kenyan primary school teachers. In K. Ferrara, B. Brown, K. Walters, & J. Baugh (Eds.), *Linguistic change and contact. Texas Linguistic Forum* (Vol. 30, pp. 232–239). Austin, TX: University of Texas, Dept. of Linguistics.

Messerschmidt, J., Ramabenyane, J., Venter, R., & Vorster, C. (2009). The facilitative role of adults in the language development of Afrikaans and Sesotho-speaking preschool children. *European Early Childhood Education Research Journal, 16*(3), 283–296.

Mifflen, F. J., & Mifflen, S. C. (1982). *The sociology of education: Canada and beyond*. Calgary: Detselig Enterprises.

Milesi, C., & Gamoran, A. (2006). Effects of class size and instruction on kindergarten achievement. *Education Evaluation and Policy Analysis, 28*(4), 287–313.

Miller, J. R. (1996). *Shingwauk's vision: A history of native residential schools*. Toronto: University of Toronto Press.

Ministry of Women and Child Development, Government of India. (n.d.). *Monitoring in ICDS*. Retrieved from http://wcd.nic.in/icdsformat/ICDSMONITORINGMANUAL.doc

Miskimmin, S. (2007). When Aboriginal equals "at risk": The impact of institutional discourse on Aboriginal Head Start families. In B. S. McElhinny (Ed.), *Words, worlds, and material girls: Language, gender, globalization* (pp. 107–130). New York: Mouton de Gruyter.

Mkosi, N. (2005). Surveying indigenous knowledge, the curriculum, and development in Africa: A critical African viewpoint. In A. A. Abdi & A. Cleghorn (Eds.), *Issues in African education: Sociological perspectives* (pp. 85–100). New York: Palgrave-Macmillan.

Mohatt, G. V., & Erickson, F. (1981). Cultural differences in teaching styles in an Odawan school. In H. T. Trueba, G. P. Guthrie, & K. Au (Eds.), *Culture and the bilingual classroom: Studies in classroom ethnography* (pp. 105–119). Hillsdale, NJ: Lawrence Erlbaum.

Mohite, P. (1993). Early childhood care and education: Emerging issues in research. In T. S. Saraswathi & B. Kaur (Eds.), *Human development and family studies in India: An agenda for research and policy* (pp. 221–232). New Delhi: Sage.

Montessori, M. (1912). *The Montessori method* (A. E. George, Trans.). New York: Frederick A. Stokes.

Montie, J. E., Xiang, Z., & Schweinhart, L. J. (2006). Preschool experience in 10 countries: Cognitive and language performance at age 7. *Early Childhood Research Quarterly, 21*, 313–331.

Moore, G. T. (1986). Effects of the spatial definition of behaviour settings on children's behaviour: A quasi-experimental field study. *Journal of Environmental Psychology, 6*(3), 205–231.

REFERENCES

Moss, P. (1994). Defining quality values, stakeholders and processes. In P. Moss & A. Pence (Eds.), *Valuing quality in early childhood services: New approaches to defining quality.* New York: Teachers College Press.
Moss, P. (2005). Making the narrative of quality stutter. *Early Childhood Education and Development, 16*(4), 405–420.
Moss, P., & Petrie, P. (2002). *From children's services to children's spaces.* London: Routledge.
Mullis, I. V. S., Martin, M. O., & Foy, P. (2008). *TIMSS 2007 international science report: Findings from IEA's trends in international mathematics and science study at the fourth and eighth grades.* Chestnut Hill, MA: IMSS & PIRLS International Study Center.
Murray, C. (2000). Learning about children's social and emotional needs at snack time-nourishing the body, mind, and spirit of each child. *Young Children, 55*(2), 43–52.
Myers, R. G. (1992). *The twelve who survive.* New York: Routledge.
Myers, R. G. (2001). Globalization, care and educational services for children under six in urban areas. In N. del Rio (Eds.), *La infancia vulnerable de Mexico en un mundo globalizado* (pp. 169–193). Mexico, DF: Universidad Autonoma Metropolitana.
Myers, R. G. (2005). *Moderating tensions between modern and post-modern views of education quality: Notes on indicators of preschool quality in Mexico.* Paper prepared for CIES conference, Stanford.
Myers, R. G. (2007, March). *Seeking quality in Mexican preschools.* Paper presented at the Society of Research in Child Development Biennial Meeting, Boston.
Myers-Scotton, C. (1993). *Dueling languages: Grammatical structure in code-switching.* Oxford: Claredon Press.
National Campaign for Sanitation and Hygiene Promotion with focus on Hand Washing, Department of Drinking Water Supply, Ministry of Rural Development, India. (n.d.). Retrieved from http://ddws.gov.in/handwash/contentpage.aspx
National Focus Group on Early Childhood Education. (2006). *Position Paper (3.6) National Council of Educational Research and Training (NCERT).* New Delhi: NCERT.
Native Council of Canada. (1990). *Native child care: "The circle of care."* Ottawa: Author.
Nayak, N. (2006). Disintegrated services. *Infochange Agenda.* Retrieved from http://infochangeindia.org/200610065675/Agenda/Hunger-Has-Fallen-Off-The-Map/Disintegrated-services.html
Niles, M., Byers, L., & Krueger, E. (2007). Best practice and evidence-based research in indigenous early childhood intervention programs. *Canadian Journal of Native Education, 30*(1), 108–138.
Niles, M. D., & Byers, L. G. (2008). History matters: United States policy and indigenous early childhood intervention. *Contemporary Issues in Early Childhood, 9*(3), 191–201.
Nsamenang, A. B. (2004). *Cultures of human development and education: Challenge to growing up in Africa.* New York: Nova.
Nsamenang, A. B. (2006). *Cultures in early childhood care and education.* Background paper prepared for Education for ALL: Strong foundations: Early childhood, care and education. Paris: UNESCO.
Nsamenang, A. B. (2007). A critical peek at early childhood care and education in Africa. *Child Health and Education, 1*(1), 1–12.
Nsamenang, A. B. (2008). Agency in early childhood learning and development in Cameroon. *Contempory Issues in Early Childhood, 9*(3), 211–223.
Odora-Hoppers, C. A. (2002). *Indigenous knowledge and the integration of knowledge systems: Towards a philosophy of articulation.* Claremont, South Africa: New Africa Books.
Ogbu, J. U. (1991). Low school performance as an adaptation: The case of blacks in Stockton, California. In M. A. Gibson & J. U. Ogbu (Eds.), *Minority status and schooling: A comparative study of immigrants and involuntary minorities* (pp. 249–285). New York: Garland.
Ogunniyi, M. (2005). Cultural perspectives on science and technology education. In A. Abdi & A. Cleghorn (Eds.), *Issues in African education: Sociological perspectives* (pp. 123–140). New York: Palgrave Macmillan.
Ong, W. J. (1991). *Orality and literacy: The technologizing of the word.* New York: Routledge.

Organisation for Economic Cooperation and Development, Directorate for Education. (2004). *Early childhood education and care policy. Canada, country note.* Paris: Author. Retrieved from http://www.oecd.org/dataoecd/42/34/33850725.pdf

Pacini-Ketchabaw, V. (2007). Biculturalism. In R. New & M. Cochran (Eds.), *Early childhood education: An international encyclopaedia* (Vol. 1, pp. 72–75). Westport, CT: Praeger.

Packer, S. (2000). The effects of scarcity and abundance in early childhood settings. *Young Children, 55*(5), 36–38.

Parten, M. (1933). Social play among preschool children. *Journal of Abnormal and Social Psychology, 28*(2), 136–147.

Peacock, A., & Cleghorn, A. (2004). *Missing the meaning: The development and use of print and non-print text materials in diverse school settings.* New York: Palgrave.

Pence, A., Garcia, M., & Evans, J. (2008). *Africa's future, Africa's challenge: Early childhood care and development in sub-Saharan Africa.* Washington, DC: World Bank.

Phatudi, N. C. (2007). *A study of transition from preschool and home contexts to Grade 1 in a developing country.* Doctoral dissertation, University of Pretoria, Pretoria.

Phatudi. (2007). *A study of transition from pre-school and home contexts to grade 1 in a developing country.* Doctoral dissertation, University of Pretoria.

Phillipson, R. (1992). *Linguistic imperialism.* Oxford: Oxford University Press.

Planning Commission, Government of India. (2008). *Eleventh Five Year Plan, 2007–2012. Vol. II: Social Sector.* New Delhi: Oxford University Press.

Powell, D. R. (2007). Families. In R. S. New & M. Cochran (Eds.), *Early childhood education: An international encyclopaedia* (pp. 352–355). Westport, CT: Greenwood.

Prinsloo, M., & Breier, M. (1996). *The social uses of literacy and practice.* Philadelphia: Sacched.

Prochner, L. (1992). Early childhood education in the late-20th century: A cross-national analysis. In G. Woodill, J. Bernhard, & L. Prochner (Eds.), *International handbook of early childhood education* (pp. 11–19). New York: Garland.

Prochner, L. (1996). Quality-of-care in historical perspective. *Early Childhood Research Quarterly, 11*(1), 5–18.

Prochner, L. (2002). Preschool and playway in India. *Childhood, 9,* 435–453.

Prochner, L. (2004). Early education programs for Indigenous children in Canada, Australia, and New Zealand: An historical review. *Australian Journal of Early Childhood, 29*(4), 7–16.

Prochner, L. (2009a). *A history of early childhood education in Canada, Australia, and New Zealand.* Vancouver: University of British Columbia Press.

Prochner, L. (2009b). Playway in India. In P. Mohite & L. Prochner (Eds.), *Early childhood care and education: Theory and practice* (pp. 16–39). New Delhi: Concept Pub. Co.

Prochner, L., & Cleghorn, A. (2005). Cross-cultural research as a lens on early childhood thought and practice. In V. Pacini-Ketchabaw & A. Pence (Eds.), *Reconceptualizing early childhood education and development in Canada. Canadian Child Care Federation Research Connections Series.* Ottawa: Canadian Child Care Federation.

Prochner, L., Cleghorn, A., & Green, N. (2008). Space considerations: Materials in the learning environment in three majority-world preschool settings. *International Journal of Early Years Education, 16*(3), 189–202.

Prochner, L., & Kabiru, M. (2008). "ECD in Africa: A historical perspective." In M. Garcia, A. Pence, & J. Evans (Eds.), *Africa's Future, Africa's Challenge: Early Childhood Care and Development in Sub-Saharan Africa* (pp. 117-133). Washington: World Bank.

Prochner, L., May, H., & Kaur, B. (2009). 'The blessings of civilisation': Nineteenth century missionary infant schools for young native children in three colonial settings – India, Canada and New Zealand 1820s–1840s. *Paedagogica Historica, 45*(1/2), 191–210.

Public Health Agency of Canada. (1999). *Aboriginal Head Start: Biennial report, 1998–99.* Ottawa: Author.

Public Health Agency of Canada. (2000). *Aboriginal Head Start initiative.* Retrieved from http://www.phac-aspc.gc.ca/dca-dea/publications/pdf/cmacw_final_e.pdf

REFERENCES

Public Health Agency of Canada. (2002). *Aboriginal Head Start: Biennial report, 1998–1999, 1999–2000.* High/Scope training. Retrieved from http://www.phac-aspc.gc.ca/dca-dea/publications/biennial-eng.php

Public Health Agency of Canada. (2004a). *Aboriginal Head Start: Program overview.* Mission. Retrieved from http://www.phac-aspc.gc.ca/dca-dea/programs-mes/ahs_overview-eng.php

Public Health Agency of Canada. (2004b). *Aboriginal Head Start: Program overview.* AHS factsheet. Retrieved from http://www.phac-aspc.gc.ca/dca-dea/programs-mes/ahs_overview-eng.php

Raibmon, P. (2003). Living on display: Colonial visions of Aboriginal domestic spaces. *Journal of BC Studies, 140,* 69–89.

Ramanathan, V. (2005). *The English-vernacular divide: Postcolonial language politics and practice.* Clevedon, Avon, UK: Multilingual Matters.

Relph, D. (1976). *Place and placelessness.* London: Pion.

Republic of South Africa. (1996). Chapter 2, section 29 (a) Bill of Rights. *Constitution of the Republic of South Africa.* Pretoria: Author.

Republic of South Africa. (2004). Revised National Curriculum Statement. Pretoria: Department of Education.

Republic of South Africa (2009). National Curriculum. R to Grade 9. Pretoria: Department of Education.

Rich, N. H. (n.d.). Remembering Avima Lombard. In *the NCJW Research Institute for Innovation in Education, Professor Avima D. Lombard (1926–2008) and the HIPPY program* (Avima D. Lombard tribute brochure) (p. 4). Retrieved from http://www.hippyusa.org/site/view/148153_ATributetoAvima Lombard.pml;jsessionid=1p0jrxy7ayjcb

Ritzer, G. (1993). *The McDonaldization of society: An investigation into the changing character of contemporary social life.* Newbury Park, CA: Pine Forge Press.

Roberts, S. K. (2003). Snack math: Young children explore division. *Teaching Children Mathematics, 9*(5), 258–261.

Sanders, M. (1999). Implementing outcomes-based education in South Africa. In *Proceedings of the 7th Annual Southern African Association for Research in Mathematics, Science and Technology Education conference,* Harare.

Schissel, B., & Wotherspoon, T. (2003). *The legacy of school for aboriginal people.* Don Mills, ON: Oxford University Press.

Schneider, B. H. (1993). *Children's social competence in context: The contributions of family, school and culture.* New York: Pergamon.

Schweinhart, L. J., Barnes, H. V., & Weikart, D. P. (1993). *Significant benefits: The High/Scope Perry preschool study through age 27.* Ypsilanti, MI: High/Scope press.

Scrase, T. J. (1993). *Image, ideology and inequality: Cultural domination, hegemony and schooling in India.* New Delhi: Sage.

Semali, L. M., & Kincheloe, J. L. (Eds.). (1999). *What is indigenous knowledge? Voices from the academy.* New York: Falmer.

Senate Committee on Labor and Human Resources & Senate Committee on Indian Affairs. (1994). Indian issues regarding Head Start reauthorization. Joint Hearing To Expand the Provisions of Head Start Services and To Improve the Overall Quality of Head Start Programs, before the Committee on Indian Affairs and the Committee on Labor and Human Resources. United States Senate, One Hundred Third Congress, Second Session. Washington, DC. (ERIC Document Reproduction Services No. ED374939)

Serpell, R. (1992). African dimensions of child care and nurturance. In M. E. Lamb, K. J. Sternberg, C. P. Hwang, & C. P. Broberg (Eds.), *Child care in context: Cross-cultural perspectives* (pp. 463–476). Hillsdale, NJ: Lawrence Erlbaum.

Serpell, R. (1993). *The significance of schooling: Life-journeys in an African society.* Cambridge, UK: Cambridge University Press.

Seto-Thomas, L. (1990). *Native child care: The circle of care.* Ottawa: Native Council of Canada.

Shallwani, S. (2009). *Releasing confidence and creativity: Early childhood development programme in Pakistan. A collaborative and localized model of ECD programme development and implementation.* Ottawa: Aga Khan Foundation.

Sharma, A. (1998). Opportunity, challenges and vision. In M. Swaminathan (Ed.), *The first five years: A critical perspective on ECCE in India* (pp. 285–301). New Delhi: Sage.

Sheila Clark & Associates. (1995). *Literature review: A reference for Aboriginal Head Start project operators.* Ottawa: Health Canada.

Sheridan, S., Giota, J., Han, Y.-M., & Kwon, J.-E. (2009). A cross-cultural study of preschool quality in South Korea and Sweden: ECERS evaluations. *Early Childhood Research Quarterly, 24*(2), 142–156.

Shizha, E. (2005). Reclaiming our memories: The education dilemma in postcolonial African school curricula. In A. A. Abdi & A. Cleghorn (Eds.), *Issues in African education: Sociological perspectives* (pp. 65–84). New York: Palgrave-Macmillan.

Shumba, O. (1999). Critically interrogating the rationality of Western science vis-à-vis scientific literacy in non-Western developing countries. *ZAMBEZIA, 26*(1), 55–75.

Silin, J. G., Schultz, S., Bevacqua, S., Laslocky, J., Tobin, J., Taubman, P., et al. (2005). Rethinking resistance in schools: Power, politics, and illicit pleasures. Occasional Paper Series, no. 14, Bank Street College of Education. (ERIC Document Reproduction Service No. ED491763)

Sinha, S. R. (1988). Childrearing practices relevant for the growth of dependency and competence in children. In J. Valsiner (Ed.), *Child development within culturally structured environments* (Vol. 3, pp. 105–137). Norwood, NJ: Ablex.

Small, G. (1979). Remote battlegrounds: The Office of Special Feld Projects. In E. Zigler & J. Valentine (Eds.), *Project Head Start: A legacy of the war on poverty* (pp. 339–348). New York: The Free Press.

Smith, M. K., & Smith, M. (2002). Globalization. In *The encyclopaedia of informal education.* Retrieved from www.infed.org/biblio/globalization.htm

Smith, P. K., & Connolly, K. J. (1980). *The ecology of preschool behaviour.* Cambridge: Cambridge University Press.

Snider, V. E., & Roehl, R. (2007). Teachers' beliefs about pedagogy and related issues. *Psychology in the Schools, 44*(8), 873–886.

Soja, E. W. (1996). *Thirdspace: Journeys to Los Angeles and other real-and-imagined places.* Malden, MA: Blackwell.

Somjee, S. (2000). Oral traditions and material culture: An East African experience. *Research in African Literature, 31*(4), 97–103.

Soudien, C. (2007). *Schooling, culture and the making of youth identity in contemporary South Africa.* Capetown: David Philip.

Spodek, B. (1988, April). *Early childhood curriculum and the definition of knowledge.* Paper presented at the annual conference of the American Educational Research Association, New Orleans. (ERIC Document Reproduction Services No. 293657)

Spreen, C. A. (2001). *Globalization and educational policy borrowing: Mapping outcomes-based education in South Africa.* Doctoral dissertation, Columbia University.

Steiner-Khamsi, G. (Ed.). (2004). *The global politics of educational borrowing and lending.* New York: Teachers College Press.

Stephens, D. (2007). *Culture in education and development: Principles, practice and policy.* Oxford: Symposium books.

Street, B. V. (2001a). Academic literacies: A critical perspective. *Ways of Knowing Journal, 1*(1), 19–23.

Street, B. V. (Ed.). (2001b). *Literacy and development: Ethnographic perspectives.* London: Routledge.

Street, B. V. (2003). What's new in the new literacy studies? Critical approaches to literacy in theory and practice. *Current Issues in Comparative Education, 5*(2), 77–91.

Street, B. V. (2004). *Understanding and defining literacy: Scoping paper for EFA global monitoring report 2006.* Unpublished manuscript.

REFERENCES

Strong-Wilson, T., & Ellis, J. (2007). Children and place: Reggio Emilia's environment as third teacher. *Theory into Practice, 46*(1), 40–47.

Stroud, C. (2007). Bilingualism: Colonialism, postcolonialism and high modernity. In M. Heller (Ed.), *Bilingualism: A social approach* (pp. 205–229). New York: Palgrave Press.

Super, C. M., & Harkness, S. (1986). The developmental niche: A conceptualization at the interface of child and culture. *International Journal of Behavioral Development, 9*, 545–569.

Swaminathan, M. (1998). Current issues in early childhood care and education. In T. S. Saraswathi & B. Kaur (Eds.), *Human development and family studies in India: An agenda for research and policy* (pp. 221–232). New Delhi: Sage.

Swaminathan, M. (1993). *The first five years: A critical perspective on early childhood care and education in India*. New Delhi: Sage.

Sweller, J. (1994). Cognitive load theory, learning difficulty and instructional design. *Learning and Instruction, 4*, 295–312.

Terbasket, K., & Greenwood, M. (2007). British Columbia First Nations Head Start program: An overview of policy development, 1998–2007. *Canadian Journal of Native Education, 30*(1), 75–84.

Thirumalai, M. S. (2003). Understanding proxemic behaviour. *Language in India, 3*(11). Retrieved from http://www.languageinindia.com/nov2003/proxemicbehavior.html#point4

Tobin, J., Wu, D., & Davidson, D. (1989). *Preschool in three cultures: Japan, China, and the United States*. New Haven, CT: Yale University Press.

Tobin, J. (2005). Quality in early childhood education: An anthropologist's perspective. *Early Education and Development, 16*(4), 421–434.

Tobin, J., Hsueh, Y., & Karasawa, M. (2009). *Preschool in three cultures revisited: China, Japan, and the United States*. Chicago: University of Chicago Press.

Tollefson, J. W. (1991). *Planning language, planning inequality: Language policy in the community*. London: Longman.

Trawick-Smith, J. (2006). Social play in school. In D. Fromberg & D. Bergan (Eds.), *Play from birth to twelve: Contexts, perspectives, and meanings* (2nd ed., pp. 173–180). New York: Routledge.

Trudeau, P. (1971, October 8). Policy on multiculturalism. House of Commons Debates, p. 8545–8548.

Tuan, Y. (1977). *Space and place: The perspective of experience*. Minneapolis, MN: University of Minnesota Press.

United Nations Educational, Scientific and Cultural Organization. (2006). *South Africa early childhood care and education progrmmes. Country profile prepared for the Education for All Global Monitoring Report 2007, Strong foundations: Early chidhood education*. Paris: Author.

United States Department of Health & Human Services. (n.d.). Indian Health Service: Head Start program: Mission statement. Retrieved from http://www.ihs.gov/nonmedicalprograms/headstart/index.cfm?module=main&option=main

Vandenbroeck, M. (2006). The persistent gap between education and care: A "history of the present" research on Belgian child care provision and policy. *Paedagogica Historica, 42*(3), 363–383.

Vargas-Baron, E. (2009). *Going to scale and achieving sustainability in selected early childhood programs of Latin America*. Washington, DC: The RISE Institute.

Waldrip, B. G., & Taylor, P. C. (1999). Permeability of students' worldviews to their school views in a non-Western developing country. *Journal of Research in Science Teaching, 36*(3), 289–304.

Warner, L., & Sower, J. (2005). *Educating young children form preschool to primary grades*. Boston: Pearson.

Washington, V., & Oyemade, U. (1987). *Project Head Start: Past, present, and future trends in the context of family needs*. New York: Garland.

Weasel Traveller Inc. (1995). *Calgary Native Head Start program: Project planning and information package*. Calgary: Author.

Webb, V. N. (2002). Language policy development in post apartheid South Africa. In J. W. Tollefson & A. B. M. Tsuie (Eds.), *Medium of instruction policies: Which agenda? Whose agenda?* (pp.). Mawah, NJ: Lawrence Erlbaum.

Weikart, D. (2003). Overview and policy implications. In D. P. Weikart, P. P. Olmsted, & J. Montie, with N. Hayes & M. Ojala (Eds.), *A world of preschool experience: Observations in 15 countries.* The IEA Preprimary Project Phase 2 (pp. 242–264). Ypsilanti, MI: High/Scope Press.

Weikart, D., & Schweinhart, L. (2005). The High/Scope curriculum for early childhood care and education. In J. L. Roopnarine & J. Johnson (Eds.), *Approaches to early childhood education* (4th ed., pp. 235–250). Upper Saddle River, NJ: Pearson.

Weststat, Xtria, & the CDM Group. (2003). *Head Start FACES (Family and child experiences survey) 2000: A whole-child perspective on program performance.* Washington, DC: Administration for Children and Families, U.S. Department of Health & Human Services.

White, C. S., & Coleman, M. (2000). *Early childhood education: Building a philosophy for teaching.* Upper Saddle River, NJ: Merrill.

Wien, C. A. (1996). Time, work, and developmentally appropriate practice. *Early Childhood Research Quarterly, 11*(3), 377–403.

Wien, C. A., & Kirby-Smith, S. (1998). Untiming the curriculum: A case study of removing clocks from the program. *Young Children, 53*(5), 8–13.

Wien, C., Coates, A., Keating, B., & Bigelow, B. C. (2005). Designing the environment to build connection to place. *Young Children, 60*(3), 16–24.

Woodhead, M. (1996). In search of the rainbow: Pathways to duality in large-scale programmes for young disadvantaged children. *Early childhood development: Practice and reflections no. 10.* The Hague: Bernard Van Leer Foundation.

Working Group on Development of Children for the Eleventh Five-Year Plan. (2007). *Working Group on Development of Children for the Eleventh Five-Year Plan (2007–2012). A Report* (Vol. 1). New Delhi: Ministry of Women and Child Development, Government of India.

World Health Organization. (2001, November 24) *Report on rise in deaths in bottle fed infants in Africa.*

Yan, W., & Lin, Q. (2005). Effects of class size and length of day on Kindergartners' academic achievement: Findings from early childhood longitudinal study. *Early Education and Development, 16*(1), 49–68.

Zan, B. (2005). NAEYC accreditation and high quality preschool curriculum. *Early Education and Development, 16*(1), 85–104.

Zastoupil, L., & Moir, M. (1999). *The great Indian education debate: Documents relating to the Orientalist-Anglicist controversy, 1781–1843.* Richmond, UK: Curzon.

Zvoch, K., Reynolds, R. E., & Parker, R. P. (2008). Full-day kindergarten and student literacy growth: Does a lengthened school day make a difference? *Early Childhood Research Quarterly, 23*(1), 94–107.

INDEX

CPSIA information can be obtained at www.ICGtesting.com
Printed in the USA
LVOW081708131111

254761LV00005B/7/P

9 789460 910999